THE SEARCH FOR A CIVIC RELIGION:

A History Of The Character Education Movement In America, 1890-1935

Stephen M. Yulish

University Press of America

University Press of America, Inc.™

4720 Boston Way, Lanham, MD 20801

ISBN: 0-8191-1174-0
Library of Congress Number: 80-5619

To Clarence, friend and mentor.

iii

ACKNOWLEDGMENT

The author wishes to express his sincere appreciation to Jim Anderson, Paul Violas, and Tom Hastings for their invaluable assistance and fruitful dialogue in the preparation of this book. The editorial and typing assistance of Ruth Tager was also most appreciated. To Clarence Karier, the author is deeply indebted for his constant encouragement and friendship, but most of all for his insightful comments and criticisms.

Finally, appreciation is affectionately extended to Debi for her unending patience and understanding.

TABLE OF CONTENTS

vii

PREFACE

The breakdown of the influence of the
Church and the Family as sanctioning institutions
of morality was a very significant part of the
growing industrialization and urbanization of the
late nineteenth century in America. Gradually,
the State, via the educational system, assumed
the burden of moral and character education. It
is the purpose of this study to examine the resulting character education movement during the
period 1890-1935.

First, it will be necessary to analyze the
antecedents of character education, namely, moral
and ethical education. These concerns will be
examined, not only in terms of the influential
educators in this country who espoused their
virtues, but also in terms of the influence of
European thought on its development. Consideration will be given to the psychological justification for moral education derived from Herbart
and the view of the State as a divine institution
as derived from Hegel.

Once the antecedents of character education
have been analyzed, and the historical perspective thus developed, the relationship between the
character education movement as a movement and
World War One will be discussed. The War generated a great deal of nationalistic jingoism as
well as a genuine concern with character which
helped perpetrate the character education movement. The moral center of gravity appeared to be
shifting from the individual to that of the
state. The moral concern generated was mostly
in the form of a political conscience. The distinction between the good man and the good
citizen became blurred.

Character education programs sprang up all
across the country. Many of these programs will
be described and analyzed, from the inclusive

Iowa and Utah Plans, down to the arrangements of individual communities. The impact of character education programs on the structure and function of schooling in America will be considered. New programs were instituted, new grading procedures adopted, and new personnel were added to the school staff. Character education programs were concerned with education for values and conduct, not skills or intellect. Once again the distinction between moral training and citizenship training as it manifested itself in character education programs will be examined in all its apparent haziness.

Another crucial aspect of character education in American was the development of the quantification, objectification, and standardization of character traits. Since the I Q tests were seen to have been inconclusive in predicting one's success in life or in a vocation, many psychologists turned to study of character and personality factors. The origins and rationale of the character testing movement will be examined with special consideration of the results obtained in terms of immigrant groups, Blacks and Jews. Most psychologists involved in character measurement agreed that the correlation between character and intelligence, while positive, was nonetheless low. The way this finding influenced the growth of character education as well as vocational education will also be examined. Finally, the correlations of character with the variables of feeblemindedness, delinquency, criminality and success in school and life will be discussed.

Several character tests will be examined and analyzed in terms of the inherent value assumptions of the testers. The tests will further be scrutinized to identify ethnic, racial, or cultural bias. Character or moral tests were supposed to be aptitude tests of a person's general character or sometimes of specific character traits like honesty, deceit, submissiveness, or cooperation.

Many questions need to be asked about
these tests. Were they tests of moral character
or tests of knowledge of morality or the law?
Were they good predictors of conduct? Why did
the Southern European immigrant, the Black and
the Indian often test lower than the Northern
European immigrant or the nativeborn white American? Finally, many of the early character
tests were actually variations of psychoneurotic
questionnaires developed during the war. Why was
it that certain pupils tested were more paranoid
and psychotic than others? A careful analysis of
the test questions involved will be shown to be
very revealing in terms of the questions raised.

The purpose of this study then is to give
the reader a perspective on the development of
character education and character testing in
America during the period 1890-1935. The issues
and problems raised during this time period are
still very much with us today. The role of the
historian not only entails providing one's contemporaries with a perspective on the past, but
also by its very nature, contributes to the
solution of present-day problems.

Hayden V. White grasped this notion accurately when he wrote:

The contemporary historian has
to establish the value of the study
of the past, not as 'an end in itself,' but as a way of providing perspective on the present that contributes to the solution of problems
peculiar to our own time.[1]

NOTES

[1]Hayden V. White, "The Burden of History,"
History and Theory, 5, No. 2, 1966, p. 125.

I. THE INFLUENCE OF MORAL AND ETHICAL EDUCATION
    ON THE DEVELOPMENT OF CHARACTER EDUCATION

A.

The concept of moral education has always
been a crucial underpinning of the American notion of a virtuous republic. Throughout its
development, American leaders in education have
strenuously sought to condemn mere intellectual
training. Whether it was the phrenological justifications of Horace Mann for training pupils
in proper laws of health and morals[1] or the
widespread perception of a need for moral training to inculcate respect for authority and law
and order,[2] the notion of moral education has
historically been a crucial factor in the
American experience. The deepfelt need to control behavior and conduct by moral training was
undertaken by the schools alongside the instruction of the church and the home.

The latter part of the nineteenth century
was a time of turbulence and change in American
society and its values. The mass onslaught of
urbanization, mechanization and industrialization broke apart the security of small towns,
driving many into crowded cities. With the
increasing revolution in means of transporta-
tion and communication, the isolation of a more
peaceful existence was continually threatened.
Former centers of community life, namely the
church and the family, found their previous
moral control jeopardized by the growing imper-
sonality of a technological urban society.

Notions such as faith and dogma by which
the church had helped maintain order and control
in the community were shattered by the evolu-
tionary doctrine and the rise of the new faith
in Science. Many clergy who saw their status
jeopardized, regenerated their concern for salvation, not so much through the scriptures as
through the social gospel.[3] As Richard Hofstadter pointed out:

1.

The social gospel movement arose
during the years when evolution was
making converts among the professional
clergy, and since ministers who were
liberal in social outlook were almost
invariably liberal in theology, also,
the social theory of the movement was
deeply affected by the import of
naturalism upon social thought. The
growing secularization of thought
hastened the trend among clergymen
to turn from the abstractions of
theology to social questions. The
liberalization of theology broke down
the insularity of religion.[4]

While many clergy saw their new mission as
to provide for the evolution of society here on
Earth with all the implied notions of progress,
purposeful social action and reform, it seems
clear that they were not only motivated by a concern with their fellow man but they were also
suffering from a loss in power and prestige in
the community. Hofstadter saw the clergy thus
often joining ranks with the emerging reformers
in an attempt to recover their power and influence in the community.[5]

The tremendous concern with ethics and
moral education during this period was due not
only to the loss of faith in the church but was
also a result of the new crowded conditions in
the cities which bred vice and disease. Also
the tremendous variety in culture and language
of the new immigrants was seen by many to mandate a common ethical base. W. C. Larrabee,
Superintendent of Public Instruction in Indiana,
wrote:

Our policy as a State is to
make of all the varieties of population among us, differing as they
do in origin, language, habits,
modes of action, and social customs,

2.

one people with one common interest.[6]

The notion of purity and unity provided
the impetus, not only for Americanization, but
for moral education as well. While American
education always had a moral tone, the changing
conditions of the late 19th century sparked the
moral flame anew in the attempt to rid the
country of poverty, disease, crime and disunity.
The goal was the Kingdom of Heaven on Earth.
Salvation was seen to be possible in the social
setting. What was needed was an ethical stance
removed from theological myth and dogma. The
Ethical Culture Society arose to meet such a
demand.

B.

Felix Adler, the son of a Rabbi, founded
the Ethical Culture Society in New York in 1876
with the intent of separating value considerations from "outworn myths and accreted metaphy-
sics."[7] Adler stressed the importance of moral
living and moral acting as the bases for a true
religion rather than the theological dogma. The
movement brought together diverse groups,
(radicals, atheists, deists, agnostics), into
a new movement of ethical humanism. The stress
for unity, so much a part of American thought,
was clearly evident. Many members obviously of
a religious persuasion attempted to transfer religious or moral ethics into a social gospel.
The social gospel was based, however, on pragmatic, not mythological considerations.

The concept of unity played an important
role in the rationale for Americanization of
immigrants. Adler felt that assimilation of
aliens was crucial to national unity, and while
he recognized the fact that certain of their
traits would enter the national character, many
of them would have to be eliminated. For Adler
the "Anglo Saxon race had the lead and would

3.

doubtless keep it."[8] For Felix Adler as well as
other moral and ethical educators, purity, as
well as unity, was a potent concept in the drive
for a perfect society. The Ethical Culture
Society was very interested in maintaining the
values of "purity of women, good deeds, and
celibacy during bachelorhood."[9] Drawing heavily
from Kantian ethics, the Society sought a morality independent of theology. While moral law was
seen to be imposed upon man by his rational
nature and thus needed no religious dogma to
bolster its efficacy, it is quite clear that
the moral tone advocated was not incongruous with
the Judeo-Christian ethic. Religious values had
become secularized but they still encouraged a
movement for purity in a context of a common
unified creed.

Besides the strong moral tone of the Society, it also dealt directly with the pressing
social problems of the time. It worked very
closely with the poor and the immigrant in an
attempt to make them into "useful" members of
society. The Workingman's School was founded in
1878 and one of Felix Adler's former students,
(Adler taught for a while at Columbia University)
Stanton Coit, founded the Neighborhood Guild in
1886, which was the first Settlement House in
America. The Society was not interested in
"glorifying" the worker, as they saw the
Marxists doing; they wanted to provide him with
the skills to transform his low station.

To those involved in the Society, education for the poor and the immigrant was defined
mainly as manual training, a procedure which
more often than not froze them at the bottom of
society and denied them the chance to acquire
or develop other abilities or interests. This
was the case not only because the immigrant was
thought to be in most cases intellectually
inferior but also because he was a threat to
the unity and cohesiveness of the society.
Manual training provided him with certain semi-

4.

mechanical virtues which aided his efficient assimilation. Also American industry was at that
time in need of an ever-expanding source of cheap
labor whose requirements the immigrant and the
poor fulfilled nicely.

The Society also created free kindergartens (the first in 1878) for the poor and helped
set up Sunday School curricula in an attempt to
create a system of education which included moral
and ethical training for the young. Ethical Culture Schools were also instituted which stressed
character formation, ethics, and social services.
Character formation was the naturalization of the
old dream of salvation.[10]

The Ethical Culture Society put an inordi-
nate stress on the influence of manual training
on character building as well as on moral training. While Adler advocated manual training for
all classes of people, it apparently served as a
justification for the socio-economic system.
Manual training for delinquents was seen not only
as a means to strengthen the will power between
good feeling and the realization of good feeling but to also cultivate the property sense of
the child. A feat that Adler saw as no small
advantage.[11]

By use of manual training Adler also
hoped to bring the classes of society together
and show the dignity of labor. He advocated
some manual training in all schools so that the
son of the rich man, learning side by side with
the son of a poor man, would learn to understand
what the dignity of manual labor really meant
and "the two classes of society, united at the
root, will never therefore entirely grow
asunder."[12] What exactly Adler meant by this
is not clear, but it is certain that the notion
of respect had a higher premium placed on it
than did social or economic equality.

This concept of respect was not the only
value which Adler stressed. Play schools and

housekeeping classes were set up to channel the
energy and build the character and responsibility of the newcomer and the poor. Adler felt
that education was the key to the moral strength
of society. One of the founding principles of
the Ethical Culture Society states in part that:

> We agree that the greatest stress
> should be laid on the moral instruc-
> tion of the young, to the end that in
> the pure hearts of childhood may be
> sown the seeds of a higher moral
> order.[13]

The ultimate grounds of moral obligation
were not to be discussed in school. The business of the public school was to deliver to the
pupils the common fundamentals of moral truth
but there was no obligation to justify these
values.[14] This notion of unquestioning respect
for authority and the supremacy of law became
an important part of moral education. A certain
body of doctrine was presented which was then
fixed into habit. Adler summarized his views on
the moral instruction of children in the following manner:

> To recapitulate briefly the
> points which we have gone over, regu-
> lar habits can be inculcated and
> obedience can be taught even in in-
> fancy. By obedience is meant the
> yielding of a wayward and ignorant
> will to a firm and enlightened one.
> The child between three and six years
> of age learns clearly to distinguish
> self from others and to deliberate
> between alternative courses of action.
> It is highly important to control the
> elements which enter into the concept
> of self. The desire to choose the
> good is promoted chiefly by the sen-
> timent of reverence.[15]

Thus Felix Adler and the Ethical Culture

6.

movement sought to perfect society by inculcating the ethical values of society without question into young children. The values were a common secularized creed which were in the best interests of the unified society. A social gospel was generated which attempted to solve the "sublime problem of the perfect civilization, the just society, the 'Kingdom of God.'"[16]

C.

The nineteenth century was not only a time for the movement for a secularized, unified morality, it was also the breeding ground for the rise of scientific methodology and expertise. While the generation of a social gospel provided the rationale for the upswing in emphasis in moral and ethical education, the growth of a scientific expertise provided the methodology. The great influx from German universities of the works of Pestalozzi, Froebel, and Herbart stimulated the growth of a scientific pedagogy in the budding American Universities. The development of a scientific curriculum flooded the system, not only raising the status of teachers and educators, but also creating curricula based on the nature of the child.

The new authority on human nature was the University. The deification of science and scientific method placed it in the new role of defining human nature and morality. A role formerly held by the church or the home. It seems clear that this new power served to legitimize education. Robert Wiebe wrote:

By 1900, universities held an unquestioned power to legitimize, for no new profession felt complete or scientific without its distinct academic curriculum; they provided centers for philosophizing and propagandizing and they inculcated apprentices with proper values and goals.[17]

7.

The growing educational bureaucracy, gaining status along with the emerging sciences of psychology, child study and sociology, saw their primary function, according to Wiebe, to rationalize, uphold, and conserve the existing order of things.[18] The new faith in science and scientific method permeated society and manifested itself in the need for the bureaucratic ideals of order, continuity, and regularity. Swept up in a march for progress, the nation saw the educational system as the prime mover. Wiebe wrote:

> In fact an uncritical faith in 'education' almost matched the devotion for science with which it was closely identified, and extraordinary hopes for an alert and informed citizenry were invested in its promise.[19]

Much of the insistence upon moralized education during the late nineteenth century found its psychological warrant as well as its historical background and justification in the psychology and pedagogy of Johann Herbart and the subsequent work of Herbartians in Europe and America. While early in the nineteenth century Pestalozzi had influenced Horace Mann and other educators with his stress on stimulating the senses with object lessons, the latter part of the century saw the influx of the ideas of Herbart and Froebel.[20] Herbart's scientific pedagogy was to have a strong influence on the growth of many moral educators including Felix Adler, Charles De Garmo, William T. Harris, and Charles McMurry. Herbart's notion of "building up a firmly established self-contained moral character through the operation of the enlightened will"[21] would have a far-reaching effect on American moral educators.

Henry Felkin in his Introduction to Herbart's Science and Practice of Education published in 1898, wrote

8.

Herbart was the first to base pedagogy, the science of education, directly on ethics and psychology, and this is his great work for and service to mankind. From ethics he derived the end and aim of all teaching: virtue; from psychology, the means whereby it is compassed.[22]

The school had a duty to train the disposition and store the mind with knowledge. When instruction had generated knowledge that incited to a volition that is controlled by ethical ideas, the task of education would be complete. Once again the notion of an enlightened moral will molding the youth was apparent. Moral education did not attempt to generate an independent critical conscience but rather inculcate the prevalent ethical ideas of the society and fix them into habit. Herbart stressed the importance of not only increasing the perception of knowledge data, in thus apparent agreement with Pestalozzi, but also developing their apperception, their assimilation with memory contents, feelings and desires as well. The teacher was to impart the high ideals found in history, literature, and science, depending upon the cultural stage of the child, so as to secure their proper apperception and assimilation which would generate good thoughts and desires which would seek their satisfaction in the deeds arising from volition.[23]

Herbartian thought summed up the one and the whole work of education in the concept, "morality,"[24] with the means of achieving this goal by way of psychological theory. Felix Adler was not the only educator to make use of Herbart's cultural epoch theory and his concept of training the will. William T. Harris, U.S. Commissioner of Education, wrote the Introduction of Adler's Moral Instruction of Children. In it he stated that "right ideas are necessary to guide the will, but right habits are the product of the will itself."[25] While he stressed the need for development of an enlightened moral sense, Harris still saw good in "old-fashioned, implicit obedience."[26] The values Harris saw that needed development in the school were what he called the "semi-mechanical virtues of regularity, punctuality, silence, and industry."[27]

This new secularized morality was to make social efficiency the cornerstone of moral education. The moral obligation of the school was to impart values, not foster a sensitive moral judgment. Charles De Garmo, President of Swarthmore College and a dedicated Herbartian, also called for a non-sectarian teaching of morals in the schools. The teachers' goal, according to De Garmo, was to "bring about a permanent harmony between the individual subjective disposition of the heart and the laws that condition the stability and progress of human society."[28] The concept of service was important to moral educators and frequently justified the status quo. De Garmo wrote:

> We sometimes complain that our railroad magnates accumulate great wealth but what are the most magnificent private fortunes ever amassed in comparison with the vast service these road builders have rendered the country by opening up to settlement everywhere by developing its boundless resources, by bringing a market to every door, in short by rendering cooperation possible among a great people.[29]

De Garmo was clearly against a subjective and individual morality or conscience. He maintained the tradition of moral education of implanting a certain body of doctrine and their fixing of appropriate habits. The society was the authority and it sanctioned the morality. The National Herbart Society dedicated its Third Yearbook in 1897 to moral education. De Garmo spoke of the need to rid society of

the passive non-social individuals (the emotional
type, the aesthetic type, the philosopher, the
pioneer), in favor of a thoroughly socialized
individual. While he chastized the individualistic spirit of classical liberalism and the
American frontier, he maintained the need for
private property and private means of production.
His goal was social unity. It was no longer the
fear of evil that brought men together, but the
opportunity for good. The goal of moral education was to create the socialized person by
furnishing him with efficient social ideals,
fostering a desire to reach them, and fixing them
in habit.[30]

William T. Harris, on the other hand,
reiterated his concern for discipline, order,
self-control and subjugation of the child's will.
"Order," wrote Harris, "is heaven's first law."[31]
Children were to be obedient to the word of command. He also felt that the new machine age
required man to adopt new semi-mechanical virtues
which had to be trained into habits. The Herbartian notions of control, obedience to
authority, and molding of the child's will by an
enlightened one were very influential in the
development of moral education in the late nineteenth century.

Charles McMurry, an American Herbartian,
although stressing the importance of gathering
into the school course as much of the world's
accumulated store of culture as possible, in
order to exert educative influence upon growing
children, saw the best materials of culture which
history, literature and social and scientific
progress had to offer as "thoroughly domestic
Anglo-Saxon, American."[32] He also felt that
moral and social culture with all its humanizing
influence was contained in the choicest literature of America and Europe. There was no
perceived need for anything foreign or exotic.
The great body of doctrine from history, literature and science to be implanted in the children

would create a unified Anglo-Saxon heritage and outlook.

Merle Curti seemed to grasp the shortcomings of Herbartianism when he wrote:

> The Herbartians were foremost among educators who believed that the reform of the individual was the chief task of the school and that individual morality would be an all-sufficient cure for the social injustice of the day . . . It also oversimplified the relation of the good citizen to social and economic forces in the face of which he, as an individual, was impotent, in spite of his knowledge and goodness . . . By centering attention upon the development of moral quality in men and women, it overlooked, of course, the possibility that the existing system itself might be immoral.[33]

Criticisms of Herbartianism, however, were not limited to the historian. John Dewey, apparently opposed to the idea of training of the will, wrote:

> Herbartianism seems to me essentially a schoolmaster's psychology, not psychology of a child. It is the natural expression of a nation laying great emphasis upon authority and upon the formation of individual character in distinct and recognized subordination to the ethical demands made in war and in civil administration by that authority. It is not the psychology of a nation which professes to believe that every individual has within him the purpose of authority and that order means coordination, not subordination.[34]

While Dewey felt that training of the will should be supplanted by independence and firmness of action, conjoined with sincere deliberation and reasoned insight, his ideals were put to the crucial test with the onset of the First World War. The rational insight that he held so strongly would however eventually subordinate itself to the ethical demands of the wartime State.

John Dewey epitomized the educator who sought "scientific principles of conduct."[35] He was interested not only in the psychological influences on ethical behavior but the sociological influences as well. Interestingly enough, however, Dewey also bridged the gap between the new secularized morality and the social gospel dream of a kingdom of God on Earth. In his exposition entitled, "My Pedagogue Creed," written in 1897, he wrote:

> I believe that every teacher should realize the dignity of his calling, that he is a social servant set apart for the maintenance of proper social order and the securing of the right social growth. I believe that in this way the teacher always is the prophet of the true God and the usherer in of the true kingdom of God.[36]

D.

The development of moral education in the United States was greatly influenced by the secularization of morality, the growth of the social gospel and the scientific methodology and justification that it received from psychology. With the decline of the power of the Church and the family, the State assumed a much greater stature. The concept of the State as a divine institution was bolstered in this country by the influence of Hegelianism in the latter part of

13.

the nineteenth century.

Hegelianism not only justified the existing order but subordinated the individual to the
existing social institutions by maintaining that
his true, spiritual self, which was constantly
in conflict with his natural or physical self,
would be realized only by adjusting himself to
the divinely appointed environment and institutions that were in actual existence. In his
Philosophy of Right, Hegel wrote:

> The State finds in ethical custom
> its direct and unrelated existence and
> its indirect and reflected existence
> in the self-consciousness of the indi-
> vidual. The State . . . is the realized
> substantive will, having its reality
> in the particular self-consciousness
> raised to the plane of the universal
> . . . The individual has his truth,
> real existence, and ethical status
> only in being a member of it.[37]

William T. Harris was influenced deeply by
Hegelian thought which he discovered after
migrating from New England to St. Louis in 1857.
He felt that the Church, together with the State,
civil society, the family and the school was a
necessary and beneficent institution. From
Hegelian philosophy he obtained an optimistic
and idealistic social thought. All the world
was infused with a divine purpose which endowed
the individual with a noble and immortal destiny.
It also justified the existing order and authorities by maintaining that the present social
system was the inevitable stage in the unfolding
of objective reason and was therefore right.[38]

The notion of the State as the highest
manifestation of reason and therefore of right
was not limited to Harris. Felix Adler wrote in
his Moral Instruction of Children in 1892, that

14.

The present system of rights,
imperfect as it is, is the result
of social evolution and denotes the
high water mark of the average ethical consciousness of the world up to
date. Respect for the existing system of rights, however imperfect as
it is, is the prime condition of
obtaining a better system.[39]

The direct example of the link between the
social gospel movement and the influence of
Hegelian thought was a paper read by Washington
Gladden at the Fifth General Convention of the
Religious Education Association in Washington,
D. C., in 1908. Gladden insisted on the reinsti-
tution of moral aims in the public schools, which
he saw as chiefly intellectual. According to
Gladden's belief, unless the schools could produce good men and women they would be deemed
failures. Gladden then proceeded to describe
the State as "first of all a religious, a
divine institution, since it springs out of an
impulse divinely implanted in the human soil."[40]
Since its function was admitted to be the establishment of justice, Gladden agreed with Hegel
that it must also be a moral organization
because the primary element of morality is justice.

That is moral conduct by which
man realizes himself, completes his
manhood; and the rights which the
State maintains and protects are simply the opportunities of self-
realization.[41]

Thus it is clear that the conservative
right wing Hegelianism, which influenced Harris,
Adler, Gladden and others, permitted the exploitation of science for social and economic
purposes without sacrificing religion and the
concerns of the spirit as ultimate values.
It paid tribute to the cult of individuality

and self-realization, while at the same time
subordinating the mass of individuals to existing institutions. While often questioning the
morality and conduct of individuals, it seldom
ever criticized the social structure. The concepts of evolution and progress in an Hegelian
perspective dictated that the present State was
the highest manifestation of the divine spirit
in man. Moral education aimed at "getting the
right ideas into the minds of the people, to
teach them to see things as they are, and to
deal with them intelligently."[42] A person could
reach his true calling only if he aligned himself
with the rational dictates of the State. To follow these dictates was deemed the appropriate way
to accomplish self-realization and individuality.

The N E A Committee on Moral Education
reflected the concerns of moral educators in
maintaining that moral criticism was "education
of conscience."[43] Joseph Baldwin, the Committee's
1892 Chairman, stated that a rational act done
from a sense of duty was a moral act. Such moral
acts, rooted into habits and ingrained into character, would become moral virtues. The end
product of moral education, namely, moral virtue,
was perceived as the succession from "It is
right" to "It is my duty," to "I ought."[44]

Once again it is clear how the educational
State was to dictate morality by making duty the
key concept and using it as the rationale to fix
the actions of the child into habits which reflected the ideals of the State. Moral education
was not development of a critical, intellectually
sensitive conscience, but the training and control of the child's emotional conscience in the
best interests of the existing order.

Emerson White continued this emphasis in
his Report of the Committee on Moral Education
Report of 1896. Moral training was defined as
will training. The aim of moral education was
the training of the will to act habitually in

free obedience to duty. In an Herbartian perspective, White called for moral knowledge to
awaken feeling which would solicit the will that
would determine conduct.[45]

While William T. Harris advocated the
school virtues of regularity, punctuality, silence, industry and obedience; others stressed
the drive for purity and exactness. W. O. Thompson, President of Ohio State University, not only
felt that the "recognition of authority (was)
essential in education,"[46] but he also referred
to the worthiness of the "habit of accuracy, the
uncompromising attitude toward error, the
insistence upon exactness, neatness and cleanliness."[47]

Throughout the discussion of moral educators there was the constant reiteration that no
one could or should, for that matter, force a
student to be moral. A student could be educated
in an atmosphere conducive to morality and
taught all the ethical precepts but still may
choose to error. Thus a tremendous emphasis was
put on self-government and personal choice, so
that the student would of his own accord choose
the good. The opportunity for choice then became an important part of certain calls for moral
education. The power to choose wisely, however,
was seen to be acquired by the constant exercise
of the will. Thompson explained:

We are disposed, therefore, not
only to educate the intellect but to
train the will and to cultivate the
emotions, to bring into our educational processes an opportunity for a
rational choice, and to bring to the
younger pupils such opportunities as
they are capable of using.[48]

On the one hand, Thompson called for self-
reliance, self-direction, and self-determination,
while on the other he stressed the importance of

17.

training the will and cultivating the emotions. He states that "there can be no such thing as self-government until people have been trained in decisions and choices."[49] The concept of the good man had been redefined to become synonymous with that of the good citizen, and good citizens needed to be trained to make the right decisions. When an individual's conscience and will coincided with the dictates of society, then and only then was he considered free and able to make his own decisions wisely. Moral education would train pupils to become the best possible citizens.

This training was differentiated according to the cultural epoch that the child was thought to be in. The psychic corollary of the biological law that ontogeny recapitulates phylogeny stated that as the child matured he passed through the cultural epochs of the race. Thus the young child was at an early age put under the influence of a school whose moral code was deemed the highest before evil habits had become fixed and there, inspired by a spirit of order, patience was cultivated and habits of persistence were acquired. Upon entering adolescence at ages 11-15, the powers of self-control and self-direction were seen to take a rapid growth. It was during this crucial period that moral authority was supposedly switched from external control to self-control, but it actually seemed to be only an internalization of external authority. Moral education seemed to advocate an internalization of social control. One was deemed free to act in a moral and wise manner when he had internalized the dictates of the social system.

The issue of moral training in the public schools often instigated essay contests in an attempt to discover the best programs and justifications for moral education. These contests were usually sponsored by businessmen in the community who in most instances preferred to remain anonymous. Such a contest took place in

18.

California in 1907, with five hundred dollars do-
nated for first prize and three hundred dollars
for second prize. The judges were Rev. Charles
R. Brown of Oakland, California; Dr. David Starr
Jordan, President of Stanford University; and
Prof. Fletcher Dresslar of the Department of
Education of the University of California.[50]

Charles Rugh, Principal of Bay School in
Oakland, California, won the first prize while
Rev. T. P. Stevenson of Philadelphia won the
second prize. It is quite evident that the link
between scientific pedagogy and social gospel was
still strong. Whenever the discussion centered
around moral education, one could expect to find
not only clergy and educators but psychologists
and sociologists as well.

Rugh at the outset described the intellectual and scientific progress of society and how
the doctrine of evolution had transferred men's
thoughts and interest from the supernatural to
the natural. While "historically the church was
the mother of schools, by support and control
the state was now the father."[51] Rugh saw the
separation of Church and State and the raising
of the State into the place of supreme power as
a mandate for the State to train its children in
morality. The justifications used were the
evident moral decline in society which manifested
itself in an increase in the number of divorces,
dependent children, suicides, murders, robberies,
sales of intoxicating beverages, tobacco, coffee
and candy, as well as a disgust with the methods
of Standard Oil and the insurance companies.

Once again the attack of moral education
was aimed at individual persons and specific
methods employed, rather than a careful analysis
of the system itself. Also much of the evidence
of moral decline was once again concerned with
the purity ethic. Eating candy, smoking, and
drinking coffee were not viewed as physically
harmful, but were seen to indicate a growing

19.

desire for mere stimulation of the nervous system and thus morally wrong.[52]

Differing from some of the other moral educators, Rugh believed that all human development had its roots and life principles in the instincts and impulses of the individual. Thus the inherent seeds of morality and religion were in each child. Rugh disagreed with Felix Adler when he stated that moral instruction should give pupils a clear understanding of what is right and what is wrong, but it should not question why the right should be done and the wrong avoided. It was felt that the child would ask why and he had every reason to do so. He had to be given a chance to bring his instincts under rational control.

The move was from blind instinct to moral insight, with the school aiding this transition by training the judgment in later years and relying on obedience to authority in childhood. That same notion of implicit obedience found in Harris and White was echoed by Rugh:

> Fear is not a final principle for the government of intelligent beings, but it is a primary native instinct and must be employed as a primary principle of control . . . In this stage the inner law of the learner's life answers back to the moral order of the universe and the soul has discovered absolute authority under which freedom is achieved by joyous obedience.[53]

Rugh made use of the racial stage theory to explain and justify this use of obedience and authority at the early stages of youth, while calling for development of insight and reason later on. Rugh, however, felt that the authority of the parent and teacher went far deeper than "ipse dixit." Once again the notion of moral character as obedience to authority and to law was made evident. The moral man was the good citizen. The goal was to make teacher, parent and statute unnecessary. The moral soul would see that it was a law unto itself because it identified itself with the universal will and order, "Thy will be done in earth as it is in heaven."[54]

For Charles Rugh the standard of selection and the test of goodness was the unity of individual life with the unfolding, moral purpose of the world. The Hegelian perspective is clear. To be a true, free individual was to have internalized the dictates of the higher moral order. The whole of existence, nature, society and the child, was viewed as a progressive moral order developing according to inherent laws and principles. Education was the progressive development of the child in response to the order in nature and society. For Rugh, "the result of this adjustment of individual life to the order of nature and society (was) a moral person."[55] Thus, while the child is by essence moral, "moral training brings this unfolding child of God into progressive adjustment with the moral order of the universe by the knowledge of the truth."[56]

It is interesting how the goal of moral training, namely, the free moral agent, could be reached by joyous obedience to the laws of life and the State in general and the educational system in particular, was taken without question to reflect the universal absolute Truth. The State and the educational system, according to Rugh, had become the bearers of Truth. The view of the necessity of moral training was shared by Rev. T. P. Stevenson. He felt that if one wanted to eradicate moral evils and shape American society into a purer and nobler national character, that moral training of citizens through public education was a necessity. Stevenson also felt that "it was the unquestionable right

21.

and the imperative duty of the nation to perpetuate her moral character by training her
citizens into that character.[57]

This right of the nation to transmit its
national character to its new citizens clearly
manifested itself in Stevenson's feelings about
the immigrants. After describing the hetero-
geneous multitudes of immigrants who flocked to
America (1,026,499 in 1906 alone), and sympathiz-
ing with their flights from oppression and
burdensome social conditions, he recognized that

. . . Many of them are not in
accord with the distinctive moral
features of our national character.
Many of them antagonize laws designed
to elevate the character and improve
the morals of the people. Their
attitude makes slower and more difficult the uplift and moral progress of
the whole nation.[58]

Training the immigrant child in moral elements and national character (these terms were
slowly becoming equivalent) was deemed the duty
of the public school. Stevenson wanted moral
perfection, a nobler race. He also once again
reflected Hegel in his belief that the "State,
as well as the Church and the family (was) an
independent and divinely instituted society."[59]
This entitled the State, according to Stevenson,
to an independent responsibility and her own
unquestionable rights. The State was becoming
stronger and more powerful, not only in avenues
of social control expertise and bureaucratic
grasp, but it also seemed to be gaining a divine
justification as the highest manifestation of
the evolution of the divine spirit. It is then
clear how Rev. Stevenson could state that:

The effort should be to convince
every child of the wisdom, justice,
necessity, and goodness of every moral

law on the statute books of the
State, to make him feel that it is
an evil and shameful thing to
break any one of these laws; and
so to win his intelligent, reso-
lute and unquestioning loyalties
to them all.[60]

The notion of training the child's emotional life became increasingly important as the
discrepancies between school education and social
efficiency became clear. Cases were often cited
where college graduates became criminals and il-
literate men became useful citizens. Henry
Suzzallo, Adjunct Professor of Elementary Education at Teachers College, Columbia University,
wrote in 1907:

So long as such examples of the
lack of correlation between education
and character exist, the educator who
is trying to control human nature
through the school must take note of
a problem which questions the assumption that a mere intellectual training
is adequate for character-building.[61]

Suzzallo felt that the school's business
was to make sane, wholesome, responsive and
vigorous men and women, and thus the directions
of control were not to be restricted to the
intellectual but had to include the emotional
as well.

John Dewey stated that

To suppose in other words that a
good citizen is anything more than
a thoroughly efficient and service-
able member of society is a
hampering superstition which it is
hoped may soon disappear from educational discussion.[62]

23.

Dewey believed that social goals were needed and all that moral training really entailed was development of social intelligence. His criticism of moral education as "too narrow, too formal, and too pathological" seems to agree with Suzzalo's viewpoint exactly. Dewey was interested in social progress and thus moral laws had to be translated into the life of the community. To teach morality apart from the social system that the students had to act in every day, was useless.

> These moral principles need to be brought down to the ground through their statement in social and psychological terms. We need to see that moral principles are not arbitrary, that they are not 'transcendental;' that the term, 'moral,' does not designate a special region or portion of life. We need to translate the moral into the conditions and forces of our community life, and into the impulses of habits of the individual.[63]

F.

The Religious Education Association was organized by the Convention for Religious and Moral Education which met in Chicago February 10-12, 1903. The movement was initiated by the Council of Seventy on August 20, 1902. Six weeks later the movement received an overwhelming public endorsement and the support of more than four hundred eminent representatives of religious and moral education. The purpose of the association was to "promote religious and moral education."[64]

The threefold purpose of the Association, as stated in its first Journal volume was to

1. inspire the educational forces of our country with the religious ideal,

2. to inspire religious forces of our country with the educational ideal,

24.

3. to keep before the public the ideal of
   Religious Education and the sense of its
   need and value.[65]

Throughout the period of moral education and on
into the development of character education, the
Religious Education Association was an influential organization.

The organization's Journal, Religious
Education, echoed the prevalent opinion that
mere intellectual training was not sufficient to
develop character. Moral training was viewed as
a necessity, both in the Church and Sunday School,
as well as in the public schools. Nathaniel
Butler, Dean of the College of Education at the
University of Chicago, wrote in 1906 that

> Everybody assents to the gen-
> eral proposition that the ultimate
> values of education are to be
> expressed, not in terms of intellect
> but of character. And the final
> fruit of the educative process is
> intelligence and moral conduct. We
> seek the trained intelligence and
> the good will.[66]

The concepts of morality and moral training were greatly influenced by the findings of
psychology and religious pathology. It is clear
that the Journal of the Religious Education Association was a platform for the liberal clergy as
well as the scientist and businessman. The social
gospel goal of a kingdom of Heaven on Earth was
presented in various contexts which were consistent with scientific methodology and expertise.
The bond between religion and science was strong
and resilient in the articles represented in
Religious Education.

Elmer Ellsworth Brown, the U. S. Commissioner of Education in 1907, wrote of the bond
between education and science. He not only felt

that science ruled the thoughts of men but that
its pure devotion to truth made it moral. In this
way the findings of the scientific community
would give the moral tone to educational endeavors. Brown wrote:

> The best that education draws
> from the scientific alliance is not
> even the perfected method which
> science has to teach, but its moral
> elevation, its power to awaken a
> new devotion to truth.[67]

This new devotion to truth unfortunately
was not as objective as it was described. Value
considerations and social context played important roles in guiding the formulation of problems
to be solved and likewise structured the answers
that were eventually found. Religious Education
contained articles on the racial theory of emotions and instincts;[68] the necessity of eugenics;[70] and the sociology of moral education.[71]
All of these articles seemed to foster the notion
that the religious impulse was instinctual and
part of man's racial heritage. It likewise used
psychological and sociological dogma to replace
the theological dogma which it thought was out-
dated. The ideals of progress and perfectability
of man when coupled with the desire for purposeful social action made the reformer, whether the
clergy of the social gospel or the scientific
psychologist, susceptible to eugenics. It was
not incompatible with his theoretical framework
or much sought after goal of a perfect society.

Another notion that was prevalent in the
Religious Education Journal was the relation of
industrial and commercial training to the development of character. Vocational schools were
seen to fit a man better to do some work in
which he would take pride and from which he
could earn a livelihood. The main value to be
instilled was pride. If the worker had pride in
his job, no matter how menial a task it was, he

26.

would be safeguarded from the temptations that
beset the idle and would have a constant incentive to better achievement. James Russell, Dean
of Teachers College at Columbia, wrote:

> Insofar as this training af-
> fords an understanding of scientific
> principles and gives an insight into
> the conditions that justify the ex-
> penditure of human labor and explains
> the motives that control social
> conduct, it makes for social service
> and intelligent citizenship.[72]

The relationship between character training and industry was a bond that would grow
stronger with time. Not only was manual training
in the schools viewed as a favorable means to
"train the will, judgment and perseverance,"[73]
but also moral or character training itself was
a valuable way to make better workers and con-
sumers.

Marshall Field and other prominent Chicago
merchants wanted to re-establish religious instruction in the city's public schools because
boys and girls were less dependable and less
reliable.[74] The pressures for a more adequate
citizenship training had now been joined by the
industrial and merchant group.

The notion of being a good moral person
had come not only to mean being a good citizen
but a good worker and consumer as well. The
values that one appealed to in describing and
justifying the good man became the values of the
State and Industry. Concepts such as patriotism,
social efficiency and good citizenship were
slowly evolving out of the concept of the moral
man. To be a moral man was to be a patriotic,
obedient, socially efficient worker.

At the New York Conference of the Religious
Education Association in 1911 a set of resolutions
were adopted regarding the moral phases of public

27.

education. The members believed "that the moral aim, i.e., the formation of character, should be treated as fundamental in all education."[75] The resolutions included recommendations for more teacher opportunity for personal contact and influence as well as a call for direct moral instruction to develop the power and habit of moral thoughtfulness. This question of direct versus indirect instruction would continue to be a battleground for years to come. Resolution number nine "approved of the greatly increased emphasis in the teaching of the biological sciences laid upon personal and institutional hygiene and in particular upon sex-hygiene and eugenics." [76]

G.

The National Education Association was also very influential in the growth of moral education and its gradual transformation to citizenship training. In its declaration adopted in 1905,

> The Association regrets the revival in some quarters of the idea that the common school is a place for teaching nothing but reading, spelling, writing and ciphering; and takes this occasion to declare that the ultimate object of popular education is to teach the children how to live righteously, healthily, and happily and that to accomplish this object, it is essential that every school inculcate the love of truth, justice, purity and beauty through the study of biography, history, ethics, natural history, music, drawing and manual arts. . . The building of character is the real aim of the schools and the ultimate reason for the expenditure of millions for their maintenance.[77]

In 1906 the National Education Association published a list of 58 papers on moral and religious education presented at their conventions in the 47 years from 1859-1906.[78] A short bibliography, prepared especially for Europe in 1908, contained nearly 100 titles for Great Britain and 300 for the Continent.[79] In 1908 the N.E.A. appointed a committee of its National Council to investigate and submit a "Tentative Report on a system of teaching morals in the Public School." The report, submitted in 1911, reflected the evolution of moral education into training for citizenship and social efficiency.

The Committee described the great scientific progress and accumulation of wealth over the preceding decades, but it also pointed out the new problems which had arisen; these included public health, food adulteration, exploitation of labor by capital, industrial safety, boycotts, lockouts, and strikes. In addition, the Committee reiterated the nation's continuing concern with the increases in vagrancy, pauperism, drunkenness, gambling, licentiousness, divorce, fraud, theft, arson, assaut and murder.[80]

It was clearly evident to the Committee that the chief problems in society were ethical problems and what was needed most was a common morality. While it was recognized that a high percentage of crime was due to ignorance and inefficiency, it was also seen that learning and skill training would not solve the most pressing economic, social and political problems. What was needed was the awakening of moral conscience, the development of moral judgment, and the guiding of moral principles.

Not only was it important to fix society's virtues into habit; it was deemed necessary to inculcate a proper regard for law and order. The notions of purity and unity secularized into a common morality were the continuing emphasis of moral education. The virtues stressed, however, included obedience, honor, truthfulness, cleanliness, honesty, self-control and justice; in addition, it reflected the growing nationalistic fervor as represented by such virtues as patriotism, heroism and duty.[81]

The school's function was seen to include the creation of an intelligent, knowledgeable populace, as well as having a mandate to train obedient, law-abiding citizens.

Proper regard for law and
properly constituted authority
should be inculcated in the child
from the time he enters the public
school, to the end that, when he
leaves it, he will continue to respect and obey the law and endeavor
to have others do likewise. The
public school which fails to inculcate proper regard for law and order
had failed in one of its chief duties.[82]

Moral education continued to reflect the values of respect for authority, law and order, discipline, duty, service, formation of good habits, social efficiency and training of the will. The goal of moral education, as stated by M. C. Brumbaugh, Superintendent of Schools, Philadelphia, was to enable the pupil of his own will to choose, and then to do, the right thing. If this could be accomplished, then the work of the school had been justified in the most direct way. Brumbaugh felt, however, that the pupil had to be taught to be right as well as to think right. The source of the sanction for right moral discipline for Brumbaugh, as well as other moral educators, was the State. He believed in a state-sanctioned morality founded directly upon Hegel's analysis of moral disci-pline which he used to provide the theoretical framework for his study. It was clear to him that guidance would only be effective when a goal was visioned so "for this reason it is

30.

necessary to construct in the soul of the child
a standard of moral and spiritual excellence
toward which all the objective forces at work
upon the child may move."[83]

The concern with the school as a training
institution for social efficiency was gaining
in momentum. The purpose of the school was
viewed by many as training men and women in useful skills which would make them good workers
and happy citizens. A connection between
immorality and industrial efficiency was frequently pointed out. Vocational training was
seen to be the base of necessity which would also
affect the life of the people industrially,
socially and morally. John W. Carr wrote:

Girls of all classes should have
the opportunity to learn domestic art,
domestic economy, the nurture and
care of children--in short, how to be
home-keepers. Every boy should have
an opportunity, at least, to begin
the preparation for some kind of a
vocation by which he can become a pro-
ducer of something society needs and
which will enable him to support a
family.[84]

This statement is significant for many
reasons. It points out how those concerned with
moral education felt that the main problems in
society were due to inefficiency and individual
maladjustments and how if everyone had a job
and was an obedient, respectful citizen, everything would be stable. Moral education never
challenged the basic values of society (the
obvious sex-role stereotyping in this case),
but instead tried to inculcate them on a wider
basis.

Also, this statement reflects the growing
concern with the moral man as the good worker.
Notions of individual dignity and self-worth

melted away in the hot pursuit of the goal of the good citizen and the good worker. A man was seen to be moral if he would produce something valuable to society and which enabled him to support a family. Moral education was also becoming more concerned with civic patriotism as expressed in obedience to law and faithful discharge of public duty.[85]

James M. Greenwood, Superintendent of Schools in Kansas City, Missouri, was the Chairman of the N.E.A. Committee on Moral Education in 1911. His report stressed the importance of habit formation, so that the "habits should sink somewhat below the plane of consciousness so that one acts automatically and in the right direction as the result of physical and mental control.[86]

Morality was thus defined in this case as an automatic response to the fundamental principles of society. The teachers were viewed as the molders of public opinion who, since they possessed the highest ethical principles, could lead the pupils into the habits and practices which would make them into good breeders in society.

Obedience once again was put forth as the supreme ideal. Greenwood saw man's freedom consisting of his "obedience to laws which he cannot change."[87] Obedience marked the difference between the savage and the civilized man. It also was seen to prepare the way for sympathy and usefulness. Greenwood not only defined the moral man as useful, sympathetic and obedient, but he also stressed the importance of purity and cleanliness as well as the habits of industry and strict attention to business.

Once again the moral deficiencies in society were seen to be a result of individual maladjustments. It was the purpose of the school to make problem children over, to remodel them by means of "educational surgery."[88] The school

was seen to be designed to take care of the
child's body, to expand his intellect, to control
his emotions, and to regulate his will. The assumption that a man had to find all meaning and
justification for his existence in his role or
work in society was once again prevalent.
Greenwood wrote, "When one has found his place
of work for life, it is his duty to adhere to
it, otherwise life is meaningless."[89]

Clifford Barnes, Executive Chairman of the
International Committee on Moral Training, felt
that a new era was coming, which he called the
children's age. He saw a movement for a new
sense of responsibility for the right development of child life.

> But most significant of all the
> signs which herald the coming of this
> new age is the earnest effort being
> made by educational authorities to
> increase the efficiency of the public
> schools as an agency for the develop-
> ment of character.[90]

Barnes accurately described the breakdown
of the authority of the church and the home and
pointed out how the school was becoming more and
more in loco parentis, both as regards the soul
and the mind of its pupils. The cry was raised
to make the school a greater safeguard of the
nation's virtue, and to increase its efficiency
as an agency for moral training and the development of character.[91]

The personality of the teacher was seen
to be the strongest influence on the development
of the pupil's character. The teacher was seen
to have a high calling, probably because many
teachers had been clergy in the nineteenth century and as the role secularized it replaced the
clergy as moral educator. The home life of the
pupil on the other hand was generally condemned
as a hindrance to the teacher in the development

33.

of student character.

H.

Moral and ethical education were greatly
influenced by the rise of the social gospel and
the secularization of morality so prevalent
in the latter part of the nineteenth century.
The State in general and the educational system
in particular were seen to be the new bearers of
morality. In order to generate a common ethical
base, a perfect civilization, a just society, a
kingdom of God on Earth, it was necessary to
naturalize the old dream of salvation into the
new dream of character formation.

Moral education drew heavily from the
psychological theory of Herbart and its reliance
upon respect for authority and supremacy of law.
It also placed a high value on purity and unity
as well as upon obedience. Hegelian thought
gave it the rationale for a state-sanctioned
morality. The State became recognized as a
divine institution and thus was entitled to sanction the appropriate morality and justice.

The values promoted by moral educators
included regularity, punctuality, silence, order,
industry, obedience, purity, exactness, neatness
and cleanliness; values which reflected not only
the demands of the social gospel but ones which
enabled man to function in a semi-mechanical
way in an industrial society. Also important
were the values of discipline, self-control and
subjugation of the child's will.

Gradually the concept of the good man
became redefined to mean the good citizen, the
good worker, the good consumer, and the good pro-
ducer. The social gospel virtues of the liberal
clergy were infused with the values of the State,
industrial and mercantile sectors.

Social efficiency was a key concept and

value assumption of moral education. The good man was judged by his social efficiency and his obedience to the authority of the State. It was felt that a man could only be truly free when he acted in joyous obedience to the absolute authority. Hegelian thought greatly influenced the assumption of the State as the highest form of social evolution. When the pupil learned to internalize the values of society and act from habit alone, then and only then would he be free to realize his own individuality. Freedom was defined as obedience to law.

Moral education as well as the character education which followed tended to blame the problems of society upon individual maladjustments or defects. In the beginning moral educators sought to retain the purity and unity ethic in their drive for a secularized morality, while gradually morality became redefined to represent social efficiency, patriotism, good citizenship, and a strong work ethic. In either case, the inefficiencies found or the moral decline evidenced was seen to be caused by individuals or groups and thus needed remedial treatment. The basic value assumptions and the structure of society were seldom if ever questioned.

With the onset of the First World War, the nationalistic, jingoistic fervor in America would strengthen and greatly influence the generation of a concern for character education. Character education would also define the good man as the good citizen and the good worker, but with a stronger emphasis on patriotism, duty and civic training. The evolution of morality into civic responsibility would be complete. The concept of the good man was redefined to become synonymous with that of the good citizen. While a person was thought to have good character in the nineteenth century if he was moral, just, and kind, in the twentieth century good character meant loyalty, citizenship, and obedience.

[1]The essence of phrenology was that there were unique differences in the propensities of individuals and thus men were not created with equal intellect or moral capacity. For Mann this gave education a mandate to nourish the propensities that expressed themselves in righteous and human behavior and restrain the ravenous and tyrannizing ones that led to selfishness and indifference to human suffering.

[2]See Jacob Abbott, The Teacher, Moral Influences Employed in the Instruction and Governance of the Young (New York: Harper and Brothers, 1856), pp. iii-iv, 70.

[3]The notion of social gospel has traditionally been understood to refer to the moderate progressive school of Christian social theory which developed out of the teachings of such men as Washington Gladden, and Walter Rauschenbush. (See Henry May, Protestant Churches and Industrial America (New York: Harper and Row, 1967) and Charles Hopkins, The Rise of the Social Gospel in American Protestantism, 1865 - 1915 (New Haven: Yale University Press, 1967). In this presentation the concept will be expanded to include other aspects of secularized morality which also sought a kingdom of Heaven on Earth, including areas of Reform Judaism, Unitarianism, and Catholicism.)

[4]Richard Hofstadter, Social Darwinism in American Thought (New York: Beacon Press, 1955), p. 107.

[5]Richard Hofstadter, Age of Reform (New York: Vintage Press, 1955), p. 135.

[6]W. C. Larrabee, Second Annual Report of
the Superintendent of Public Instruction, Indiana,
1853, p. 31.

[7]Howard Radest, Toward Common Ground
(New York: Ungar Co., 1969), p. 1. Similar
societies sprang up in Chicago (1883), Philadelphia (1885), and St. Louis (1886).

[8]Felix Adler, The Moral Instruction of
Children (New York: D. Appleton and Co., 1892),
p. 243.

[9]Radest, op. cit., p. 31

[10]Ibid., p. 97.

[11]Adler, op. cit., pp. 266-267.

[12]Ibid., p. 270.

[13]M. W. Meyerhardt, "The Movement for
Ethical Culture at Home and Abroad," American
Journal of Religious Psychology and Education, 3,
May 1908, p. 78.

[14]Adler, op. cit., p. 15.

[15]Ibid., p. 58.

[16]Ibid., p. 30.

[17]Robert Wiebe, The Search for Order (New
York: Hill and Wang, 1967), p. 121.

[18]Ibid., p. 153.

[19]Ibid., p. 157.

[20]Both stressed the importance of recognizing the fact that the child recapitulated the
cultural epochs of the race. Herbart studied the
child to find the best that could be done for it,

while Froebel studied it to work out its best development. Herbart was more coercive and used a larger amount of compulsion to secure reform and progress than did Froebel. Herbart studied the child to mold it; Froebel studied the child to guide it in growth. Herbart saw the need of control much more clearly than the need of freedom while Froebel sought a harmony between the two. Froebel saw the human soul as divine, while Herbart saw its function solely as a means of entering into relations with the external world. For further information see James L. Hughes, "Comparison of the Educational Theories of Froebel and Herbart," NEA Proceedings, 34, 1895, pp. 538-545.

[21] Henry Felkin, An Introduction to Herbart's Science and Practice of Education (Boston: D. C. Heath and Co., 1898), p. 5.

[22] Ibid., p. 7.

[23] See Felkin, op. cit., also Johann F. Herbart, The Science of Education and the Aesthetic Revelation of the World (Boston: D. C. Heath and Co., 1893).

[24] Herbart, op. cit., p. 57.

[25] William T. Harris, "Introduction," to Felix Adler, Moral Instruction of Children (New York: D. Appleton and Co., 1892), p. v.

[26] Ibid., p. vi.

[27] Ibid., p. vii.

[28] Charles De Garmo, "Ethical Training in the Public Schools," Annals of American Academy of Political and Social Science, 2, 1891-1892, p. 579. See also De Garmo's "A Basis for Ethical Training in Elementary Schools," NEA Proceedings, 30, 1891, pp. 179-177.

[29]Ibid., p. 596. For another plea for service, see G. Stanley Hall, Educational Problems II (New York: D. Appleton and Co., 1911), pp. 667-682.

[30]Charles De Garmo, "Social Aspects of Moral Education," National Herbart Society Yearbook, 3, 1897, pp. 35-56. See also De Garmo's Herbart and the Herbartians (New York: Charles Scribner's Sons, 1896) and Principles of Secondary Education--Ethical Training (New York: MacMillan Co., 1910).

[31]William T. Harris, "The Relation of School Discipline to Moral Education," National Herbart Society Yearbook, 3, 1897, p. 59.

[32]Charles McMurry, "Round Table Report to the National Council of the Influence of Herbart's Doctrine on the Course of Study in the Common Schools," NEA Proceedings, 34, 1895, p. 475.

[33]Merle Curti, Social Ideas of American Educators (Patterson: Littlefield Adams & Co., 1959), p. 254.

[34]John Dewey, "Interest as Related to Will," Second Supplement to National Herbart Society Yearbook, 1895, p. 29.

[35]John Dewey, "Ethical Principles Underlying Education," National Herbart Society Yearbook, 3, 1897, p. 7.

[36]John Dewey, My Pedagogue Creed (Chicago: A Flanagan Co., 1897), p. 17.

[37]Found in Joseph Kinmont Hart, A Critical Study of Current Theories of Moral Education, Ph.D. Dissertation (Chicago: University of Chicago Press, 1910), p. 32-33. Dr. Hart also explains the psychological, sociological, ethical

39.

and logical implications and debates in the
development of moral theory.

[38]Curti, op. cit., p. 313. See also John
S. Roberts, William T. Harris, A Critical Study
of His Educational and Related Philosophic Views
(Washington, D. C.: National Education Association, 1924), William T. Harris, "Social Culture
in the Form of Education and Religion," Educational Review, Vol. XXIX, 1905, pp. 18-37.

[39]Adler, op. cit., p. 223.

[40]Washington Gladden, "Bringing All the
Moral and Religious Forces Into Effective Educa-
tional Unity," Education and National Character
(Chicago: R. R. Donnelly and Sons, 1908), p. 35.

[41]Ibid.

[42]Ibid., p. 38.

[43]Joseph Baldwin, "Report of the Committee
on Moral Education," NEA Proceedings, 31, 1892,
p. 761.

[44]Ibid., p. 762.

[45]Emerson E. White, "Moral Instruction in
Elementary Schools," NEA Proceedings, 35, 1896,
pp. 407-410.

[46]W. O. Thompson, "Effect of Moral Education in Public Schools Upon the Civic Life of
the Community," NEA Proceedings, 1906, p. 44.

[47]Ibid., p. 45.

[48]Ibid., pp. 46-47. Emphasis added.

[49]Ibid., p. 47. See also "The Means Afforded by the Public Schools for Moral and
Religious Training," Thomas A. Mott (Superintendent of Schools, Richmond, Indiana), NEA
Proceedings, 1906, pp. 35-42. Mott stressed the

importance of self-control, discipline, and training of civic morality. He also described the use of the playground, gymnasium, manual training courses, and the kindergarten in the development of moral training.

[50] Moral Training in the Public Schools, The California Prize Essays (Boston: Ginn and Co., 1907).

[51] Ibid., Charles Rugh Essay, p. 4.

[52] Ibid., p. 5.

[53] Ibid., pp. 14-15.

[54] Ibid., p. 17.

[55] Ibid., p. 51.

[56] Ibid.

[57] Ibid., Rev. T. P. Stevenson Essay, p. 58.

[58] Ibid., p. 61.

[59] Ibid., pp. 63-64.

[60] Ibid., p. 79-80.

[61] Henry Suzzallo, "The Training of the Child's Emotional Life," NEA Proceedings, 45, 1907, p. 906.

[62] John Dewey, Moral Principles in Education (Boston: Houghton Mifflin Co., 1909), p. 9. See also "Ethical Principles Underlying Education," National Herbart Society Yearbook, 3-4, 1897-1898, p. 11.

[63] Ibid., p. 58.

[64] The Religious Education Association Handbook, 1903-1904, Chicago, p. 5.

[65]Religious Education, 1, 1906, p. 2.

[66]Nathaniel Butler, "The Moral and the Religious Element in Education," Religious Education, 1, Aug. 1906, p. 89.

[67]Elmer Ellsworth Brown, "Some Relations of Religious Education and Secular Education," Religious Education, 2, Oct. 1907, p. 124.

[68]See John Dashiell Stoops, "Psychological Bases of Religious Nature," Religious Education, 1, Oct. 1906, p. 123, 127. Stoops was a Professor at Iowa College who wrote about the instinctual racial nature of emotions as opposed to intellect and will which were seen as individualistic. Women were seen as more racial and less individual than men. Stoops also described various personality types as well as maintaining that religion was instinctive and thus did not need to be created or proved, but the necessity was in training and developing an already existing impulse.

[69]See John Dashiell Stoops, "The Emotional Element in Religious Education," Religious Education, 2, Aug. 1907, p. 96.

[70]See G. Stanley Hall, "Eugenics," Religious Education, 6, 1911, pp. 152-166. Hall wrote of relationship of sex and eugenics to essence of Christianity. He wanted to find out practical ways of improving the human stock and helping the world on towards the kingdom of some kind of superman (p. 159).

[71]Edwin Starbuck, "Moral and Religious Education--Sociological Aspect," Religious Education, 3, Feb. 1909, pp. 203-217. Starbuck also wrote of the instinctual religious impulse. He was a student of G. Stanley Hall.

42.

[72]James E. Russell, "The Relation of Industrial and Commercial Training to the Development of Character," Religious Education, 3, Oct. 1908, p. 132. See also Charles Zeublin, "The Relation of Commercial and Industrial Training to the Development of Character," Religious Education, 3, 1908-1909, pp. 135-137.

[73]Samuel Dutton, "Religious and Ethical Influence of Public Schools," Religious Education, 1, 1906, p. 50.

[74]Charles Williams, "Patriotism as an Instrument for Moral Instruction in the Public Schools," Religious Education, 2, June 1907, p. 58.

[75]"Resolutions on the Moral Phases of Public Education," Religious Education, 6, 1911-1912, p. 117.

[76]Ibid., p. 118. The importance of sex education and eugenics to the R.E.A. is evidenced by the statement in Henry F. Cope's Ten Years Progress in Religious Education, the Religious Education Association, Chicago, 1913, p. 20.

[77]Declarations, NEA Proceedings, 45, 1905, p. 43.

[78]Fiftieth Anniversary Volume, NEA Proceedings, 1906, p. 715.

[79]Michael Ernest Sadler, Moral Instruction and Training in Schools (London: Longmans, Green, and Co., 1908).

[80]"Tentative Report of the Committee on a System of Teaching Morals in the Public Schools, NEA Proceedings, 49, 1911, p. 343.

[81]Ibid., pp. 344-345.

43.

[82] Ibid., p. 345.

[83] M. C. Brumbaugh, "Moral Education: The Problem State," NEA Proceedings, 49, 1911, p. 349.

[84] John W. Carr, "Moral Education Thru the Agency of the Public Schools," Nea Proceedings, 49, 1911, p. 373.

[85] Ibid., pp. 373-374.

[86] James M. Greenwood, "The Home and School Life," NEA Proceedings, 49, 1911, p. 381.

[87] Ibid., p. 382.

[88] Ibid., p. 386.

[89] Ibid., p. 397

[90] Clifford W. Barnes, "Status of Moral Training in the Public Schools," NEA Proceedings. 49, 1911, p. 401.

[91] Ibid., p. 402.

II. THE IMPACT OF THE FIRST WORLD WAR ON THE NATIONALISTIC STRESS ON CHARACTER OVER INTELLECT

A.

The turn of the last century marked the entrance of America into the international community. The crucial concepts of order, stability and law, which were so vital to moral educators in this country, were translated into notions of international brotherhood and world peace. While the American Ethical Union was formed in New York in 1889, Ethical societies were subsequently founded in Great Britain, Ireland, France and Germany. An International Union of Ethical Societies was founded in 1893 and International Conferences on Moral Education were held in England in 1908 and 1911 and in Holland in 1912.[1] As Robert Wiebe pointed out, the American drive for peace abroad was but a projection of its desire at home.

> In place of a European policy, Americans pursued peace. A word of manifold meanings, it managed to encompass most of their sssumptions about modern civilization. Peace connoted order and stability, the absence of violence, the supremacy of reason and law. It suggested the disappearance of militarism and all other vestiges of a barbaric past. It implied, in other words, a world operating from the same general precepts so many Americans were trying to realize at home.[2]

The American drive for peace manifested itself in the National Peace Congress, held in New York in 1907. A direct outgrowth of this Congress was the formation of the American School Peace League. The League stressed the necessity of beginning early in life to "inculcate the broad ideas of international justice, universal brotherhood, and world organization."[3] The American School Peace League soon became a familiar organization to all teachers in both public and private schools. The League's objective, as stated in its Constitution, was to "promote through the schools and educational public of America, the interests of international justice and fraternity.[4] Dr. James H. Van Sickle was the first President of the League and served until 1913, when Dr. Randall J. Condon replaced him. The movement expanded rapidly and by 1919 it had branches in 45 states. Like the Ethical Culture Society, this peace movement also spread across the Atlantic to England and Ireland.

The American School Peace League maintained a positive relationship with the National Education Association. In 1909 the N.E.A. meeting in Denver passed the following resolution:

> The National Education Association endorses the purpose of the American School Peace League. The Association believes that the principles of the League will make for effective citizenship and urges all teachers to acquaint themselves with the work of the League and to cooperate with it.[5]

The League sponsored oratorical contests, state-wide essay contests and even offered peace medals in the pursuit of order, stability and peace. While these goals were in many ways synonymous with those of moral education, they gradually moved away from a personal morality towards social responsibility, citizenship, and patriotism. The good man was no longer seen as merely one who obeyed the precepts of the secularized, unified morality and was thus socially efficient, but he/she was also defined as the good patriotic citizen. The gradual change in emphasis from moral education to character education was manifested in this evolution of the moral person into the good citizen.

As a result of its joint sessions with the
annual conventions of the American Institute of
Instruction, the League published a course of
study in History for elementary grades (5 vols.)
and later a course in Citizenship and Patriotism
(grades 1-8). The League held to the view that:

> Surely a child who receives
> instruction from this book through
> all the elementary grades will enter
> upon life with a broad view of citi-
> zenship and patriotism and an
> appreciation of law, justice and
> government.[6]

The League's commitment to peace and brotherhood seemed foreshadowed by the drive for
patriotism and citizenship. In order to be a
good moral person one had to be an obedient,
faithful citizen. It was thus not inconceivable
for the League, like many of the academic community who were also committed to rationality,
progress, and peace, to eventually side with
President Wilson when World War I broke out.[7]
In 1917 the League announced its policy to co-
operate with the President in his aims to
safeguard the principle of democracy throughout
the world and to lay the foundation for a durable
peace. Thus demonstrating the flexibility of
American pragmatic thought and the perceived
need of remaining in an influential power position, the League changed its emphasis from
international justice and brotherhood to training
in democracy and citizenship.

The implicit concerns with order and
stability, once manifested in a drive for international peace, now became the rationale for war.
The American School Peace League issued a "Call
to Patriotic Service," which sought:

1. To maintain a civic and moral stability

47.

among the youth of the country.

2. To inspire anew a love of American institutions and American ideals.

3. To foster civic service appropriate to youth, consciously entered upon for the nation's welfare.

4. To hold to the ideal of the ultimate triumph of democracy.[8]

The notions of international justice and universal brotherhood melted away in a wave of nationalistic jingoism as the nation engaged in a mission to "save the world for democracy." Citizenship training played a strong role, not only in maintaining belief in American values and institutions during the war, but it also attempted to dispel any dissent or criticism.

The Schools sought to instill in school children the desire to help win the war by heightening the general morale, calling for food conservation and by encouraging hatred of the Germans and devotion to the Stars and Stripes. There was ample evidence of the undiluted patriotism of the teachers and educators.[9]

The schools were to bear the burden of maintaining the ideals of democracy at home.   In 1918 the N.E.A. appointed a Commission on the National Emergency in Education to coordinate the various types of war-time service work assigned to the schools, to find the means of alleviating the teacher-shortage problem, and to study the relationship of the educational system to the weaknesses of our national life, which the war crisis had revealed.[10]

The N.E.A., in a resolution typical of the extreme nationalistic thought at the time, demanded the employment of only those teachers who proved their loyalty to our national ideals.[11]

While the more hysterical aspects of this patriotism subsided after the war, the impetus given to the patriotic, nationalistic function of the schools remained a persistent influence on American education.

After the War, the American School Peace League changed its name to the American School Citizenship League to emphasize the "new obligation of the citizen in the new world order."[12]

The need was seen for the schools to mold the thought of children to a new light, namely, to reconstruct education so as to weld together divergent interests of the many races represented in this vast country into a "solid phalanx for democracy and justice throughout the world."[13] America was perceived as an active member of the international community, whether in peace or war. For those in the American School Peace League, America had arisen to shape the affairs of the struggling nations throughout the world. Inextricably tied up in this notion were the haughty American beliefs in our Manifest Destiny, and our duty to Save the World for Democracy. The American School Citizenship League continued to mold character by the use of courses in Patriotism, Citizenship and History, as well as the promotional use of contests and awards.

The Committee on Democracy, headed by A. Duncan Yocum of the University of Pennsylvania, had previously been a sub-committee on curriculum of the Committee on Superintendents' Problems, but the outbreak of the First World War turned its attention to the existing democratic factors in American life and education. A product of the N.E.A. Commission of Emergency in Education, the Committee created a Democracy Questionnaire to be sent to a selected group of cities. This project was subsequently adopted as a research project by the U.S. Bureau of Education. The Committee also studied the increasing compulsion exercised as a result of the War by the State and society upon the individual, and finally attempted to study the subject and strengthen the contribution to democracy made by several school subjects and forms of school work.[14]

Interestingly enough, Yocum's Committee found that religion should play an even greater role in the teaching of democracy. The growth of a secularized morality had manifested itself in a state-sanctioned ethic, namely democracy. The social gospel had found a new secular religion, one whose laws and duties were laid down by the State. This strong bond between secularized religion and the State in the maintenance of order, stability, and control was clearly evident in the following resolution made by Yocum at the 1921 meeting of the National Council of Education. It was endorsed by the Council.

> In view of the dependence of democracy upon religion, and the attacks to which all churches and all democratic governments are alike being subjected by radicals and the emissaries of nations now under radical control, it is the duty of all churches, irrespective of differences in creed, to unite in an effort to make religious education more universal and efficient, to emphasize democratic elements in religious instruction, and to correlate religious instruction with all the elements in public school education helpful to religion. It is the duty of public school authorities to emphasize all non-religious elements in instruction which tend to make religious education more intelligent and efficient and to organize some systematic form of moral instruction in every public school.[15]

B.

In theory, the American concept of a meritocracy entailed rule, not by the privileged or the rich, but government by the moral and intellectual elite. Social inequalities were to be eliminated so that natural inequalities could best manifest themselves in a hierarchical democracy based on merit. Edward Ross summarized this belief in the following manner:

Socially, democracy insists that the grading of folks on the basis of birth or rank or calling or cash is course and barbaric. It does not deny that men are as gold, silver and copper in relative worth. But it wants men rated not by place or trappings, but by essential things--wisdom, character, efficiency . . . democracy, at its best, substitutes the direction of the recognized moral and intellectual elite for the rule of the strong, the rich, or the privileged.[16]

The importance of both character and intelligence had been stressed throughout the American educational experience. It was clearly seen how intellect alone was insufficient for success in life. The First World War, however, greatly accentuated this distinction and generated a movement for Character Education. Character Education not only stressed development of social responsibility, good citizenship, and patriotic fervor, but it also was in agreement with Ruskin's statement that "education is not to teach men what they do not know, but to teach men to behave as they do not behave."[17] This quote seems to summarize nicely the clear distinction put forth between intellectual training and emotional or conduct training. As the understanding of the mind and its control became more secure during the twentieth century, education for control of behavior became more prominent.

America's confrontation with Germany during the War was undertaken with a certain uneasiness. Americans had borrowed freely from Germany's rich cultural heritage and many reformers in this country had praised its neat, efficient ways. Furthermore, many Americans had German ancestors.[18] The problem was how to criticize the rational, scientific, efficient culture that we had borrowed from so freely. The belief in progress and growth to perfection was dealt a terrible blow by this new appraisal of the German nation. The ultimate problem of the Germans was finally determined to be not their intellect but their character. Guy Fernald wrote:

> It is not the intellect but the character of our efficient enemy in Germany that we despise . . . While it is our own intelligence that dictates our instinctive contempt for the Kaiser's principles, the dictation would be void without our character to express and enforce it.[19]

This distinction between thought and character was, as previously pointed out, crucial to character education. It was not enough to encourage growth and development in intellect without the corresponding development of moral ideals and conduct. This revelation was seen by many as a tremendous insight into educational aims and procedures and thus quickened our progress towards perfection. In describing "Education after the War," Nicholas Murray Butler wrote:

> It (war) has shortened by many years, perhaps by a generation, the path to progress to clearer, sounder, and more constructive thinking as to education, its processes, and its aims than that which has occupied the center of the stage for some dozen years past.[20]

The German people were described as having developed a psychology without a soul. The
gospel of efficiency without a moral idea evidenced by Germany supposedly taught us the
lesson that efficiency apart from a moral ideal
was an evil and wicked instrument which could
only end in disaster.[21] We chastized Germany
for its lack of moral purpose and then picked up
the banner of moral righteousness and carried it
all over the globe to make the world safe for
democracy. There is little doubt that the
entrance of the United States into the war had
strong religious overtones and was not instigated
merely as a result of our perception of Germany
as an economic threat.

It was seen as a crusade to make the world
safe for the development and spread of the new
faith in democracy. Wiebe stated that the "war,
now sanctified, had become the necessary prelude
to mankind's salvation."[22] While the belief in
progress had been shaken in 1914, it had acquired new life through "the sublimation of war
into an Utopian agent."[23] Thus, after the war,
the emphasis on character and moral training was
greatly increased in the hopes of averting the
disastrous course embarked upon by the Germans.
Training in behavior and conduct were stressed
over and beyond mere development of intellect.

As evidenced by A. Duncan Yocum's previous
call for a bond between religion and the State
in the face of radical intrusion, the "Bolshevik
Coup" of November, 1917, also greatly affected
the American consciousness, especially the concern with law and order. The revolution in
Russia was viewed as not only motivated by
anarchy, thus leading to chaos, but those in
power in this country feared that it would cause
unrest here, especially among the immigrant
working population. While prominent Americans
joined Europe's leaders in "praying for its
demise,"[24] American soldiers, along with French

and English personnel, entered Russia to support briefly the counter-revolutionary movement. This fear of instability, anarchy and chaos, with the accompanying breakdown of law and order, greatly influenced the growth of character and moral education and was reflected in their value orientation.

The War and the Russian Revolution were not the only traumatic experiences that the country faced at this time. Crime was skyrocketing in the crowded cities, and the moral standards of an agrarian society were constantly threatened by the new urban industrial centers. While as early as 1907 the public schools were criticized for not doing enough to stop the steady increase in crime,[25] the War only heightened the attack. The schools were seen as the only institution which could maintain stability, order, and morality in the midst of these developments. C. N. Jensen, State Superintendent of Instruction in Utah, wrote:

> . . . The increase in juvenile delinquency and unstable conditions of society since the World War has led some of us to hope that the public school might become a greater force than it has been in the past for training morality.[26]

William Bagley summarized the feelings of most Americans when he stated that the crime ratios in this country were much higher than in any other comparable nation, and the ratios of serious crime seemed to be increasing over a period that has witnessed a marked decline in serious crime in practically every nation with which we would wish to be compared. In other words, the situation faced in the United States seemed quite peculiar to our own country. Bagley was quick to point out, however, that this was not due to other nations sending their criminal classes to our shores.

Insofar as the homicide rates
can be considered an index of the
prevalence of serious crime, the
American states that have the largest proportion of foreign-born
population are actually among the
states that have the lowest crime
ratios.[27]

The high crime ratios in America were seen
to be a result of increased mobility, diversity
of standards of conduct, the American tradition
of lawlessness and individualism, as well as the
increased material prosperity. But for whatever
reason, the schools took on the burden of
building a more orderly society. The best way
to eliminate crime and disorder was seen to be
to educate children in the Golden Rule, and provide them with a code of ethics and uplifting
ideals, and train them in character.[28]

The feeling of a general breakdown in the
structure of society and its norms and sanctions
continued for many years and was still viewed
as serious in 1932, when the Department of
Superintendence devoted its Tenth Yearbook to
the question of Character Education. They concluded that:

Under the conditions of freedom and plenty generated by industrial
society, the youth of the country are
abandoning the severe sex taboos of
the past; the sanctity of the marriage
relationship is being challenged; the
dogmas and ceremonies of the church
are losing their power and traditional
purposes of living fail to satisfy.[29]

The changes taking place in society at this
time instigated a casting away of old values and
morality. The Superintendents saw this as a

55.

"form of social and mental disease and obviously in (that) age of rapid social transition the problem of moral education (required) very fundamental analysis."[30]   The goal was not only moralization but socialization as well.   The whole concept of democracy was seen as more moral than intellectual.

For men like Edward Ross the concept of democracy in early twentieth century terms manifested itself in the social sphere as a belief in a meritocracy. It did not deny that men were as gold, silver, and copper in relative worth but it wanted men rated not by place or trappings but by wisdom, character, and efficiency. Likewise in the political sphere democracy meant sovereignty not of the average man but of a matured public opinion. Democracy at its best was seen to substitute the direction of the recognized moral intellectual elite for the rule of the strong, the rich or the privileged. Unfortunately these two groups were not so easily separated in the society of that day. Those in positions of power and authority were thought to be there because they were morally and intellectually superior.

Ernest Smith, in his call for compulsory Character Education, reiterated the aim of moral education, namely that a duty could never become a vital energizing force until it (was) fixed in habit.[31]   This notion of fixing one's actions and duties into habits played a strong part in character education and helped make for an obedient, patriotic person.

C.

The generation of a new social order was welcomed not only by those interested in the social gospel concept of a Heaven on Earth, but also by the State in its push for a controlled, planned society. Character Education was

welcomed by both sides, since it attempted both
to inculcate the notions of purity, morality and
service in a social setting, and to legitimize
the actions of the State in the name of evolution, progress, rationality and science. The
gospel of salvation and the sanctity of heaven
had been replaced by the possibility of a Heaven
on Earth, a true Utopian democracy, where all
men would be free of disease, crime, sin, and
suffering; what was needed was the controlling
of behavior and the fixing of it into habits
which promoted good citizenship and civic responsibility.

David Snedden felt that progressive democracy needed new types of Character Education.
He believed that this new type of education
would include the largest practicable numbers of
individuals who

> According to their natural
> powers and probable responsibilities
> be predisposed and fitted in this
> conforming behavior as well as their
> self-initiated activity, to serve
> the ends of the higher social well-
> being.[32]

While the first step in the development of
a liberal education was seen by Snedden to be
the creation of vocational schools, the next step
was the development of a moral education which
could produce a moral character required to meet
the needs of a highly developed democracy in the
twentieth century.

> The demands of the war have
> simply made more clear what many
> have surmised before, namely, that
> any people who wish to preserve demo-
> cracy of social organizations, while
> at the same time becoming more so-
> cially efficient in meeting the
> contingencies of twentieth century

57.

civilization, are confronted by
problems of character education of
the most difficult kind.[38]

Character Education thus was a means of pre-
serving democracy and furthering social efficiency. The schools were mandated to preserve the
new social order by instilling the values of
order, stability, patriotism, duty, and citizenship. America was perceived as having a mission,
a destiny, not only to make the world safe for
democracy but we also had the responsibility to
make democracy safe for the world. This entailed
the socialization of all children for the responsibilities of modern life in the American Republic.[34] Children had to learn to be obedient
as well as to respect authority and law and order
or face the chaos of anarchy. In order for
democracy to be safe for the world it had to be
stable, orderly, and under the control of the
moral and intellectual elite.

Social psychology developing at this time
also affected the development of character and
moral education. According to its theory,
morality was instinctive to man in the form of
a herd preservation instinct. It manifested
itself in the social forces by which the mores
of society were organized and enforced. Joseph
Folsom wrote:

> To a social psychologist, the
> very intensity of conviction with
> which we believe in national honor,
> in the ultimate righteousness and
> divine sanction of monogamous wed-
> lock, in masculine courage or femi-
> nine chastity--the resentment we
> show when these propositions are
> critically analyzed--all this is
> evidence that these beliefs rest not
> upon any rational appreciation of the
> actual value or utility of the ideals

58.

in question but rather upon our
instinctive sensitiveness to the
voice of the herd.[35]

Folsom disagreed with the notions of social control advocated by Edward Ross. Ross
spoke of the need for social control and the
need to assimilate and reconcile the members of
the all-inclusive group by weakening the ties
that bound men into minor groups which inter-
rupted the social order. For Ross the
improvement in the means of social control had
facilitated the formation of large, orderly
societies.[36]

Folsom saw Ross's idea as too purposive
rather than genetic. Changes in custom were not
caused by a change in needs for control or by
a presence and possibility of another means of
control, but by new conditions that caused man's
instinctive emotional tendencies to become at-
tached to new types of conditioned stimuli,
rendering impossible their continued attachment
to the old.[37]

Folsom felt that social control was not the
goal, social progress was. He wanted to get away
from the use of control for its own sake or for
the sake of society as advocated by Ross. For
Folsom, social control should make use of man's
best instinctual elements. The ideas expressed
by Folsom represented the drive for a new
scientific rational order. He did not wish for
the new education to destroy the herd instinct,
only shift it to another stimuli. The concern
voiced by Folsom to objectify the sentiments so
that man could reject the irrational ones and
retain the rational ones, generated the concern
as well as the need for analysis and quantification of character traits.

Irwin Edman was another social psychologist
who stressed the importance of education as the
means by which the adult members of society

"impress upon the plastic minds of the immature those habits of thought and action which are currently recognized as desirable."[38] Social psychology provided a new discourse and investigation into the problem of the nature of the social relationship in man. It attempted to alleviate the inequities and injustices in society by putting the herd instinct under rational control.

According to the social psychologists, the rational stimuli of the new enlightened society, governed by the dictates of reason and science, would replace the irrational stimuli of wealth and power which were seen to have been governing society. By objectifying the sentiments, the social psychologist could sort out the rational stimuli influencing people from the irrational. According to his expertise, the habits of thought and action of children could be shaped and molded into the desirable form. This new rational, scientific control did not suggest an elimination of the herd instinct. It merely attempted to replace the irrational bases for the status quo with a rational one. The voice of the herd may have told the Black in the "irrational system" that he was not human, not equal to other members of society and therefore should remain separate from them. In the "rational system," the voice of the herd might have told him that according to the findings of science, he was best suited for vocational or manual work. The possibilities for injustices and inequities existed in either system. Rational maintenance of the status quo by scientific expertise was in many ways no different than irrational control by the wealthy or the powerful.

The dangers of the voice of the herd were clear to William Trotter when he wrote:

He (man) is more sensitive to the voice of the herd than to any other influences. It can inhibit or stimulate

his thought and conduct. It is the
source of his moral codes, of the
sanctions of his ethics and philosophy. It can endow him with energy,
courage and endurance and can as
easily take these away. It can make
him acquiesce in his own punishment
and embrace his executioner, submit
to poverty, bow to tyranny and sink
without complaint under starvation.
Not merely can it make him accept
hardship and suffering unresistingly,
but it can make him accept as truth
the explanation that his perfectly
preventable afflictions are sublimely
just and gentle.[39]

The influence of social psychological theory
was important to the development of character
education. The herd instinct was perceived as
being under rational control and thus would make
for a stable, rational, just society. All the
efforts at citizenship training and character
development were at the instigation of the preservation of the social body. The new secularized
moral ethic, generated in the genuine concern for
creation of a rational, scientific new order,
acted to cement the society together and maintain
an uncritical, obedient, patriotic citizenry.

D.

One of the leading proponents of a secularized moral ethic was Milton Fairchild. He founded
the Moral Education Board in 1896 and became the
director of the National Institution for Moral
Instruction in 1911. Later, after the War, the
Institution was changed to become the Character
Education Institution. This organization was
significant not only as a leader in character
education, but it also showed the transition from
moral training to citizenship training which occurred during this period. Although Fairchild in
1908 scorned the unsatisfactory evidence that

61.

came from sociology as being too narrow and unmindful of the great beliefs so important to human beings[40] by 1916 he was writing Edward Ross seeking support for moral education from sociology. Fairchild listed ten reasons why moral or character education should be in all public and private schools.[41] The plea for support manifested itself in a tremendous obsession not only with unity and purity (so vital to moral education), but also with the necessity of developing strength of character, educating public opinion and preventing crime (so vital to character education).

The Institution also received a great deal of support from the business community, especially from an anonymous "Donor."

> In the winter of 1914, by chance it became known to educators interested in a movement for character education in American public schools that a businessman of wide experience and thoughtful attitude towards the needs of his Nation had made up his mind that the fundamental necessity for success with popular government was moral education of all the children. As a result they would have such character development when they came to exercise their rights as citizens among a free people, as would insure loyalty to the true purposes and traditions of the Nation. As true citizens they would solve the problems of life in the interests of all and for the general good.[42]

The move from teaching a secularized morality in the schools to developing character in order to create good citizens is clear. The Donor created a $5,000 prize for the best Children's Code of Morals. The contest ran from

Washington's Birthday, 1916 to Washington's
Birthday, 1917. The judges were Professor
George Trumbull Ladd of Yale University, Justice
Mahlon Pitney of the United States Supreme Court,
and Mrs. Philip North Moore, who was President
of the National Council of Women.[43]

The best code was that submitted by William
Hutchins. The Code stressed the values of obedience to law, self-control, clean thoughts, and
good workmanship. Hutchins called his code,
"Ten Laws of Right Living," and that summarized
the intent and force of its compulsion. The
child was not only to "obey the laws of right
living which the best Americans have always obeyed,"[44] but he was also to "try to find out what
my duty is, what I ought to do, and my duty I
will do, whether it is easy or hard; what I ought
to do I can do."[45] The sequence of knowing one's
duty, and then doing it was as important to
character education as it was previously to moral
education.

The duty was no longer merely towards a
secularized religious morality, but was now
directed towards generating a greater America by
creating good citizens and good workers. The
moral values of purity and kindness were no doubt
still there, but the power and influence of the
State were slowly gaining momentum.

In the Law of Good Workmanship, the future
worker was told not to be envious of those who
got a larger reward from their labors because
it would spoil the work and the worker alike.
Loyalty to family, school, town, state, country
and above all, humanity, was seen as the greatest
law, since "he who obeys the law of loyalty
obeys all the other nine laws of the good
American."[46] While no mention was made of what
to do when these loyalties conflicted, since the
general concensus of the character education
movement seemed to center on the uniting of individual needs with the society's demands, it is

not difficult to see how patriotism might win out.

Later in 1919, Milton Fairchild's National Institution for Moral Instruction drew up a list of the characteristics of a perfect human being. While it included 91 virtues, the list centered on the nuclei of character, including intellectual character, working character, personal character, social character, emotional character, and physical character. Each center had four or five traits listed after it. This list reflected the growing tendency after the war to objectify and quantify character traits.

While this move will be discussed later, it is necessary to mention it in this context because Fairchild felt that this analysis was vital to educational planning. Fairchild believed that nature did not make the happiness and satisfaction of the individual its fundamental objective and thus it was up to the education system to develop these virtues so that the resulting human being would be "a great success as a citizen of a democratic state and worthy of life among a free people."[47]

Man was thus viewed as unable to find happiness and satisfaction within himself and only through the educational system could he find the successful citizenship and worthiness to live in a free democratic society. The immediate aim, once again, was the creation of citizens worthy of the social order, but since the ultimate goal was the perfect society it is little wonder that those concerned sought to mold perfect human beings.

The Morality Code was subsequently deemed to be insufficient, and the "Donor" created a $20,000 research prize for the best public school plan for character education of children and youth . . .

64.

> Because, while intellectual
> education is fairly well developed,
> vocational and physical education
> are only partly provided, and charac-
> ter education on human motives, cover-
> ing the wisdom of human experience,
> although recognized by school authori-
> ties and by parents as the supremely
> important phase of public education,
> is underdeveloped and often neglected.[48]

The contest ran from October 1, 1919 to
February 22, 1921, with the winning plan coming
from the State University of Iowa[49] under the direction of Dr. Edwin Starbuck. The Character
Education Institution published and distributed
5,000 copies (and over 10,000 by the late 1920's)
of the Iowa Plan both nationally as well as
internationally.

As shall be developed later on, the Iowa
Plan was used as a model for character education
programs across the country. Starbuck was a
student of G. Stanley Hall and was deeply committed to religious education, as well as to the
beliefs in recapitulation, eugenics, inner development of the child and child study, racial
traditions and sex education. Once more it is
evident how the religious social gospel merged
with the developing science of child nature to
provide the rationale for control and molding of
human character. This shaping of the child and
control of his environment was viewed as not
only consistent with his inner nature but also
was in the best interests of the rational scientific evolution of the race--an upward march
to purity and unity.

By the mid-1920's, the Character Education
Institution (formerly the National Institution
for Moral Instruction, reincorporated February 2,
1922), was allocating $15,000 per year for re-
search and was seeking a $300,000 maintenance
fund and an independent endowment of one million

65.

dollars. It was organized as a non-commercial research institution with no copyright privileges, no lecture fees, and nothing for sale. Its membership included State Commissioners of Education, State Superintendents of Education, the Federal Commissioner of Education, the Superintendent of Schools of the Nation's Capitol, the Secretary of the N.E.A., the Secretary of the National Council of Parents and Teachers, the Dean of the School of Education of George Washington University, some research specialists chosen from the staff of the Smithsonian Institute, and the Chairman of the Character Education Institution, Milton Fairchild.[50]

In 1924 Fairchild set out to take the Hutchins Morality Code which had previously won the Donor's $5,000 prize for best Children's Code of Morals and on which $25,000 had been spent on its verification, as well as the Iowa Plan which was the winner of the Donor's $25,000 prize for best character education program, and sort out the best features of each into a program for character education. The result was known as the Five Point Plan. It made use of morals leaders in the classroom, called Uncle Sam's Boys and Girls, who wore badges and acted as officials moderating conduct.

The Five Point Plan also made direct use of the Hutchins Morality Code which was discussed every day in the classroom for ten minutes and from which character projects were instigated in the hopes of creating good habits. The last two points included a type of subtle coercion by the teacher, by the use of argument and personal appeal to influence the pupils' motives, as well as the use of character charts and school records to keep a permanent record of the character development of the individual child.[51]

The Five Point Plan encompassed the values of leadership, habit formation and guidance,

66.

mingled with a patriotic zeal and a psychological legitimation. Fairchild was also greatly
influenced by the science of eugenics. He saw
it as one of the background sciences for education and combined this appeal for eugenics with
the recurring notion of being worthy of citizenship. This haughty notion of having to be
worthy of being an American and worthy of being
a member of mankind shows to what limits those
in character education were willing to go, in
search of the perfect state. Fairchild concluded:

> The problem of character edu-
> cation is to succeed in discovering
> ways and means and methods by which
> the inherited capacities of each and
> every child shall be stimulated and
> guided to development into adult
> character worthy of citizenship in
> our nation and of participation in
> our human civilization.[52]

E.

The first World War reaffirmed the necessity for teaching moral values in the schools.
It not only necessitated a cooperative collective
action but it mandated a reply to the claim that
only autocratic governments were efficient. The
Commission on the Reorganization of Secondary
Education of the N.E.A. reported in 1917 that
"our newly reanimated pride in our country
should therefore spur us to fresh concern for
the type of personal character which democratic
living is especially commissioned to promote."[53]
The greatest need of all children was unquestionably agreed upon to be character, which was
defined as the "habitual disposition to choose
those modes of behavior that do honor to human
dignity."[54] The Commission concluded that the
leading mission of the school was not only to
promote character because it signified the
democratic notion of a type of worthy living, but

in the process to assist in "purifying and ele-
vating the ideal itself."[55]

In its July, 1921 report the National
Council of Education recommended the appointment
of a permanent Committee on Character Education
to work closely with its Committee on Democracy
in Education and the American School Citizenship
League. The Committee, which existed until its
final report in 1926, was under the chairmanship
of Milton Bennion of the University of Utah. In
its preliminary report to the Council, the Committee set out three aims of research. The
first was a determination of objectives of
character education, including primary and secondary virtues; next was a study of the various
methods of character education, including
instruction and training; and finally the question of teacher training was pursued.[56]

Interestingly, the Bennion's home state,
Utah, had enacted a law in 1919 which required
all boys and girls up to eighteen years of age to
register once a year for a twelve-month enrollment program including both school and work but
with year-round supervision. Much use was made
of community groups and agencies, including the
Boy Scouts, Red Cross, Y.M.C.A. and Campfire
Girls in the pursuit of character building.[57]

In 1923 the Committee on Character Education submitted a list of theses to be discussed
before the National Council of Education at its
July meeting. The theses presented reflected the
concern with development of character (which was
seen as a synthesis of simpler units) inductively
by modifying the original nature and impulses of
the child, using habit formation, development of
ideas, intellectual discussion, and creation of
standards of choice of action by means of teacher
selection and control of the child's life experiences. The Committee also put forth the need
for professional staff to make a complete scientific diagnosis of each child and the possibility

of using a case-method-like approach.[58]

The Committee report for that year (1923) stressed the necessity of attracting better teachers by increasing the pay and status of teachers and raising the standards in the teacher colleges. It also spoke highly of the use of the case-method approach and of behavior clinics. Bennion reported that, promoted by the Commonwealth Fund Program for Prevention of Delinquency, the National Committee for Mental Hygiene had undertaken a nation-wide campaign for the establishment of child-behavior clinics in cities over 100,000 in population.[59] The Committee also commended the work being done by the Boy Scouts, the Committee on Essentials of Democracy, the American School Citizenship League, moral code writers and the Iowa Plan. Finally, they advocated the incorporation into teacher training of such areas as psychology, hygiene, ethics, character education methods, education for democracy, habit formation, training in use of conduct clinics, and even training of religious school teachers. Teacher training was also to instill the necessity of cooperation with community agencies and the importance of self-government.[60] The goal of the Character Education Committee was the making of the "thoroughly socialized individual."[61]

The Committee was unquestionably out not only to control behavior and conduct, but it also set out to acquaint the teacher with the new tools of scientific education, a move which no doubt enhanced their status, especially in the eyes of the church and the home.

The schools had taken over the responsibility for inculcating the values of hygiene, ethics and conduct which were to be formed into habit. The educational system as the backbone of the society had usurped much of the power and influence of the church and the home and mingled it with its democratic ideals and rationalizations.

69.

The new social gospel issued forth from the mouth
of the educator in the new sacred language of
science.

The Committee on Democracy, headed by A.
Duncan Yocum, attempted to bond democracy not
only with character education but with religion
as well. The new social gospel of democratic
faith permeated this bond. Yocum wrote:

> Superthreats to civilization and
> democracy require super education that
> is necessarily complex. But through
> its very complexity, the character
> education which makes a few virtues
> controlling will through the interde-
> pendence of one virtue upon another,
> insure control of all; and through
> this interdependence in their elements
> teach morality through religion, reli-
> gion through morality, and democracy
> through both.[62]

The Character Education Committee's report
of 1926 stressed the two goals of social progress
and the development of personalities. The two
were inextricably interrelated since outstanding
personalities caused social progress which was
then passed on in the form of social inheritance
by the schools which in turn helped form personality. While the report stressed love of God,
love of fellowmen, morality, truth, goodness and
beauty, it nevertheless revealed its true inspiration and guiding light in the following passage:
"Faith in and reverence for power that makes for
righteousness is a moral force that should not
be ignored in any phase of character education."[63]

While Bennion put forth ten objectives for
character education,[64] the inherent conflict between morality and patriotism was not addressed.
The difficulty in reconciling love, justice, and
reverence for good with defense of right, service,

70.

and loyalty was never considered. When morality was dictated by the State, it could not help but compromise its high ethical standards. The notion that Americans had a monopoly on the power for righteousness which enabled us to inevitably do what was moral was a haughty belief; a belief nonetheless which fueled the fires of character education.

Milton Bennion continued to lead his Committee to a greater responsibility in character education. In 1924 he set up five sub-committees to make a thorough scientific study of different aspects of a complex problem. The sub-committees included curriculum and materials, teaching procedure, school organization, character tests and measurements and teacher training.[65]

Edwin Starbuck, who was both a member of the N.E.A.'s Character Education Committee and the Chairman of the Subcommittee on Tests and Measurements, reported frequently to the N.E.A. He was very interested in setting the educational house in order, and this he believed required both training for character and moulding of personality. The present system he saw as plagued by "four fools hiding in the basement." The first of these was mechanism which threatened to make education merely concerned with training in skills. Next came information which represented the anemic highbrow who was merely interested in assembling facts and describing laws. Institution was seen as the third fool which sought to surround everything with bureaucratic statistics, rules, and programs. Finally there was tradition which knelt in a state of reverence but constantly gazed backwards over his shoulder in obeisance to the wisdom of generations gone by. The goal was not to eliminate these hindrances but to instead counter their self-serving tendencies and conventions and to integrate them into the everyday life of the child. Mechanism could make of the school houses of efficient service rather than shops of devices. Information

71.

could convert schools into temples of wisdom rather than museums of curious knowledge. Institution could see that its true function was socialization and not organization, and tradition could open up the rich treasures of the past in order to give spiritual orientation to the pupils so that they could meet their present work in a spirit of reverence.[66]

Starbuck was distressed by the factory model of education and instead agreed with Froebel that the school was a garden for the nurturing of personality. Character was viewed as something that grew, not something that could be produced in a factory by machine methods. His approach was also goal-oriented and heavily laden with the value of socialization. Character education, according to Starbuck, should not merely inculcate "The Virtues" apart from the real world of the child, but instead should substitute objectives and situations for these virtues. The entire school program was to be geared to the child's outward adjustment to society, to his socialization. School morality was mandated to widen its range to include the concerns of the home, the State, the Church and the industrial order. Starbuck wished to bond the morality of the industrial order with the school's function to instill meaning and significance in the routine, often menial, tasks involved.[67] The schools promulgated a secularized morality, a morality representative of the virtues needed to maintain the orderly, stable, workings of society. One part of such an ethnic was the generation of happy content workers. Workers who not only found fulfillment in their menial tasks but who also recognized the need for the present distribution and conservation of wealth.

It requires but little imagination to hear in the hum of the wheels of industry a song of human improvement and fulfillment. It takes now but a tiny bit of wit to appreciate

72.

the gain to every one--even the
international benefits--of saving
and earning and spending and rightly
conserving the wealth of the world.[68]

Starbuck also put forth the growing interest in the scientific investigation of human
character. He was confident that "we shall be
able to analyze out the elements of character,
define its types, and discover the limits within
which it is possible to cultivate it."[69] If one
believed in the perfectability of man and the
desirability of human progress, coupled with a
program of purposive social action, then the

Future of humanity, the destiny
of nations, the direction of human
progress are in the hands, not so
much of makers of laws or captains of
industry, as of teachers who are shaping the citizenry of the world.[70]

The educator thus receiving new knowledge
about the hidden springs of conduct, the unex-
plored reaches of personality, could consciously
control human development as he had done with
plants and animals. Scientific investigation of
the nature of the child provided not only the
methodology but the rationale as well for the
shaping and molding of human personality.

The final report of the Committee was
published in 1926 by the U.S. Bureau of Education.
Its general objectives for Character Education
were as follows:

1. To develop socially valuable purposes
   leading in youth or early maturity to
   development of life purposes

2. To develop enthusiasm for realization of
   these purposes and coupled with this
   enthusiasm, intelligent use of time
   and energy

3. To develop moral judgment--the ability to judge what is right in any given situation

4. To develop the moral imagination--the ability to picture vividly the good or evil consequences to one's self and to others of any type of behavior

5. To develop all socially valuable natural capacities of the individual and to direct the resultant abilities towards successfully fulfilling all one's moral obligation.[71]

Once again the important conceptual change occurring was the redefining of the moral person as the socially valuable citizen. This equivalency is crucial to an adequate understanding of character education. The good person was one who was responsive to the social maintenance of the State. One had to develop socially valuable purposes and socially valuable natural capacities in the name of one's moral obligation to the system.

Character Education set out to inculcate a State sanctioned morality, a secularized ethic, in the hopes of preventing delinquency and improving behavior by the use of educational guidance, child guidance clinics, personal counseling as well as character education per se.[72] Morality and life purpose were no longer supplied by the Church, the home or the individual but by the social valuableness to the State.

It is also important to remember that in most cases the creation of a socially valuable citizen was not to be accomplished through coercion or repression which were seen to cause a loss in moral potency. The child had to desire and will the desired ends for himself. This child, "to be really moral, must not only see the right, he must also love it, and habitually respond to it in appropriate action."[73] If, however, that was not possible to accomplish, other methods were considered'. The possibilities for character alteration, while frighteningly possible today, were only wished for then.

Long ago surgical interference
in the brain was proposed as a means
of controlling character; it seemed
then a wild idea, yet even that is by
no means unthinkable now, although
certainly not yet practicable.[74]

It is interesting to note how the only drawback to such "interference" was seen to be the practicality of such a technique which had not as yet been perfected. The morality of such a procedure was never questioned. The view of the enlightened scientist as expert on character was indicative of the power and influence of scientific pragmatic justifications.

F.

Two other influential organizations in the furtherance of character education were the Character Education Inquiry and the American Social Hygiene Association. Both reflected the increasing secularization of morality and the growing importance of the scientific community in providing new insight into moral issues which could be put forth in the schools.

The first proposal for creation of the Character Education Inquiry came from the Religious Education Association. At its 1922 meeting a resolution was adopted to attempt a careful and scientific investigation of the question, "How is religion being taught to young people and with what effect?"[75] In May of 1922 they wrote to the Institute of Social and Religious Research at Teacher's College, Columbia University, seeking assistance. In October of the same year the Committee on Curriculum of the

International Lessons Committee asked the Institute to provide funds for a critical study of curriculum material, while in November the Bureau of the Research Service of the International Council of Religious Education requested a grant for three successive years. Pressed by these three separate requests, the Institute called a conference of representatives of the three petitioning organizations for January 6, 1923. The following recommendations were adopted:

1. Study the actual experiences of children which have moral and religious significance and the effects for periods of time of the moral and religious influences to which children, youth, and adults have been exposed.

2. Apply the objective methods of the laboratory to the measurement of conduct under controlled conditions.

3. Engage one or more full-time investigators and associate advisors and assistants with them.

4. Secure collaboration by various institutions and groups.

5. Make results of the study available in both technical and popular forms.[76]

The men chosen to head the investigation were Dr. Hugh Hartshorne, Professor of Religious Education at the University of Southern California, and Dr. Mark A. May, Professor of Psychology at Syracuse University. At the same time, Teacher's College agreed to undertake the project as "an inquiry into character education, with particular reference to religious education."[77] The Character Education Inquiry was placed under the immediate supervision of Dr. Edward Thorndike and ran from 1924 until 1929, when May and Hartshorne went to Yale University to create the

Yale Institute of Human Relations.

The striking compatibility of psychology and a secularized religion in the service of character education and study is apparent once again; of the two directors in the inquiry one was a psychologist and one a religious educator. While secularized religion provided the ethical and moral standards, psychology provided the experimental methodology and gave the movement status and influence. The Character Education Inquiry classified its work as involving the following areas of interest:

1. Mental content and skills--so-called intellectual factors

2. Desires, opinions, attitudes, motives-- so-called dynamic factors

3. Social behavior--the performance factors

4. Self-control--relation of these factors to one another and to social self-integration.[78]

As shall be discussed in a subsequent chapter, the Character Education Inquiry developed an entire battery of character tests to analyze and objectify all aspects of human personality and conduct.

The American Social Hygiene Association, under the direction of Thomas W. Galloway, also provided material for character education, especially in the area of sex education. Galloway believed that the phenomena of sex and reproduction and the educative use of these phenomena "must loom large in any character education which pretends to fit for a real, present life."[79] In any attempt to control an individual's conduct and mold him to develop in the best possible manner, there is the need for control over his sexual behavior. Galloway wrote:

To supply this need is the core of the proposal for social hygiene and sex education. It is to develop all the qualities in character and to relate these specifically and consciously by the widest use of the project method to the dilemmas of sex, so that sex behavior may be most wholesomely adjusted to the most significant needs and happiness, both of the individual and of society.[80]

Galloway was also a member of the N.E.A. Committee on Character Education and the subcommittee on Character Tests and Measurement. He brought to the movement the concern with the ductless glands (endocrine glands) and the influence of their hormones on the determination, not only of sex but of personality type as well. Knowledge of endocrines, according to Galloway, would enable man to supplement his neuro-muscular and intelligent tests for vocational and other guidance.[81]

The sex education advocated by Galloway as a necessity for social health and character adjustments was heavily laden with sexist, role-stereotyped overtones. Man was described as highly physical in sexual desire, ready at any time to be roused, while the woman was described as less intense with a more intermittent quality of sexual arousal, "apparently with a slight fortnightly or a monthly rhythm."[82] Feminine qualities due to hormonal secretions were seen to involve the extremes of softness, tenderness, compassion, patience, and maternal devotion on the one hand, closely flanked by quick changes in temperament, touchiness, spitefulness, nagging and tears on the other.[83]

Man's sexual nature and love was seen as more simple, passionate and self-seeking, more animal than the shy, spiritual nature of the female. These great physical elements of man's

78.

love were seen to often turn the aesthetic,
spiritual love of women into indifference and
cold or even antagonism to the physical aspects
of love.[84] The importance of sex education was
to help both sexes adjust to the differences
between them, which meant, in other words, to
promulgate the stereotypic views of the over-
sexed animal male and the cold, aesthetic,
spiritual female. No attempt was made to examine
the bases of such distinctions in the social
framework or mores of the society.

Although Galloway felt that marriage was
the legalized form of indulgence, he nevertheless
believed that even in marriage sex should be
limited as much as possible to the process of
reproduction, because women were less erotic and
more spiritual than men. He also called for a
dropping in the age at which persons could marry
because "anything which increases the time from
sexual maturity to marriage makes more difficult
the problem of continent sex behavior and is
socially unsound and injurious.[85]

Character education in the form of sex
education attempted not only to maintain the sex
roles as determined by the social fabric of the
times but also set out to educate youth in the
responsibilities of marriage and the necessity
for a voluntary, positive eugenics program.[86]
In order to perfect the race and further the
adjustment of individuals to the social order,
much care and concern had to center around sex
education. Galloway and his association wanted
to bring sex education out into the open, so
as to create an enlightened population which
would not only recognize the "inherent" differences between the sexes, but one which would
funnel all their "indulgences" into marriage,
solely for the purpose of reproduction of the
race, a race which understood social hygiene,
eugenics and endocrinological differences between
human beings.

The tremendous drive for moral education
and character education after the First World
War was steeped in a nationalistic, patriotic
fervor. The good person became the good citizen
and the schools were given the ultimate responsibility of stopping the increase in the rise
of crime and delinquency by creating good,
socially efficient, and patriotic Americans.
These views did not go unchallenged, however, as
many people of the time recognized the inherent
difficulties of such viewpoints and the undesirable potentialities for an unquestioning obedience that they often fostered.

Edward Sisson of Reed College did not
believe that the roots of juvenile delinquency
and crime lay in the school or the moral terpi-
tude of the rising generation. He felt that
the method of instruction in morals which seemed
so effective to most laymen was in reality hedged
about with perplexities and had shown little
evidence of possessing educative potency.
Finally, he stressed the point that the moraliz-
ing of the rising generation must begin in the
world of action and not in the school.[87]

Sisson saw delinquency and crime in most
cases to be caused by broken homes, slums, and
unjust working conditions. Teaching moral precepts would never work until these values were
reflected in the world of the outside society,
the world of action. Sisson saw the contradic-
tory aspects of teaching the evils of wealth in
school, while those in the world of action
continued to hoard it; or to teach freedom of
speech while police harassed protesting miners.
He felt that "in morals the world is always
educator-in-chief."[88] Moral education began and
ended in the world of action, not in the classroom.

The most indispensable change
needed in the case of moral education
is the change of venue; we must move
the main battle from the quiet pre-
cincts of the school to the energetic
and often stormy arena of the world of
action. The primary task is not with
children at all, but with men and
women, with the generation now in
power, ruling the world and setting
standards of right and wrong. The
world is the Supreme Court in practical
ethics and its decisions are final.[89]

In battles of moral conviction with individuals, the world, according to Sisson, always
won out. Those who attempted to teach otherwise,
like Socrates or Jesus, were done away with.
Action and not words, Sisson saw as playing the
decisive role in moral training. The world had
to clean house but the "main battle against
sin (was) to be fought among men and women and
not among children."[90]

The persistent nationalistic fervor in
America after WWI was also seen by many as undesirable. Nationalism was seen to have become
a religion with its own processions, holy days,
saints, temples and icons.[91] When this secularized religious fervor was applied to education,
it was

Often at the ceremonial level
and (preferred) the flights of jingoism and self-glorification, as if it
feared the more sober exam of the
alleged advantages or traits of the
particular state or area or group.[92]

The First World War saw a drive for censorship of textbooks.[93] Any textbook that falsified
the facts regarding the War of Independence or
the War of 1812 or which defamed our nation's
founders or misrepresented the ideals and causes

or which they struggled and sacrificed, or which
contained propaganda favorable to any foreign
government was to be censored according to the
1923 ruling of the Commonwealth of Wisconsin.[94]
Ironically, Bessie Pierce's study of American
School Textbooks not only found that the Germans
were portrayed as crafty, cruel, militaristic
and egotistical, but that much of the stories
about American History were chiefly about political and military matters as well. Pierce found
that none of the authors had adopted "a revision-
ist point of view regarding war guilt"[95] and
furthermore, she found that the war stories were
not only often overblown and incorrect, but some
of the school histories were ridiculous, absurd,
and stupid.[96] Pierce concluded by stating that:

> Each nation engages in self-
> praise and asserts its superiority to
> other peoples in all lines of endea-
> vor. Above all, the U.S., like other
> nations, ascribes peaceful inclinations
> to itself and denies any militaristic
> tendency.[97]

The debate over censorship and overt nationalistic fervor continued and in 1923 the
American Historical Association voiced vigorous
protest against an official censorship which
would, they felt, inevitably bring about a
ruinous deterioration both of textbooks and
teaching. The Association demanded a truthful
picture of past and present, not based upon
grounds of patriotism but upon grounds of faith-
fulness to fact. It was also resolved that
"attempts, however well meant, to foster national
arrogance and boastfulness and indiscriminate
worship of national 'heroes' can only tend to
promote a harmful pseudopatriotism."[98]

The comparison of nationalism to a religious
movement persisted in the decade after the War.
The school system, often viewed as the church of

the new secular religion, was thus held to be strictly accountable for any lapse from the official theology or for any slur upon the popular mythology.[99] Character education as well as civic training were perfect examples of nationalistic outgrowths of a new secularized religion. Their duty was to create good citizens who were obedient, patriotic and loyal. Every good American was supposed to believe that the United States was in every respect the greatest and best country in the world, and particularly that it was morally superior to any other nation and was the natural mentor of mankind.[100]

J. Montgomery Gambrill, Assistant Professor of History at Teacher's College, recognized the dangers of a rampant nationalistic fervor. He pointed out how in the recent world tragedy, Germany was singled out as the villain and America was the Sir Galahad that came nobly and unselfishly to the rescue of civilization. Gambrill wrote in apparent disdain:

> In all our wars and international controversies since the nation began, we have been wholly in the right; we always are right and by plain implication we never can be anything but right . . . 'The Founding Fathers' were divinely inspired and wholly above such sordid human motives as a desire to extend the opportunities for profitable investment . . . The Constitution is a sacred scripture, not to be criticized; the school should cultivate toward it an attitude of veneration while the 'good citizen' will view with horror any proposal to change our form of government. . . It is not only our right but our duty to place American interests above all others. 'America First' is a good maxim to teach American children, though 'Deutchland Uber Alles' is an outrageous song for

young Germans. 'My country right or wrong' is the only sound principle for us, though it is particularly reprehensible for the people of Germany, who fully deserve the ruin that came upon them for loyally following their government. The German Kaiser was at once dangerous and ridiculous when he assured his people that 'We are the salt of the earth,' but when the American President informs his people that 'We are the flower of mankind,' it is a dictum to be complacently received and to pass unquestioned.[101]

Gambrill concluded with the earnest plea for Americans to seek a rational, tolerant and constructive nationalism, one which condemned the excessive nationalism as demonstrated by the Germans, as opposed to its apparent emulation. Americanism would become only what Americans chose to make it, and therefore it was for Americans to say whether "the historian of some future day shall record that Prussia lost the War, but Prussianism won it."[102]

Character Education set out to inculcate a state-sanctioned morality. The good man was defined as the good citizen. The training of citizens by the State, however, precluded the development of free judgment upon the State itself. This criticism was voiced very strongly by George A. Coe who was Professor of Religious Education and Psychology at the Union Theological Seminary and one of Character Education's most severe critics. Coe wanted to counteract the universal tendency of institutions to mechanize life and prevent variation. Instead he wanted to train the individual not to take customs, even good customs, as finalities, but instead to foster the habit of freely judging society, the State included, from ethical standpoints.[103]

Coe disagreed with Snedden, that the teacher must uphold the will of the majority, but instead agreed with Professor Davidson that the teacher was the servant of truth and not of the majority.[104] Since the public schools were always in danger of becoming agents for the maintenance of the status quo, Coe saw the need for them to be supplemented by a schooling that was free from political control and that represented a super-political standpoint in morals.

He saw the growing social philosophy of education and the subsequent move from individualistic to social ends in education, while necessary, still tending to elevate the authority of the State to a new position. This tendency, however, was not only found in Snedden. Coe saw Cubberley as treating the social ends of education as ends prescribed to the schools by the State, for the ends of the State with a capital S, without the idea that criticism and improvement of the State's purposes are likewise a necessary objective.[105]

Coe also criticized Bagley's exaltation of the sense of duty and stated that the concept contained nothing that would have been objectionable to Prussia, or even to our own social conservatives who were willing to perpetuate the present inequality between classes.

> On the whole, the present demand
> for a duty-pedagogy plays into the
> hands of the political orthodoxy of
> the movement, which would gladly use
> the schools to perpetuate its author-
> ity . . . Thus the State, Hobbes's
> Leviathan, looms as sovereign not only
> of territory but also of conscience.[106]

Coe granted that while religious institutions themselves tended to become mechanized, conventional and repressive, nevertheless they were the only teaching bodies which were committed to the conviction that there was a super-political law. The aim of religious education in the training for citizenship was, for Coe, "Habituating the young to judge all social relations, processes and institutions, the State included, from the standpoint of the command, 'Thou shalt love thy neighbor as thyself.'"[107] Coe reaffirmed this belief two years later:

Let the churches re-assert that the State is not a final moral authority for the citizen. This is an ancient doctrine but it has fallen into disuse among Protestants. It is high time to recover the old position and to teach children freely to judge from their religious standpoint the policies and acts of their own government. A super-political conscience must be developed in and through church schools.[108]

George Coe saw the problems of a secularized morality, a State-sanctioned morality. It prevented a critical appraisal of the values and actions of the State itself. This problem surfaces especially in character education which received a scathing attack by Coe.[109] Coe saw the distinction between moral training and civic training obliterated in character education. For Coe character education resulted in the good man being redefined as the good citizen. One was to be a good neighbor, which meant don't consider class stratification; one was to have respect for property, which meant respect the property of the elite. Coe saw all this as a means of adjusting the individual to the industrial system rather than adjusting the system to individuals.[110]

The political aspect of character education was also clearly evident to Coe. He stated that "at the heart of the whole agitation for character education is the concern, expressed or

86.

unexpressed, for appropriate use of authority and appropriate response to authority."[111] The good citizen was seen by Coe to be one who willingly signed a blank check upon his ethical reserves and placed it in the hands of government officials, whoever they happened to be.[112] Character education by its very concept was unable to avoid being propaganda, since it sought to make up the mind of the student, develop habits, automatic processes, imitation and unquestioning obedience to command.

Coe saw this propaganda promulgated by business interests as well as by the nationalistic desires of the State. But no matter what the form even for good, Coe was against propaganda as a methodology.

> Propaganda on its own behalf, that is practiced by every modern State in its schools, is directed towards a limited, often merely specious good and thus unevenly distributed. The kind of good that some dominant class has experienced in its own limited environment is prescribed as the common good.[113]

The naivete of many legislators was criticized by Coe. They actually thought that the way to make good citizens was to tell the young this or that fact or alleged fact, expatiate upon this or that virtue, praise our country and its heroes and require this or that ceremonial act.[114] For Coe the problem of citizenship was summarized in the following statement: "Citizens have no duties to the State; rather acting as the State, they have duties to persons."[115] This notion of responsibilities to persons rather than to the State set Coe apart from many religious educators who also backed character education programs. Coe did not see citizenship training as the ultimate goal of the State but instead saw the State as the ultimate

creation of its citizens. Persons were to create
the State rather than having the State create
citizens.

It seems quite clear that character education played a significant role in the American
experience in the decade following the First
World War. While the meritocratic ideal had
always stressed the importance of character as
well as intellect, the War bolstered the notion
that intellect without a moral ideal was poten-
tially evil. While we criticized the extreme
nationalism and goose-step obedience of the
Germans, it appeared that while "Prussia lost
the War, Prussianism may have won." The extreme
nationalistic jingoism so prevalent in this
country during and after the War manifested itself in an education for character movement that
sought to generate good citizens. The State was
to be the sanctioning agent of a new secularized
morality. A State morality which put a premium
on loyalty, patriotism, and obedience to law.
While this creation of a political conscience was
attacked by some as negating a free criticism of
the State, it continued to grow and spread in the
form of character education.

The schools were viewed as the only institution that could slow the crime rate and
create a stable, orderly populace. This tremendous burden of reforming society by inculcating
respect for law and order and the rights of others
also manifested itself in the form of character
education. In addition, character education
sought to inculcate the values of the industrial
state in the hopes of producing better workers,
ones who took pride in their work no matter how
menial the task. The notion of promulgating
values in the school which did not reflect the
real world was also criticized. Critics felt
that the battle for a better society should be
fought among adults, not children.

In spite of the critical attacks, the Character Education movement continued to grow. Programs were adopted in cities and states across the country. The next chapter will examine many of these diverse programs in an attempt to see exactly what was going on in the schools themselves in the way of character education.

[1]See Milton Bennion, "History of the Movement for Character and Citizenship Training in the Schools," Historical Outlook, May 1924, p. 204; M. W. Meyerhardt, "The Movement for Ethical Culture at Home and Abroad," American Journal of Religious Psychology and Education, 3, May 1908, pp. 71-153; also a good chronological description of the growth and achievements of the American Ethical Union can be found in Ethical Culture Fact Book 1876-1966; see also Second International Moral Education Congress (The Hague: The American Committee of the International Congress, 1912).

[2]Robert Wiebe, The Search for Order (New York: Hill and Wang, 1967), p. 260.

[3]An Eleven Year Survey of Activities of the American School Peace League from 1908-1919 (Boston: American School Citizenship League, 1919), p. 11.

[4]Ibid., p. 11.

[5]Ibid., p. 15.

[6]Ibid., p. 20.

[7]The N.E.A., after expressing opposition to military training and devotion to internationalism in its resolutions of 1915 (NEA Proceedings, 53, 1915, pp. 25-28) swung over to one hundred percent patriotism in its next two annual conventions (NEA Proceedings, 54, 1916, pp. 27-28 and NEA Proceedings, 55, 1917, pp. 26-27). See also Erwin Stevenson Selle, The Organization and Activities of the National Education Association (Teacher's College, Columbia University, Contributions to Education, No. 513, 1932), pp. 167-172. For a complete perspective of the relationship between the

academic community and the War, see Randolph Bourne, War and the Intellectuals, (New York: Harper and Row, 1964).

[8] Peace League, op. cit., p. 34.

[9] See Report of the Commissioner of Education, 1917, Vol. I, pp. 1-16; NEA Proceedings, 56, 1918, pp. 23-24; Arthur D. Dean, Our Schools in War Time and After (Boston: Ginn and Co., 1918).

[10] See Merle Curti, The Social Ideas of American Educators (Patterson: Littlefield, Adams and Co., 1959), Chapter XVI.

[11] "Report of Commission on Resolutions," NEA Proceedings, 56, July 1918, p. 25; see also "Resolutions of the American Rights League," Journal of Education, 88, 1918, p. 122.

[12] Peace League, op. cit., p. 44.

[13] Ibid., p. 45.

[14] A. Duncan Yocum, "Report of the Subcommittee on Curriculum of the Committee on Superintendent's Problems," NEA Proceedings, 58, 1920, pp. 174-176.

[15] A. Duncan Yocum, "Resolution," NEA Proceedings, 59, 1921, p. 270.

[16] Edward A. Ross, Changing America (New York: The Century Co., 1912), pp. 4-5; see also Irwin Edman, Human Traits and Their Social Significance (Cambridge: The Riverside Press, 1920), p. 213.

[17] As quoted in, Frederick Bolton, Adolescent Education (New York: MacMillan, 1931), p. 482.

[18] See Wiebe, op. cit., p. 264.

[19] Guy Fernald, "Character vs. Intelligence in Personality Studies," Journal of Abnormal Psychology, 15, April 1920, p. 8.

[20] Nicholas Murray Butler, "Education after the War," Educational Review, 57, Jan. 1919, p. 65.

[21] Ibid., p. 67.

[22] Wiebe, op. cit., p. 272.

[23] Ibid., p. 279.

[24] Ibid., p. 275.

[25] See Walter Hervey, "Moral Education in the Public Schools," Religious Education, 2, Aug. 1907, p. 81. Hervey commented that crime had increased from 1/3,000 to 1/300 in the past fifty years. Also, Walter Rauschenbusch wrote in Christianity and the Social Crises (New York: The MacMillan Co., 1908) Chapter V, that disease, crime, and poverty were the nation's most dangerous enemies.

[26] C. N. Jensen, Character Education Supplement to the Utah State Course of Study, Dept. of Public Instruction, Salt Lake City, Utah, 1925, p. 6. See also W. J. Hamilton, Supt. of Schools, Oak Park, Ill. "Character Education," Religious Education, 20, Aug. 1925, p. 263. Hamilton wrote of the problems of juvenile delinquency, crime, sub-normality, and insanity alongside the general drift toward disrespect for law and authority; Henry Noble Sherwood, "The Morals of Modern Youth," NEA Proceedings, 63, 1925, pp. 133-134. Mr. Noble, State Superintendent of Public Instruction in Indiana, called for more emphasis on character building and religious education to combat crime.

[27] William Bagley, Education, Crime and Social Progress (New York: The MacMillan Co.,

1931), p. 21. See also National Commission on Law Observance and Enforcement, Report on Crime and the Foreign Born, No. 10 (Washington: Government Printing Office, 1931), p. 134.

[28] See Sidney J. Beer, Crime . . . Character . . . Education (Los Angeles: The United Printing Co., 1935), p. 180. See also William H. Harvey, The Remedy (Chicago: The Mundus Publishing Company, 1915). Mr. Harvey wrote, "My proposition is a system of education that will create proper character in the individual and a high character of citizenship; that will get at and develop the roots of what makes character, and an ever-increasing desire for the advancement of the human race; with an organization in charge that will see continuously to its application and development," p. 19.

[29] "Character Education," Tenth Yearbook (Washington: Department of Superintendence NEA, 1932), p. 16. This notion of the immorality of youth is common in American history. See Archer Butler Hulbert, "The Habit of Going to the Devil," Atlantic Monthly, 138, Dec. 1926, pp. 804-806.

[30] Ibid.

[31] Ernest Smith, "Compulsory Character Education," NEA Proceedings, 58, 1920, p. 474.

[32] David Snedden, "Education Toward Formation of a Moral Character," Educational Review, 57, 1919, p. 287. See also David Snedden, "The Improvements of Character Education," Journal of Education, 88, 1918, pp. 144-145.

[33] Ibid.

[34] Smith, op. cit., p. 472. Italics mine.

[35] Joseph Folsom, "The Social Psychology of Morality and Its Bearing on Moral Education," American Journal of Sociology, 23, Jan. 1918,

p. 436; see also Lester Frank Ward, <u>Pure Socio-</u>
<u>logy</u> (New York: MacMillan, 1903), p. 134;
William McDougall, <u>Introduction to Social Psycho-</u>
<u>logy</u> (Boston: John W. Luce & Co., 1912),
Chapter on Gregariousness; Edward Thorndike,
<u>Educational Psychology</u> (New York: Teacher's
College, Columbia University, 1914), Vol. I,
Chap. VII.

[36]Edward A. Ross, <u>Social Control</u> (New
York: MacMillan, 1901).

[37]Folsom, <u>op</u>. <u>cit</u>., p. 469.

[38]Irwin Edman, <u>Human Traits and Their</u>
<u>Social Significance</u> (Cambridge: Riverside
Press, 1920), p. 107.

[39]William Trotter, <u>Instincts of the Herd</u>
<u>in Peace and War</u> (London: T. Fischer Unwin
Ltd., 1916), pp. 114-115. Dr. T. MacCurdy agreed
with Trotter when he wrote, "It is the herd
instinct which stones the prophets, burns
Galileo, puts convention above abstract justice,
cements the uncritical electorate, rushes wildly
into war. The world of men suffers and has suf-
fered more from such tendencies than from all
crime, insanity, or nervousness." "Synthesis
Symposium on the Relative Roles in Psychopathy
of the Ego, Herd, and Sex Instincts," <u>Journal of</u>
<u>Abnormal and Social Psychology</u>, 16, 1932, p. 268.

[40]Milton Fairchild, "Illustrated Moral
Instruction," <u>Education and National Character</u>,
V. 5, Religious Education Association (Chicago:
Lakeside Press, 1908), pp. 213-220. Fairchild
saw sociology as concerned only with the civilization of this world. He felt that an ethics
which enabled men to merely adjust to the details
of daily life would never win respect nor carry
influence because it would lack truth and wisdom.
He called for a new ethics, a natural ethics.

[41]Letter from Milton Fairchild to Dr.

Edward Ross, dated September 19, 1916. Edward
A. Ross Papers,Division of Archives and Manuscripts, the State Historical Society of Wisconsin.

[42]Character Education Methods, The Iowa
Plan (Chevy Chase: Character Education Institution, 1922), p. iii.

[43]Ibid., p. iv.

[44]William Hutchins, Children's Code of
Morals for Elementary Schools (Washington:
National Capital Press, 1917), p. 1.

[45]Ibid., p. 2.

[46]Ibid., p. 4.

[47]Milton Fairchild, "Important Centers of
Character," School and Society, 9, May 1919, p.
568.

[48]Iowa Plan, op. cit., p. iv.

[49]Studies in the psychology and pedagogy of
character and religion occupied an important
place in the Department of Philosophy and Psychology at the State University of Iowa. In
1922 there was established a Research Station in
Character Education and Religious Education
under the auspices of the Graduate College of
the Department of Philosophy and Psychology. The
Iowa Station was very influential in the beginning of character or personality, analysis,
measurement and testing, as well as in the area
of compiling bibliographies for character education programs. See Edwin D. Starbuck, "Studies
in Character at the University of Iowa," Religious Education, 22, 1927, pp. 48-49.

[50]Milton Fairchild, "Character Education,"
NEA Proceedings, 64, 1926, pp. 402-403. Each
state had its own division of the organization,
directed by the State Superintendent of

Education or by his nominee. The Institution also worked closely with Universities, National Welfare Societies, Colleges of Education and National Patriotic Societies. A flow-chart, depicting the working organization of the Institution can be found reprinted in Thomas J. Golightly, "The Present Status of the Teaching of Morals in the Public High Schools," George Peabody College for Teachers, Contributions to Education, 38, 1926, p. 30.

[51]Ibid., (Fairchild), pp. 404-406.

[52]Ibid., p. 406.

[53]Henry Neumann, "Moral Values in Secondary Education," United States Bureau of Education Bulletin, No. 51, 1917, p. 12.

[54]Ibid., p. 7.

[55]Ibid., p. 37.

[56]Milton Bennion, "Preliminary Report of the Committee on Citizenship and Character Education," NEA Proceedings, 59, July 1921, pp. 344-346; same as "Report of Committee on Citizenship and Character Education," School and Society, 14, Sept. 1921, pp. 190-192.

[57]See Ernest Smith, op. cit., Smith was Superintendent of Schools for Salt Lake City, Utah. Another concern with the necessity of coordination between community agencies in effecting Character Education was put forth by Albert Shiels of Columbia University. He sought coordination of the school, church, library, local board of trade and community council in developing high motives, intelligently interpreting the best motives, and fixing the appropriate actions in habit. See Albert Shiels, "The Coordination of the Community Agencies in Effecting Character Education," NEA Proceedings, 60, 1922, pp. 409-416.

[58]Committee on Character Education, "Theses on Character Education," Journal of Educational Method, 3, Oct. 1923, pp. 84-86.

[59]Milton Bennion, "Report of the Character Education Committee," NEA Proceedings, 61, 1923, p. 251.

[60]Ibid., pp. 491-494.

[61]Ibid., p. 253.

[62]A. Duncan Yocum, "Three Reports on Character Education Objectives," NEA Proceedings, 61, 1923, p. 253. George H. Mead also saw the connection between religion and democracy. He wrote that "the bringing together of the attitude of universal religion on the one hand and the widening political development on the other has been given its widest expression in democracy." See Mind, Self and Society (Chicago: The University of Chicago Press, 1934), p. 286. See also p. 243.

[63]Milton Bennion, "Report of the Committee on Character Education," NEA Proceedings, 62, 1924, p. 279.

[64]Ibid., pp. 281-282. The objectives were 1) personal and social responsibility; 2) self-direction and self-restraint; 3) sense of justice and honesty; 4) defense of right; 5) love; 6) goodwill and service; 7) appreciation and gratitude; 8) tolerance of opposing beliefs; 9) best achievement of person's potential; 10) loyalty, faith and reverence for the good.

[65]Ibid., p. 284.

[66]Edwin D. Starbuck, "Fundamentals of Character Training," NEA Proceedings, 62, 1924, pp. 159-160.

[67]Ibid., pp. 160-164.

[68]Ibid., p. 164.

[69]Edwin Starbuck, "Tests and Measurements of Character," NEA Proceedings, 62, 1924, pp. 159-160.

[70]Starbuck, "Fundamentals of Character Training," op. cit., p. 165.

[71]Character Education, Report of the Committee on Character Education of the NEA. U.S. Bureau of Education, 1926, No. 7, p. 1.

[72]Milton Bennion, "Report of the Committee on Character Education," NEA Proceedings, 63, 1925, pp. 182-183.

[73]Character Education, op. cit., p. 22. In the final report three new subcommittees were represented. They included one on developmental processes (where this quote was taken from), one on delinquency, and one on compiling a bibliography on character education.

[74]Ibid., p. 2.

[75]Galen Fisher, (Executive Secretary of the Institute of Social and Religious Research, Teacher's College, Columbia U.), Studies in the Nature of Character, Vol. 1 (New York: MacMillan Co., 1928), p. v.

[76]Ibid., p. vi.

[77]Ibid., p. vi.

[78]Ibid., pp. 7-8.

[79]Thomas W. Galloway, "The Bearing of Sex Education Upon Character," NEA Proceedings, 60, 1922, p. 420.

[80]Ibid., p. 421.

[81]Thomas W. Galloway, "Chemistry and Character," Journal of Educational Psychology, 13, 1922, p. 305. Galloway was very influenced by the work of Louis Berman. See Louis Berman, The Glands Regulating Personality (New York: MacMillan, 1921).

[82]Thomas W. Galloway, Sex and Social Health (New York: American Social Hygiene Association, 1924), p. 228. See also Thomas Galloway: Parenthood and the Character Training of Children (New York: Methodist Book Concern, 1927); The Responsibilities of Religious Leaders in Sex Education, Publication No. 335 (New York: American Social Hygiene Association, 1921); The Part of the Church in Social Hygiene, Publication No. 520 (New York: American Social Hygiene Association, 1925).

[83]Ibid., p. 229.

[84]Ibid., p. 231.

[85]Ibid., p. 237.

[86]Positive eugenics called for a program of breeding between the most desirable persons in society as a means of race improvement. This is in contrast to negative eugenics where race improvement was to be accomplished by sterilization of defectives. See Marc Haller, Eugenics (New Brunswick: Rutgers University Press, 1963), p. 77.

[87]Edward O. Sisson, "Moral Education Again to the Front," School and Society, 21, May 1925, p. 543.

[88]Ibid., p. 547.

[89]Ibid.

[90] Ibid., p. 548.

[91] Carlton Hays, Essays on Nationalism (New York: MacMillan, 1926), pp. 108-109.

[92] C. E. Merriam, The Making of Citizens (Chicago: University of Chicago Press, 1931), p. 338.

[93] The Lusk Law passed in 1918 in New York prohibited use of any textbook which contained statements seditious in character, disloyal to the U.S. or favorable to the cause of any enemy country.

[94] See Bessie Pierce, Civic Attitudes in American School Textbooks (Chicago: University of Chicago Press, 1930), p. 233.

[95] Ibid., p. 60.

[96] Ibid., p. 123; see also Thomas Dickson, Critique on American School Histories (New York: Military Order of the World War, 1956).

[97] Ibid., p. 124.

[98] "Resolutions of the American Historical Association," The American Historical Review, 29, April 1924, p. 428.

[99] Hays, op. cit., p. 113. Hays believed that nationalistics like religious enthusiasts has a chronic fear that the masses were on the point of losing their faith, and thus only information that strengthened their faith and promoted popular devotion to it should be imparted to them. Thus it sought to keep the minds of the young pure and uncontaminated from knowledge of the full truth which was assumed might weaken if not destroy the nationalistic faith (p. 114). Harry Emerson Fosdick, in his sermon of November 13, 1927, said, "The dogma of nationalism as it has developed in the last two

centuries has become a competing religion and Christianity's supreme rival," pp. 184-185.

[100]J. Montgomery Gambrill, "Nationalism and Civic Education," Teachers College Record, 23, Feb. 1922, p. 110.

[101]Ibid., p. 110-111.

[102]Ibid., p. 120.

[103]George A. Coe, "Religious Education and Political Conscience," Teachers College Record, 23, Sept. 1922, p. 298.

[104]Ibid., pp. 299-300.

[105]Ibid., p. 302. Ellwood P. Cubberley was Dean of Education at Leland Stanford University. See his Public Education in the United States (Boston: Houghton Mifflin Co., 1919), p. 317.

[106]Ibid., p. 303. See William Bagley, "The Place of Duty and Discipline in a Democratic Scheme," Teachers College Record, 9, Nov. 1918, pp. 419-430. Coe also criticized A. Duncan Yocum's, "What Democracy Should Compel Through Religion," Religious Education, 14, 1919, pp. 180-189. Yocum believed that if the older moralists were essential to the well-being and continued existence of democracy then religious cults should be prohibited by national law from antagonizing them.

[107]Ibid., p. 304.

[108]George A. Coe, "Shifting the National Mind-Set," Religious Education, 19, Oct. 1924, p. 321.

[109]George A. Coe, Educating for Citizenship (New York: Charles Scribner's Sons, 1932).

[110]Ibid., p. 10.

[111]Ibid., p. 21.

[112]Ibid., p. 35. See also the Macintosh decisions of the U.S. Supreme Court which ruled 5-4 that whenever Congress votes for War, the decision must be accepted as expressing the will of God, p. 183.

[113]Ibid., p. 73.

[114]Ibid., p. 105.

[115]Ibid., p. 189.

III. THE IMPLEMENTATION OF CHARACTER EDUCATION
        PROGRAMS IN THE SCHOOLS

A.

The concept of character education was well
received in the schools across the country in
the 1920's and early 30's. Although no two programs were exactly the same and a debate on the
most appropriate methods to be employed raged
throughout its implementation, character education represented a major undertaking in the
development of American education. The educational system at this time not only stressed
the intellectual development of the child, but it
also began to shape and influence his social and
moral growth as well.

Character education was a result of the concern with educating the whole child. With the
breakdown of the influence of the home and Church
in the area of moral training, the school picked
up the burden of character training and moral
education. F. Neff Stroup, Superintendent of
Schools in Newark, New York, summarized that
transition in the following manner:

> Character training has come to take
> on a new meaning. We used to look upon
> character as the moral development of
> the child and considered the home and
> the church largely responsible for this
> instruction. Now we recognize it as
> the sum total of qualities or features
> which distinguish one person from
> another. This involves not only the
> moral or spiritual growth of the child
> but the intellectual, physical and so-
> cial as well.[1]

Character education programs not only stressed citizenship training, but they often were
also concerned with preparing the child for his

future life in the society. This included
lessons in life adjustment, right living, vocational efficiency and worthy use of leisure time.
The concern with the increasing crime rate,
especially among adolescents, and the breakdown
of law and order manifested itself across the
country in programs of character education. The
schools were seen as the panacea for the social
crises of the times. The best way to alleviate
the lawlessness and breakdown in morality was
thought to be helping children acquire high
ethical standards as well as good habits of
conduct and assisting them in adjusting to the
society in which they lived.

The increasing modernization and urbanization of society witnessed the breakdown in
morality and the ethical influence of the Church
and the family. Schools were there to assume
this burden. The morality and ethics that they
fostered were the values of the dominant influences in the culture, a morality which might
have been best for the maintenance of the social
order but often was one which was in conflict
with an individual's religious, moral or ethical
conscience. The educational system thus had
control over the child's intellectual development and felt the responsibility to prepare him
for citizenship and adjustment to life, according to the precepts of right living. Character
education even made one of its most important
goals, as evidenced by its stress in programs
across the country, the education of the child
for worthy use of his leisure.

Counseling was a crucial part of character
education and possibly had the most lasting effect on the educational process. In order to
assist persons in their adjustment to life it
was often necessary for them to have the guidance
and leadership of those who could show them the
best values in society. Guidance programs,
however, had two forms which resulted in different approaches to the development of
character. The first form was group guidance

programs, such as assemblies, clubs, athletics, the concept of the homeroom, and even student government, where all students could be guided in the responsibilities of life in a group. Group participation in extra-curricular activities, such as Scouting, the Y.M.C.A., and Red Cross were similarly stressed.

Individual guidance was another aspect of the counseling influence in character education. The case method approach was often utilized in treating behavior or character problems. Psychologists and psychiatrists were brought into the schools along with nurses and psychiatric social workers to deal with the adjustment of individual problems. Individual guidance also took the form of visiting teachers, going into the homes to deal with possible parental difficulties; and of special schools for behavior problems.

Character education took the forms, both of adjusting the individual to society by guiding him in group participation and responsibility, and of attempting to alleviate his maladjustment by means of psychological guidance and counseling. The parent was often seen as totally ignorant of child development and the problems encountered therein and thus character education programs often recommended education for parenthood.

The force of character education and the tremendous influence that it exerted also manifested itself in the form of the child's report card. Most cards reflected only the student's intellectual progress, which gave an incomplete picture of the whole child. Many school systems began putting conduct or character ratings directly on the report card to augment the measure of intellect; some used a separate character-rating chart. In either case the stress on character as well as intellect was clear.

Just as it was insufficient to educate a

child merely in terms of intellect, it was likewise insufficient to report his progress only in
terms of intellectual growth. The character of
the child needed to be shaped and adjusted to the
society's ideals of right living; in addition, it
needed to be evaluated and the progress of its
development reported.

B.

The first comprehensive plan for character
education was developed by Edwin Starbuck at the
State University of Iowa. The Iowa Plan, as it
was subsequently known, won the $20,000 First
Prize in 1921 as a result of the Character Education Institution's search for the best public
school plan for the character education of
children. This plan was widely circulated and
influenced the creation and implementation of
character education programs across the country.

The Iowa Plan set forth thirteen foundation
principles which not only sought to create a
goal for character education but also attempted
to measure the progress and the product of such
an endeavor. The end product of such a program
was personal in that it sought not only to teach
good virtues but also to create good people.
The good people were to have been thoroughly
socialized, which meant they were not only made
good citizens but were made moral as well.[2] The
distinction between the moral man and the good
citizen was once again blurred. The moral man
was seen as best represented in the concept of
the good socialized citizen. This conceptual
transference was characteristic of the move for
character education. The concept of a state-
sanctioned morality had taken precedence over
the conscience of the Church, the family or even
the individual. To obey the laws of society
made one moral and good.

Starbuck's principles also stressed the
importance of conducting oneself in the practice
of the good life rather than merely entertaining

106.

thought about it, as well as the development of progressive skills in moral thoughtfulness according to the stage of development of the child. Starbuck believed in a stage theory of development as well as in a psychic law, wherein ontogeny recapitulated phylogeny. Thus, as the child grew up he passed through the cultural stages of his ancestors. According to Starbuck, these stages were those of childhood, 0-3 or 4 years (represented by the dominance of habits, instincts, precepts), boyhood, 3-7 or 8 years (dominated by desires and imagery), youth, 7-12 or 14 (dominated by sympathies and clear ideas), and adolescence, 12-maturity (dominated by moral sentiments and thoughtfulness).[3] As a result of this belief it is clear why the Iowa Plan stressed the importance of familiarizing children with the best of racial (humanity) traditions in the areas of myth, legend, poetry and drama.

The average child, according to Starbuck, needed a threefold recentering. This included a transformation of his lower selfhood of crude instincts and desires into a higher personality of refined taste in insight, outlook, and intellectual purpose; an awakening into wholesome appreciation of the interest and well-being of others and participating in their programs, customs, conventions and institutions and showing loyalty to their ideals; a disinterested administration of the non-personal values in nature and life, those that glorify both the self and other than self and culminate in a spirit of reverence.

Starbuck felt that to bring about this threefold othering of the original, unorganized life of childhood was the end and aim of character education.[4] The goal was:

. . . A person with powers proportionally developed, with mental discrimination, aesthetic appreciation and moral determination; one aware of his social relationships and happily

active in the discharge of all obli-
gations; one capable of a leisure-
loving nature, revering human beings,
their aspirations and achievements;
one observant of fact, respect of law
and order, devoted to truth and justice; one who, while loyal to the best
traditions of his people, dreams and
works toward better things; and one
in whom is the allure of the ideal
and whose life will not be faithless
thereto.[5]

The allure of the ideal did not detract
Starbuck from his concern with preparation of
pupils for life adjustment, which included the
areas of health, life in the group, civic relations, industrial and economic relations, vocation, parenthood, and tradition. The concepts of
morality, health and socio-economic relations
were all-important to character education under
the Iowa Plan.

Starbuck even presented a justification for
democracy over autocracy and Bolshevism. He was
against the centralized authority that he saw in
autocracy as well as the anarchy and nihilism
that he saw in Bolshevism,[6] but nevertheless he
saw these two elements along with the interacting
agencies for insuring adjustment of individuals
and groups into a living social whole, as the
three essentials for democracy.

"The democracy," wrote Starbuck, "has as
great a centralization of power as imperialism
but with this difference, that authority rises
from and is vested in people themselves."[7] This
concept of democracy as the centralization of
power reflected the same train of thought which
viewed the concept of morality as the centralization and standardization of state-sanctioned
behavior. In the latter case as well as the
former, the State could sanction any of its actions on the grounds the authority rose from and
was vested in the people themselves.

The concept of "education according to nature," where children would be free to develop naturally was seen by Starbuck as more fit for anarchy. Teachers who accepted this belief were seen as giving up all their responsibility for shaping the conduct, thought, and sympathies of the child. According to Starbuck, "the teacher must accept her place as a kind of leader of children and men and as a shaper of the destiny of the State."[8]

Starbuck's plan for character education involved the deliberate shaping and controlling of the child's environment according to the theory of recapitulation. From nature stories, storytelling and make-believe, to myths, legends, hero and great-man stories, to fiction and ethics, the child was seen to gradually recapitulate the life of the savage, the barbarian, and finally the moral being. Starbuck wrote:

> The proper selection of character training materials and how to use them depends somewhat upon the tastes and needs of children as determined by the period or stage of development through which they are passing.[9]

One of the previously mentioned goals of life adjustment in the Iowa Plan was the preparation of the child for family life and parenthood. Starbuck argued against repression and for the sublimation, redirecting or channeling of the reproductive passions along the lines of innocent companionship.[10] While he did not comment on the subject of sex education in the schools, he did feel that one should "approach the question of sex usually from above rather than from below, i.e., from ideal considerations rather than from practical or factual ones."[11]

Starbuck shared many of the views of his former mentor, G. Stanley Hall, who had been very concerned with the spiritualization of the concept of sex.[12] Moreover, both were very concerned with the eugenic improvement of the race. In his chart of Suggestions of Projects and Problems to Enrich a Character Training Curriculum, Starbuck provided a year-by-year project or problem suggestion in each of the seven objectives of life adjustment. Under family and parenthood, he suggested the observation of heredity in animals (Grade 6), the study of Burbank (Grade 8), a controlled experiment in cross-fertilization (Grade 9), the study of race problems (Grade 10), and the study of race improvement (Grade 11). The rationale employed by Starbuck was that:

> When in connection with the profound insights into biological progress, for example, one is able to picture possible race improvement through right breeding, it becomes as impossible for the young man to despoil the human breed through foolishness as it would be for him to destroy a highly developed breed of animals or variety of plants.[13]

The Iowa Plan was so well accepted because it was seen to be based upon a thorough knowledge of the public schools, the most accepted theories of modern psychology and the most progressive principles and methods of sound pedagogy.[14] The Iowa Plan also presented practical schemes for the rating of individuals in qualities of character and in the improvement of these qualities. Jessie B. Davis, State Supervisor of Secondary Education for Connecticut, wrote:

> The plan is clear-headed and business-like. It is national in scope. It calls for a more conscious endeavor upon the part of teachers to make each one of their pupils the sort of citizen this country must have if democracy is to be preserved,

one who is respectful of law and
order, devoted to truth and justice
and loyal to the best traditions of
the past.[15]

Another influential character education
program was known as the Utah Plan,[16] which was
devised in 1925 by a character education committee headed by Milton Bennion who, while Dean
of the School of Education of the University
of Utah, also headed the N.E.A. Committee on
Character Education. The Plan made use of the
Iowa Plan, the Hutchins Morality Code, and the
Goals of the N.E.A. Committee on Character Education.

Previously, the Utah Law of 1919 had required all boys and girls up to the age of 18 to
be at school or under supervised work for the
entire year. They would register once a year
for a twelve-month enrollment. Known as the
Rexburg Plan, this concept in year-round supervision also provided for subjects to be pursued
through summer vacation, with the work supervised
and graded by teachers. It is clear how the
State of Utah wanted to make the school a greater
force for training in morality, and character
education was a vital part of such a plan.

The goals of the Utah Plan were social
progress and the development of personalities.
Bennion, et al., felt that children should practice the good life rather than entertain thoughts
about it. It was not enough to know what the
good life was. One had to practice it in his
everyday conduct. The character developing
school had to be orderly and organized so as to
make "self-control easy and popular."[17] Once
again, the value of order was crucial for the
development of self-control. What one thought
was not nearly as important as what one did, and
thus the concern with conduct rather than with
intellect was stressed as was the necessity for
replacing external control with self-control.

111.

The new citizen would be able to control himself and willingly take his own place in society.

Bennion seemed greatly influenced by[18] George Mirick's book, <u>Progressive Education</u> and quoted from it often. Not only did Mirick call for conditions favorable in school for conduct leaders to rise to prominence (similar to Fairchild's Uncle Sam's Boys and Girls), but he also wanted a school of freedom that, according to Bennion, had conditions favorable to character education. Mirick's school of freedom was an orderly, efficient, quiet school, but one with opportunity for mischief because, if there were no such opportunities, there was no freedom of choice and of self-control and thus no morality. Once again, the goal of character education was to enable the pupil to pursue the proper conduct as a result of his own self-control and self-direction.[19]

The Utah Plan stressed the need for good food, fresh air, plenty of sleep and much play. Play was viewed as a tremendous opportunity for training in self-control, attention, training of the will, and sportsmanship for the growing child, and was advocated by Bennion because, "on the playground he not only builds up a strong body, but receives a mental and moral training that comes from no other source."[20]

Like the Iowa Plan, Bennion's Utah Plan also made use of stage theory of development. The objectives and methods used reflected the physical and psychological period that the child was thought to be passing through at that time. All the stages of development had their own characteristics, but the use of slogans, poetry, mottoes and proverbs was a constant mechanism used to develop character. Frederick Bolton attributed this to the law of ideo-motor action.

> The law of ideo-motor action
> (viz., that every idea which gains
> lodgement in the mind tends to

express itself in action), is
sufficient warrant to urge memoriz-
ing gems of poetry, proverbs, and
beautiful uplifting sayings. The
Buffalo Plan, the Utah Plan and the
Iowa Plan of character education all
urge emphasis upon this phase of
method in character building.[21]

The Utah Plan made use of literature,
mathematics, foreign languages, geography,
science, industrial education, art, music, physical education and hygiene, as vehicles for
character education. Industrial education was
deemed very important because "training for
service must finally be regarded as the chief
duty of man, and to realize that training in
industrial efficiency increases the ability to
serve home, community, and nation."[22]

In 1929 the Utah Plan was revised to include new chapters on psychological principles
and case method approaches. The new emphasis on
adjustment and psychological guidance in character education was clearly evident. The revised
plan spoke of all the new advancements in
psychological theory, including the theories of
Freud and Adler, and the acquisition of habits
by imitation, attention, and conditioned reflex.
The case method approach used in the psychological and social sciences was also adopted.

Antecedents to this approach could be
found in the National Committee for Visiting
Teachers, which in 1919 undertook a five-year
experiment financed by the Commonwealth Fund.
Beginning in 1921 the movement spread so quickly
that by the close of 1927 there were 211 visiting
teachers regularly employed by boards of education in 75 cities scattered throughout 37
states.[23]

The case-method approach was used by
teachers to visit the homes of the mentally
retarded, physically defective, the emotionally

113.

unadjusted and the morally handicapped children
in the public schools. Character education, in
terms of its new concern with individual guidance
for maladjusted pupils, had broadened its horizons
and influence. It was no longer satisfied to
work for citizenship training and preparation for
life in society, but it now concerned itself with
alleviating the problems of the maladjusted
pupils. The revised plan stated:

> According to the most reliable
> surveys of the problem, about five
> percent of the unselected elementary
> school population are so retarded
> mentally as to require more or less
> individualized guidance. Another
> five percent--making ten percent in
> all--is made up of such types as the
> epileptic, the cardiac and choreic
> children, the chronic truant, the
> stealer, the seclusive child, the
> disobedient or stubborn child, the
> daydreamer, the sexually unadjusted
> child, etc., all of whom demand special
> care and differential guidance by the
> school staff.[24]

The interesting part of the above concern
with guidance for maladjusted or unadjusted children, is not even so much that they grouped
physically handicapped persons with truants,
sexually unadjusted children and daydreamers, but
that all of these could be seen as problems for
character education. It nonetheless followed
logically from their arguments. Character education seemingly became a matter of adjustment and
all those who had trouble adjusting to society
for whatever reason, needed character education
in the form of personal guidance. The goal of
the ideal society was everpresent in the minds
of the reformers and set the boundaries of their
standards.

> For a reflective and progressive
> moral personality, there is an ideal

114.

society over and above the actual
society and it is this that sets
the standards for moral advancement.[25]

It is no small wonder that those in search
of the ideal society would attempt to isolate
those who would not or could not fit into such a
model and either rehabilitate them or put them
into custodial institutions. Character education
received its theories of personal conflicts and
maladjustment from the growing fields of psychoanalysis, psychopathology, and mental hygiene.
Character education had augmented its patriotic
socio-economic approach with psychological
guidance and counseling.[26]

As a result of a 1927 act of the Nebraska
legislature, all grades 1-12 were required to
provide for character education curricula and
development. The program was headed by F. M.
Gregg of the Psychology Department at Nebraska
Wesleyan University. Unlike the Iowa and Utah
Plans, the Nebraska Plan[27] accepted the hormic
theory of action. This theory made full use of
racial urges and instincts in its explanation of
child development. Gregg was quick to point out,
however, that this was not a belief in recapitulation, with which he disagreed, but was just a
belief that certain characteristics were dominant
at definite times of the individual's growth.
Instincts were viewed to have aspects of cogni-
tion (perception), conation (struggle), and
emotion (strong feeling accompanying the struggle). The Nebraska Plan answered the question of
how does one get pupils to do what they ought to
do, by the following:

1. control their feelings
2. direct their instincts and emotions
3. persuade their intelligence
4. influence their habits through
   a. conditioning of instincts
   b. forming of sentiments
   c. modifying their motor adjustment[28]

115.

The Nebraska Plan also had separate lists of characteristics of the various stages of development. Each period was discussed in terms of physical traits, instinctive and emotional ties, mental characteristics, and moral and religious development. From these traits, suitable character objectives were established by means of control, direction, persuasion and influence. Thus, the best way to control a person's behavior (character education) was seen to be attitude control. Paul Rankin, Superintendent and Director of Research and Adjustment of the Detroit Public Schools, also advocated attitude control, when he wrote:

> Character education is largely a matter of attitude. It behooves all of us to learn from the advertising man, the propagandist and others who are expert in determining and in modifying people's attitudes.[29]

C.

The period of the "Roaring 20's" was one of moral turbulence in American society. Not only were prohibition, flappers, and speak-easies a part of the American scene, but the debate on the rise of the crime rate was raging. Some found statistics which proved that crime of violence had been steadily increasing in the United States since 1900 while others felt that the absolute numbers of crimes were increasing but they attributed it to the increase in population. Another area of debate centered on the increase in crime among those under 34. One thing seemed sure, however, and that was the fact that the crime rate among women was increasing. The changing role of women in this period of American history also seemed to increase their susceptibility to criminal action. The crime rate of Blacks and second generation American youth was also higher than the rest of the population and was attributed either to the hostile,

116.

urban nightmares with which they had to cope or was explained by references to their inherent deficiencies.[30]

As a result of this perception of a decaying moral situation, the Department of Superintendence of the N.E.A. initiated its own Committee on Character Education. It felt that training in right conduct was one of the chief objectives of the public schools, and that a survey should be taken to determine what was being done in the schools of the United States to further the development of ethical character.

The Committee also was committed to offering suggestions as to how the efforts of the schools to provide character education could be improved. As a result of an inquiry sent to 300 cities enrolled in the Cooperative Plan of Curriculum Revision, the Committee reported its findings in the Fourth Yearbook of the Department of Superintendence published in 1926.[31]

The Committee reported that the efforts at Character Education across the country were "seemingly feverish, anxious, and even frantic in character."[32] It was impossible to discover anybody of settled convictions as to experiences needed or subject matter preferred. There was little evidence of carefully thought-out, well-tested techniques of procedure which could be employed in securing character results. Thus while the schools of the country were giving universal and definite attention to the development of good character, there was some confusion and lack of clear knowledge as to how best to go about the problem of character education.[33]

Of the 300 questionnaires sent out, 229 were returned. The majority of endeavors seemed to be directed toward utilization of regular curricular and extra-curricular activities to develop desirable habits and ideals. While only 20% of the systems used special character-

education materials (codes, plans, special
character education courses of study) and only
20% used special programmed periods for character
education, 65% of the schools reported use of the
opening exercise period for character education
purposes, such as Bible study, clubs, assemblies,
art, or music. Of the schools that did report
use of individual periods for character education,
66% were in grades K-6, 24% in grades 7-9, and
10% in High School.[34]

    As far as can be ascertained from the
questionnaires, there seemed to be no widespread
tendency to adopt the plans and codes thus far
developed. Most systems seemed content to either
develop their own course of study, or else pursue
character education results through regular school
subjects. A total of 98 references were made in
the questionnaire returns to courses of study in
various subjects which contained suggestions as
to ways for securing character education results.
Over thirty-six percent of these references were
to courses in history, civics and Americanization. English and social studies were next in
order of frequency. Character education at this
point (1926), seemed to be largely concerned with
social relations.[35]

    The debate as to the adequate methodology
being the direct teaching of character objectives
or the indirect approach through normal subject
matter, was not settled here, but an equal stress
on both was found. Some stressed specific standards while other spoke of the proper development
of each pupil as an individual. The influence
of the teacher through her proper example,
character, and attitude was named most frequently
as the chief determinant in the development of
good character in pupils. The life of the school
as a whole was next in importance, followed by
the relations between pupils and teachers, and
finally, pupil relations.

    The diversity and expanse of character

education in the schools was evidenced by the
range of pupil activities suggested as ways of
securing character education results. Physical
education activities were mentioned most often,
followed by school control activities (student
councils, student government) club activities,
activities involving individual pupil responsibility, and assembly activities.[36]

Individual personality development seemed
to be stressed in classroom relations, rather
than in other school relations. This conclusion
is strengthened by the fact that activities involving individual pupil responsibility ranked
ninth in ten classifications of school activities
outside the classroom reported as encouraged,
and seventh among the nine classifications of
activities suggested in the life of the school as
a whole. Those activities involving the greatest
social cooperation, namely, club activities,
physical education, school control, assembly,
social, welfare, journalistic and forensic activities, all ranked above activities involving
individual pupil responsibility.[37]

Since practically all the respondents
included a list of traits and attitudes which
they thought to be desirable, a list of desirable
character education outcomes was compiled. In
overall mention, the top five traits were
courtesy, honesty, cooperation, loyalty and conformity. Judgment was ranked thirteenth and
leadership was not ranked at all. In terms of
classroom recitation alone, the desirable traits
were honesty, courtesy, industry, cooperation
and independence, with initiative ranked thirteenth and leadership fifteenth. In terms of
other classroom relations, the traits most favored
included courtesy, cooperation, justice, loyalty,
and conformity. Here independence was ranked
ninth, initiative was ranked fifteenth, fraternity
fourteenth, and judgment, thirteenth.

In school life as a whole, the traits of
loyalty, responsibility, conformity, cooperation

and courtesy were most desirable.[38] From this it is evident how the social values of conformity, cooperation, courtesy, loyalty, took precedence over the values of initiative, leadership, fraternity, and independence. This, however, is not surprising, in light of the social relations approach that character education manifested itself in at this time. The goal, remember, was the "thoroughly socialized individual."[39]

The Superintendent's report also contained examples of how character education goals could be implemented through regular school subjects, such as physical training, science, mathematics, fine arts, spelling and music. Once again, the stress on right and wrong, even in the case of school subjects, was considered a moral issue. Taking spelling as an example, it was believed that "there (was) a right way to spell a word (and) all other ways (were) wrong."[40] Spelling errors were a result of a failure in conduct. One had to develop a "spelling conscience" which would not only instill an abiding desire to spell correctly but would also generate the appropriate remorse and sense of shame if the words were misspelled. Character was also to be fostered by the correct use of the dictionary.

The right spelling of words was considered an issue of one's conscience, and spelling mistakes demonstrated an unsatisfactory conduct which through the appropriate approval and disapproval of the teacher and class could be corrected. Simple cognitive skills, like memory or recall, were transferred into issues of conscience and ethical conduct, which could only be remedied by shame and remorse.

Those investigating the influence of character education also were interested in the implementation of character education in the kindergarten. A list of twenty desirable character traits, which was compiled from a report sent to parents by the Lincoln School of Columbia

Teachers College, was mailed to sixty-five
kindergarten teachers across the country. The
five most important traits to be developed in
the kindergarten were truthfulness, respect for
the rights of others, courtesy, cooperation and
obedience to authority.[41]

While the stated objectives of the kindergarten were to provide the environment which
offered the opportunity for the exercise of
desirable traits and to guide these activities
so as to enable the child to gain conscious
control of them,[42] it was likewise felt that
"psychologically the parental relation to the
child and teacher relations to the learner is
that of authority to obedience."[43] The report
continued:

> The highest form of cooperative
> conduct found where those in authority
> exhibit and exercise intelligent good
> will and the one in obedience has in-
> sight enough to recognize the author-
> ity as good will, and accordingly
> joyously cooperates in what is essen-
> tially a joint project.[44]

It was believed that this form of authority and obedience exhibited the democratic form
of authority and thus government procedure at
its best. Character education also sought this
joyous obedience to the good will of the authority of the teacher, the school and the country.
Everyone was seen to have the freedom and power
to achieve good character, but they likewise
have the possibility of failure through disobedience and wrong action. While promotion of
strength and integrity of character was crucial,
a technique for recovery from wrong conduct was
also viewed as a necessary principle.

Two breaks in character took place when
misconduct occurred. The first was the break in
the personality from within, resulting in a

fracture of the self; and the second was a break with authority or society from without. This dual aspect of wrong conduct was considered very crucial to the Superintendent's Committee. They felt that "parents and teachers may be justified in absolving themselves for any responsibility for the particular 'behavior segment' diagnosed as wrong, but they cannot be absolved themselves, from responsibility for acting as counselors in the process of recovery."[45]

Interestingly enough, the parable of the Prodigal Son was given as an example of the psychology of the whole process. Teachers and counselors were seen as the new bearers of moral judgment and forgiveness. The concept of character education not only involved promotion and development of sound character but it slowly was evolving into a process involving repentance, confession, restitution, and consecration of wrong conduct.[46] As character education developed between 1925 and 1935 it was evident that psychological guidance and counseling became an ever-important factor in character education. It was not enough to promote integrity and good conduct. One had to correct misbehavior and wrongdoing and restore the self to its psychic whole.

D.

The best way to understand what was going on in the schools in terms of character education is to examine the various procedures and objectives that were used in cities and states across the country. While no two approaches were exactly the same, many similarities and common themes recurred.

In 1925 the Character Education Committee of the New York City Board of Education submitted its Report on character education in the high school. The Committee believed that the aim of character education should be to "develop

122.

clearcut conceptions of positive virtues, to
(present) the principles of right living that
will govern boys and girls in making moral decisions rather than stressing 'thou shalt not.'"[47]
It was their feeling that citizenship training
had been neglected in favor of intellectual
attainment and there was thus a need for positive
instruction in character education. This included not only adoption of ethical codes and use of
assemblies for character education, but it also
included the training of students in the responsibility of student organizations. New York City
also adopted the use of citizenship or character
ratings on reports to parents and even revised
the wording on diplomas to include both character
and scholarship qualifications as a response to
the demand of college and business firms for
credentials of good character. Finally, they
recommended that the position of Dean be established in the high school for the direction of
character education.[48]

The Nebraska legislature enacted a Character Education Law in 1927 to provide the necessary
legal authority whereby the State Department of
Public Instruction might make available to the
teachers of the State, material necessary in setting up a program for the purpose of building
character. According to Bill 79-2131, it was
the duty of each and every teacher in the first
twelve grades of any public, private, parochial
or denominational school in the State of Nebraska
to give special emphasis to

> Common honesty, morality,
> courtesy, obedience to law, respect
> for the national flag, the Constitu-
> tion of the United States and of the
> State of Nebraska, respect for parents
> and the home, the dignity and neces-
> sity of honest labor and other lessons
> of a steadying influence which tend
> to promote and develop an upright
> citizenry.[49]

The Law was a result of the state-wide demand that something be done to check the apparent increase of delinquents among the youth of the State. Character education would reinstitute law and order, obedience, respect for authority and stability. While the debates raged on the actuality of a rise in delinquency and what segments of society were most involved and why, character education programs blanketed the country.

A part of the Nebraska Plan that attempted to cultivate right action was the Knighthood of Youth Plan. This organization was developed through the efforts of Dr. John H. Finley in New York City in 1924, but was subsequently adopted by the Nebraska Department of Public Instruction in 1933. Using capes, helmets, armbands, shields, flag salutes and other medieval ritual and pageantry, the Knighthood of Youth Club attempted to prepare boys and girls for "service with a smile."[50] The Club's objective was to develop good citizens, citizens who understood the principles of honesty, cleanliness, courtesy, respect for law and order. Along with the usual objectives in the areas of law and order, cleanliness and honesty, the value of thrift also appeared. As the economic depression of the time continued, thrift became another desirable trait for cultivation in character education.

The concern with the "growing laxity of morals, the increasing disregard for law, the lessening of home and parental authority through the conditions of modern life, the increase of crime, the breakdown of religious sanctions, hitherto such a bulwark of moral stability,"[51] was not limited to Nebraska. Pontiac, Michigan was experiencing the same situation and it also attempted to counteract the deteriorating tendencies of the time by creating in its children and youth, ideals and habits that would on the one hand built into their lives through habit, a resistance factor that would stand them in good

124.

stead in hours of temptation, and on the other hand would instill ideals of individual and social behavior. Unlike other approaches, the character education program in Pontiac schools sought to educate and train teachers to handle personnel and problem children through the case work approach with the pupils, neighbors and parents.

As stated previously, character education objectives and methodologies often differed among programs. There was no widespread agreement as to the exact objectives sought or the correct procedures to be used. According to Gordon Hendrickson of Teachers College at the University of Cincinnati, the great spiritual leaders of the race have always regarded themselves as teachers and have recognized spirituality in the task of teaching.[52] He was opposed to the factory metaphor of education and instead, favored Froebel's concept of the spirituality of the child. For Hendrickson, schools were not factories but were places in which children lived and grew. His concept of character education emphasized children's needs, pupil initiative and individual difference rather than uniformity.

Norwalk, Connecticut established a Bureau of Character Education Research on November 5, 1930. This Bureau was part of the Connecticut State Board of Education as a result of the plan of the Hartley-Jenkins Corporation for the study and development of character education. The Norwalk schools were set up as lab schools. The Bureau, under the directorship of Ruth White Colton and the supervision of the Yale School of Education, worked in the areas of a state-wide teacher training program, Extension courses and community cooperation, with such organizations as the Department of Health and Character, County Commissioner, religious societies, Boy Scouts, P.T.A., and the League of Women Voters.[53]

It was also important to the Bureau to discover the existing practices and principles

125.

in character education and to evaluate them in light of modern psychology. The Connecticut Congress of Parents and Teachers was the first State Congress to establish a common character education emphasis for the entire community. They felt that,

> In other words, it is unfair to charge failure to either home, church, school, or community, since anyone or more than one of these phases of the child's life may completely nullify the efforts at character formation put forth by other places.[54]

Norwalk schools made use of maps to give them information on physical pictures of each district in terms of the location of parks, movie houses, poolrooms, gang meeting places, Y.M.C.A., as well as the density of the child population of school age, the density of wage-earning population and the location of the foreign population. They suggested the use of guidance training for boys and girls, aged 14-16, seeking employment, and even recommended the creation of a full-time all-year-round recreation leader and a detention home modeled along the lines of the Society for the Prevention of Cruelty to Animals shelter at Mineola, Long Island.[55]

While the new State Commissioner of Education, Dr. Ernest W. Betterfield, felt that character education was the "art of living together well,"[56] the Connecticut Bureau also favorably quoted the Superintendent of Chicago, W. J. Bogan, and his concern with a factory metaphor for education:

> It is about time that we were paying direct attention to the building of character the same as we build buildings and ships, by having designs drawn and having experts do the work.[57]

The Norwalk, Connecticut teachers made 1274 visits to the homes of their pupils. Sixteen teachers visited 100% of their pupils' homes, and 88% of the teachers in Norwalk undertook the task. The concern with case-method approach and the importance of pupil as well as parental guidance by visiting teachers were both a crucial part of character education in Connecticut.[58]

The concept of adult education or education for parenthood is one which appeared often in discussion of character education. Those concerned with the "appalling prevalence of lawlessness and crime throughout the country,"[59] were opposed to the conflicting moral standards between the school and the outside world. Adults had to be educated or re-educated into the morality of the State as represented by the school. The school became the bearer of the true morality. Good character was expressed by moral conduct sanctioned by the principal and teacher.[60] Thus, morality was redefined to mean socialization. Development of character meant development of right habits of social relations. The moral man was the good pupil, the good citizen.

While many educators complained that the schools had not been very effective in citizenship training or in preparing people for the goals of right living or life adjustment, still others argued for the opposite viewpoint. Character education was necessary, not because the schools had been ineffective, but instead, "because the schools (were) so effective in their work, we naturally, at the time of many social crises, turn to the school as a panacea for all our ills."[61] In this call for character education, the Dean of the Graduate School of the University of Wichita proceeded to describe the activities in character education in several school systems across the country.

Several prominent themes recurred. A

127.

common methodology was to assign a different
character trait each month which was to be studied by each grade. The Bedford Plan of Bedford,
Indiana, stressed the qualities of industry,
courtesy, unselfishness, obedience and respect,
civics and cooperation, loyalty and patriotism,
truthfulness, honesty, sportsmanship and self-
control,[62] while the Newark Plan utilized the
traits of the Hutchins Morality Code.[63]

The Bedford Plan made use of quotations,
drama, mottos, poetry, storytelling, as well as
physical education, group activities, the Hi-Y,
and Girl Reserves in an attempt to develop civic
conduct for the right ideals and principles of
living. This concern with producing the ideal
citizen and adjusting his life work to his native
endowment was shared by the Boston Plan.[64] The
Boston Plan also stressed developing the pupils'
capacity for the right use of leisure. The
Denver Plan[65] made use of report cards, social-
civic activities, student participation in
government, advisors, the home-room and the
assembly in an attempt to generate a greater insight, a stronger will and better habits in its
pupils.

In the public schools of Missoula, Montana, report cards were constructed where pupils
could be checked as unsatisfactory in honesty,
truthfulness, thrift, self-control, good sportsmanship, school service and good workmanship.
It was felt that the emphasis on grades, rewarded
dishonesty more than honesty, and thus character
ratings were more effective.[66]

The concepts of right living, life adjustment, and right use of leisure epitomized the
moralistic zeal of character education. It was
now the duty of the school to dictate the right
way to live, to act, to relax. Even the structure and functioning of the school itself adapted
to this new goal by stressing the homeroom concept for character guidance, by creating student

128.

governments where the students could learn to
govern themselves, and finally by instituting
character ratings on report cards. All of this
was clearly at attempt to produce good citizens
who not only acted according to the right precepts of life and were well adjusted to their role
in society, but who also knew how to make the
right use of their leisure time. Character education programs fostered a civic religion that
touched every aspect of an individual's life.[67]

    The educators of Kansas City, Missouri
also had specific objectives in character building. While they wanted their students to appreciate the traits of the great men and women of
the past and present and to recognize the right
ideals of living, it was also crucial for the
students to have the opportunity to practice
the traits. True citizenship could be developed
as a result of rationalized habit formation and
automatization of the right habits. Character
educators in Kansas City were also concerned with
diagnosis and integration of personality, and use
of rating cards for citizenship. The four character building objectives were stated to be
worthy home membership, civic life, recreational
life and ethical character. Once again, the
school was seen as the bearer of the true precepts of social relations and morality, not only
for the pupil's home life and his leisure, but
for his ethical development as well.[68] The
values stressed were promptness, orderliness,
self-control and obedience, courtesy, cooperation,
honesty and health.[69]

    New York State Education Department pub-
lished a bulletin entitled, "Character Building
in New York Public Schools." It presented an
analysis of the practices of 150 city, village,
and district superintendents, as well as an
analysis of case reports submitted by some
seventy-five principals and ninety teachers,
"to give a fair picture of what New York Public
Schools (were) doing in character building."[70]

The report stressed the necessity of the guidance director, the principal and the teacher working together to perfect an organization for social and moral guidance which was viewed as "the essence of character building."[71] While New York schools made use of a variety of syllabi, outlines, codes, pupil organizations, and assembly activities for the development of character, the influence of the teacher was seen to be the most important because, "from kindergarten to senior high school, the subtle influence of 'what she is' is a powerful factor in the lives of boys and girls."[72] The "business of the school was to produce good citizens,"[73]and thus the primary consideration in character education was "not what a child learns but what he becomes."[74]

The concern with the crime situation and those forces which tended to halt human progress, disintegrate society and undermine civilization was not absent on the West Coast of America, either. The Oakland, California public schools were very concerned with maintaining stability and order and in 1923 created a character education course of study.[75] A crucial part of their program was a policy platform for parents. Modern parenthood, according to the Oakland educators, should distinctly recognize and shape a program of home training for character. Much of the crime was blamed on the over-indulgence and carelessness on the part of parents. They were accused of substituting material things for a careful program of child training.[76]

The Oakland Plan wanted emphasis placed on obedience and respect for law in the fostering of good citizenship. Activities suggested included clubs centered around achievement, cleanliness, clean news, and knights; plays on punctuality, the community chest, and the red, white and blue; as well as creation of such activities as thriftsville, honor societies, Junior police, student council, character charts and character grades on report cards. The values of law and order, stability, cleanliness, purity, thrift, loyalty, honesty, and self-control were the central objectives of character education in Oakland. In this case, the parents were blamed for much of the disorder and thus in this case the necessity for education for parenthood was clearly recognized.

Notable agreement on methods to be employed in character education was lacking, but the final product was similar in most cases. In Los Angeles, conscience was viewed as merely the individualization of long-established social codes.[77] The goal of character education was conformity to the prevailing standard of ethical conduct. Morality, in terms of rules and actions was seen to be not only empirical but tentative as well.[78] The relativity of value questions and the false notion of them being empirical, clearly demonstrated the creation of a pragmatic civic morality, a morality that could change depending upon the circumstances and needs of the society.

The objectives of character education in Los Angeles were vocational efficiency, worthy home membership, good citizenship, and worthy use of leisure time.[79] In an auto mechanic's course at Franklin High School, an interesting description of how proper attitude toward the teacher and the subject was as praiseworthy as the attained skill was justified by the fact that the objective was citizenship, not craftsmanship.[80] The traits of reliability, dependability, responsibility, honesty, neatness, cleanliness, ambition, accuracy, shop ethics, regularity and punctuality were all stressed, over and beyond craftsmanship. The worker had to be prepared for work in the factory, and the proper attitudes needed to function in a mechanized, industrial setting. The old values of craftsmanship and pride in one's work seemed to vanish in the name of vocational efficiency.

The Los Angeles program concluded with the statement:

> Moral training can never be one division in the field of education. It must penetrate the warp and woof of the whole fabric or it does not exist at all . . . character education, as far as the school is concerned, consists in creating a climate of opinion about and within the institution which will demand that pupils adapt themselves unconsciously to the wholesome moral forces of their environment.[81]

In 1929 a questionnaire was sent to the nine teacher training schools and thirty representative schools in the State of Wisconsin to survey the implementation of character education programs. Instigated by P. M. Vincent, Superintendent of Schools at Stevens Point, the study reached both small villages as well as cities of up to 40,000 persons.[82] While only three of the twenty-six communities reported that they used a separate course for character education, they all seemed to have incorporated it into all the other subjects. While they stressed the common traits of fair play, honesty, courtesy, neatness, adaptability, efficiency, initiative, and patriotism, they felt that "character (was) of the heart and not of the brain"[83] and had "to be caught and could not be taught."[84] Four of the nine teachers colleges in Wisconsin offered a definite course in character education.

By 1932, however, the Lapham School in Madison[85] set out character education as its greatest objective and attempted to shift emphasis from knowledge of fundamentals to the development of the right standard of living. The emphasis on not only knowing the right, but doing the right, was clear. The move from mere intellectual training to training for conduct was evident. A new report card was instituted

132

which evaluated students in character attitudes
and not in academic subjects. The objectives
of character education at this later time were
more geared towards self-control, adjustment and
social attitudes than they were previously. The
social psychological justification for character
education continued to gain stature in the movement.

Schools were seen to bear the burden for
the development of good character in all facets
of the child's life. With the breakdown of
the old structures of control and guidance,
namely the family and the Church, it was seen
to be the school's responsibility to develop the
whole child. As quoted in the Massachusetts
Character Education program:

During the last few decades, the
task of the public school has been
rendered more and more complex and
difficult, as the duties which in an
earlier day were discharged by the
home, have been gradually forced
upon it. Examples are to be found in
the industrial training, formerly
handled on the farm or by the ap-
prentice system in the shop, and in
the household economics, in music or
art, in games and sport, and in the
case of the body, until recently
taught at home. And now, with the
breaking up of the older form of
home life as a result of such changes
as the participation of both parents
in gainful occupations away from
home, the increase of divorce, the
compelling social activities of some
strata of society, and the commercial-
ization of amusement, the demand is
becoming more insistent that the
schools add character training to
their other responsibilities.[86]

The Massachusetts program for character education in the elementary school not only stressed the objective that the school should supply the influence of culture and refinement to pupils who were not exposed to it and needed it, but it also emphasized the need for guidance and counseling in order to develop the whole child.[87] While both hereditary and environmental factors were seen to be influential in personality development, the environment was thought to greatly outweigh heredity in determining a child's specific modes of response or conduct. The responsibility for standards and patterns of conduct in children was seen to be in the hands of those who lived and worked with them. Thus, according to the Massachusetts program, "children (were theirs) to shape and form."[88]

This concern with shaping and molding the whole child was an important part of the character education program in Massachusetts. One was shaped rather than born a desirable or undesirable citizen.[89] The ideal citizen exhibited the traits of courtesy, industry, obedience, fairness, neatness, honor, self-control, punctuality, dependability and cleanliness.[90] Since the school was dictating the moral standards of the children, it felt the need to lead the pupils to appreciate the programs of cultural value and entertainment of a high standard[91] as well as developing the worthy use of their leisure time.[92] Once again, the test of good character education was the creation of effective citizens.

The Massachusetts Report emphasized the importance of the home in forming the character of the child, both in his pre-school period as well as during his school years. Unfortunately, this tremendous influence was seen to be waning and losing its virtuous standards, due to the changing environmental and economic pressures of the day. While it was formerly said that the home was the heart of our country, many felt that this title had been lost. The educators

in Massachusetts agreed that good character was
formed in a home

> In which the family income is
> not only sufficient to cover not just
> the base necessities but a home where
> there is some degree of culture in the
> way of art, music, refinement and
> wholesome recreation; it is a home
> where all personal relations are har-
> monious; it is a home in which
> democracy prevails.[93]

Since the actual home life prevalent at
the time was plagued by poverty, lack of sanita-
tion, overcrowded conditions, divorced parents,
dependence upon charity, ineffective discipline,
lack of wholesome recreation and exemplification
of weak character, it was crucial that the home
become more efficient and realize its responsibility more keenly.[94] The school and other
community organizations, including the PTA,
Scouting and Y.M.C.A. were called upon to supplement the ineffectiveness of the home in training
for character, since the goal was unity, stability and an effective citizenry. Much of the
burden for instability and lack of respect for
law and order was attributed to the home which
justified, in the minds of the educators, the
usurping of its moral influence by the school.

Character education in the secondary
schools of Massachusetts was at least partially
a response to the increase in juvenile crime
and delinquency.[95] While the home, Church, and
community were all seen to have a responsibility
in character training, the Church and home were
seen to have a waning influence in modern
society. The parents needed to be educated to
recognize the necessity of home training.
Another of the objectives of the public schools
was training the pupils in the profitable use of
leisure. The school, in its pursuit of the goal
of good citizenry, not only attempted to control

135.

more and more of the child's actions and attitudes, but also reached into the home to re-educate the parents. In its drive to create a unified, stable, well-adjusted populace, the school gained more power over the lives of the child and his parents. The new bearer of morality was not the clergy or the parent, but the teacher.

Guidance and counseling were vital parts of character education in the secondary schools of Massachusetts because it was felt that "true success in life depends quite as much upon character as it does upon information or skill."[96] With the introduction of departmental instruction, the vital factor of the teacher-pupil relationship in the development of character had been lessened. The Home Room Organization was given prominence to re-establish the pupil-teacher relationship. The secondary schools also made use of student councils (the principal retained veto power), assemblies, radio programs, athletics and clubs in an effort to institute self-control, rather than an autocratic form of control. Control was thought to be most effective and most constructive when administered by indirect methods.

Just as an ounce of prevention is worth a pound of cure, so a system of control through wise direction of well-informed public opinion within the school excels in efficiency any system of penalties that may be established.[98]

The incentive for seeking right conduct and living standards was the approval of the group. There was no need for harsh autocratic rule when social psychological pressures could be applied. The stress on rewards instead of penalties was also utilized but the

136.

Rewards, regardless of their
nature, should be retained for
superior achievement, as otherwise
their values become lowered to the
point where incentive for possession
is lost and they fail to function as
instruments of worth in our educational program.[99]

No mention was made of the harmful effects
of the competition for such rewards in terms of
envy, jealousy, rejection, inflated ego, or
ruthlessness. People had to compete for the
rewards of society and only those with merit
would succeed. The meritocracy once again was
the form of distributive justice which the
society most sought after in spite of its inabi-
lity to take into account anything but the values
most treasured for the good and stability of
society.

The District of Columbia's Board of Education, on November 20, 1929, passed a resolution to study character-building activities in
the public schools.[100] Character education
objectives were seen in the elementary school as
fostering of ambition and enthusiasm in work and
play.[101] Behavioral objectives stressed included
cooperation, honesty, fairness, justice, self-
criticism, good workmanship (neatness, accuracy,
industry, efficiency, and self-reliance),
health, cleanliness, thrift, kindness, respect
and reverence, initiative and leadership, and
wholesome ways of using leisure.[102] Once again,
the emphasis was on conduct rather than intellect
and thus a differentiated curriculum was necessary so as to produce the best possible citizen
given the differences in native ability. The
rationale was that an intellectual program
adapted to needs of the children would promote
growth in character.

This aspect of character education has
not been discussed in great detail, but is

137.

nevertheless significant. Part of the rationale
for a differentiated curriculum was a direct
result of the concern with character education.
A definite need was seen for a differentiated
curriculum to provide for individual differences
on the secondary school level. The District of
Columbia Board called for a philosophy of education which saw vocational adjustment and economic
independence for all as one of the major objectives of education.103

        The concern with crime, especially among
teenagers, led Royal S. Copeland, Chairman of
the Senate Subcommittee on Racketeering and
Crime, to campaign to strengthen schools in their
treatment of anti-social tendencies in child-
ren.104 Senator Copeland stressed the case
method, clinical approach as the only adequate
way to meet the pupils' individual needs.
Teachers were seen as more responsible for the
social and moral adjustment of their pupils than
for their intellectual development. Senator
Copeland asked

            Educators whether it (was) not
        time for those in the educational
        system who (were) responsible for
        the health of character in children
        to give precedence to prescriptions
        for moral and social health over
        prescriptions for academic work.105

        As a result of this pressure, the Seventy-
Third Congress added $70,000 to its ten-million
dollar budget for the study of character education in Washington. Washington was chosen
because it was convenient, because the Board of
Education and the Superintendent of Public
Schools, Frank W. Ballou, were enthusiastic, and
because teachers in this area had been working
on the problem for the past five years. Five
white schools and five colored schools on
elementary, Junior high, Senior high, night

high, and vocational high levels were chosen.
The experiment utilized 175 teachers and 550
pupils.

The goal of the program was to help pupils
act correctly as well as to help them develop
a truer scale of values, by developing their
whole personality.106   Ten areas of experience
were utilized, including those of health, intellect, economics, vocation, politics, recreation,
social relations, esthetics, religion, and the
area of parenthood, family life or sex.107   The
seven group behavior patterns or traits that
were stressed, included intellect, honesty,
friendliness, efficiency, cooperation, forceful-
ness, and good taste.108   The important consideration, however, is not so much the specific
behavioral objectives or areas of concern, but
the scope of the objectives.   The character
education experiment in Washington, D. C. was
set up to fight the anti-social tendencies in
children which supposedly led to juvenile delinquency and crime.   Those involved perceived the
solution as a more complete control of the child's
moral and social growth, including a restructur-
ing of his value system.   From this program every
child was to become aware of the dignity and
importance of labor, respect for law, the intelligent use of money, wholesome leisure-time
activities, sex as one of the great moving
factors of civilization, good taste, and cogni-
zance of the economic and political institutions
of society as agencies for promoting social
welfare.109

The concern with individualized instruction
and guidance as the principle method of reaching
its stated objectives, which was deeply held by
the educators in Washington, manifested itself
in the necessity to devise machinery by which
teachers would be able to learn much about their
pupils.   This involved the collecting and record-
ing of vastly more information than was readily
available at that time.   Certain minimal facts,

139.

it was decided, should be collected on all
children. It was next decided that current records of characteristic and significant actions
of children should be collected by teachers and
officers as so-called anecdotes. Finally, it
was agreed that for problem children and for
children who were taken to court or to the judge
of the court, detailed case studies should be
made wherein all useful data that could be collected from the school records, from psychiatrists
and other specialists, should be assembled and
used in diagnosing the maladjustments of these
children and for setting up remedial procedures.
Subsequently, it was decided to add to these the
results of interviews with guidance officers.
All of these materials were to be assembled in
record folders, with the most significant data in
the folders summarized upon record cards for
ordinary use.[110]

Thus the concern with individualized instruction and guidance forced the cumulative
record card to also record behavior traits, as
they developed in the pupil from time to time.
These records of behavior traits "Will be the
basis of efforts of the principal and the teacher
for giving constructive help to the individual
pupil in the development of appropriate behavior
traits."[111]

Senator Copeland had no desire to challenge
the fact that in America we had come to expect
the teacher to instruct our children in manners,
personal hygiene, social etiquette and household
arts, and that we likewise expected the teacher
to give by precept and example that moral and
ethical training which in other times were imparted by the home and the Church.[112] He
stressed the importance of behavior records in
order to point out anti-social tendencies of certain children who may then be given special
attention and such treatment as the individual
case required. The behavior record would serve

140.

as a warning, a red light indicating the necessity to stop, look and listen. Copeland felt
that:

> If it serves to attract atten-
> tion to the need for special treatment
> and, if, as a result of collaboration
> with these scientific consultants, the
> child is returned to mental and phy-
> sical health, our first purpose has
> been accomplished.113

While Copeland wished the schools to
change their objective from purely intellectual
activity to promotion of good citizenship, he
recognized that the states never delegated to
the Federal Government any legislative or
administrative authority in the field of education. Under the Constitution, the acceptance
of a new policy and of action under such a
policy had to be left to voluntary cooperation.
Thus Copeland formed an advisory body known as
the Education and Law Conference, to press for
a new American policy in Education. Working
with the American Council of Education, the
Education and Law Conference proposed to face
the problems of local conditions, as well as
those deep-rooted traditions of States' Rights
and local autonomy, by making use of the welfare
clause of the Constitution.114

What was sought after was a "New Deal
in Education." Copeland, realizing that only
through voluntary cooperation could this new
policy be adopted, saw the need for only one
general legislative enactment. He introduced
in the Senate a Bill which was intended to serve
two purposes:

> First, it is intended to estab-
> lish a privilege status in the Federal
> Courts for teachers and their behavior
> records of the American Council type-
> records, which I hope will eventually

be established for every child of
school age in this land.

And second, I hope this bill
will establish, so far as the Federal
Government is concerned, the professional status of the teacher as
parallel with and comparable in its
dignity and authority to that of
the doctor and clergyman.[115]

The objective of education was to be re-
stated in terms of character and citizenship, as
well as content. Many of Senator Copeland's
addresses in support of a nationwide program
of character education and citizenship training
for the prevention of crime were also placed in
the Congressional Record.[116]

A survey of character education plans in
Chicago in 1931 revealed 200 plans in use--30
used direct methods, 40 an indirect approach,
70 a combination of both, and 60 had only
incidental goals. Character training in Chicago,
however, was typified by the goals of the
Doolittle School. Its goal was to make good
school citizens who were active, polite, obedient,
self-controlled, industrious, honest and loyal.[117]

Once again the concern with parenthood
education was clearly evident, as was the role of
teacher as absolver of sins. At Goethe School,
for example, when a boy or girl became a behavior problem for the class, they were sent to
the principal for investigation of the causes of
their troubles. When the parents were to blame
(corporal punishment or spoiling were examples
given), they were sent for and given one or more
lessons on how to treat their children with more
firmness, more gentleness, or more regularity of
habits of sleep and of feeding. When the cause
of the problem was found to be personal antagonism between the pupil and the teacher, the pupil
was sent back to the teacher to ask for

142.

forgiveness and to ask for punishment. The
teacher's leniency was to do the rest.118

While there were many different character
programs in the schools of Chicago, one of the
most interesting concepts developed was the creation of special schools for behavior and truant
children. The Chicago Advisory Council on
Character Education was created to study the
problem of the rise in juvenile delinquency,
truancy and vandalism. The work of its Juvenile
Delinquency Committee resulted in the establishment of Montefiore and Mosley Special schools.
Two other schools, the Chicago and Cook County
School for Boys and Chicago Parental School, were
also established as residential schools. Pupils
were sent to Chicago Parental School and to
Chicago and Cook County School through commitment
by the Juvenile Court. There was no Court action
involved in the transfer of boys to either of
the two special day schools, as pupils were
transferred by school authorities upon the re-
quest of principals and district superinten-
dents.119

The trend of all educational activities at
both the Chicago and Cook County School and the
Parental School was toward building character.
Real life situations were utilized to develop
proper conduct, as was correction of physical
handicaps, including proper care of eyes, ears
and teeth; regular meals, good food and plenty
of sleep to make children susceptible to good
influences and help to redirect their characters
in proper channels. The Parental School, whose
students were truants and incorrigibles, unlike
the delinquents of the Chicago and Cook County
School, used the self-improvement plan of Benjamin
Franklin and later, of Charles Lindbergh. Lindbergh drew up a list of what he called character
factors and marked himself each day and compared
his growth from month to month. The Parental
School used this scheme as well as the use of a
Boy Scout troop within the school as incentives

143.

for proper habit formation and better character development.[120]

The Montefiore and Mosley special schools were day schools and thus had different problems and approaches in terms of character education. These schools were for the treatment of unadjusted and problem boys and were recent additions to the Chicago Public School System.[121] Both of the schools were established to care for underprivileged and unadjusted boys, coming from the regular schools of the district. They contained pupils who were physically, educationally, emotionally, or morally maladjusted, but all of whom were seen to be greatly in need of character education. The schools had the services of doctors, nurses, dentists, psychologists, social workers, visiting teachers, and psychiatrists.

Character education manifested itself in the creation of special schools where problem children could be sent, not only to improve their character, but to withdraw them from unfavorable environments. This procedure nevertheless stigmatized students as problem cases and made no effort to provide separate facilities for persons with physical, educational, emotional or moral deficiencies. It also grouped underprivileged children with unadjusted ones, thus complicating the distinction between poor children and problem children even further. The use of social workers and visiting teachers to make contact with the homes of the children to create a proper out-of-school environment shows how character defects were seen to be partly a result of defective home discipline. The schools once again took on the responsibility for both creation of the correct habits of conduct and behavior in its students, and for the creation of a proper home environment. Education for character became a crucial part of the educational process for maladjusted children.

When seven schools, composed mostly of

immigrant and black children,[123] of manual labor-
ers and small businessmen, were compared in terms
of character education objectives, an interesting finding occurred. The teachers in these
schools listed their objectives as honesty, reliability, loyalty (patriotism), truthfulness,
industry and obedience. When the pupils were
asked what character objectives they saw as
important, they listed, kindness, honesty,
courtesy, generosity, helpfulness, and justice.
The report concluded that:

> . . . Children do not attach the
> same degree of importance to several
> greatly admired traits as teachers
> ascribe to correct character object-
> ives. The children and teachers
> agree fairly closely on the relative
> values of honesty, cleanliness and
> punctuality. However, they disagree
> sharply on the traits or objectives
> of kindness, reliability, helpfulness
> and obedience.[124]

There was also closer agreement between
the offenses recognized by children and those
observed by teachers than between traits admired
by pupils and the objectives slated by teachers.
Pupils recognized more varied forms of mischief
in destruction of property than did teachers;
however, the latter observed more personality
defects evident in bad attitudes than did the
pupils.[125]

The problem of character education for
immigrants was also dealt with in the Detroit
Plan.[126] While the immigrant was seen to have
the type of home training that forced a child
into the paths of virtue and kept him there by
forceful measures, the freer atmosphere of the
schoolroom often caused him to manifest extreme
tendencies. Special training in the fundamental
attitudes of right and wrong, property rights,
truthfulness and cleanliness were considered

essential. The subject of usefulness and constructive production was continually put before
them, with the American ideal that a man may make
of himself what he will.[127]

Once again, the basic rationale for character education was that those involved were
convinced that the strength of the nation was
dependent upon moral cleanliness in the home and
a strong character development for right living
in every citizen. Adult classes stressed re-
adjustment and education into civic, cultural,
economic and personal duties. Since the example
of the teacher was so vital to training in
character development, teachers were not only
constantly cautioned to set a 100% example in
terms of law enforcement but "no teacher who (did)
not thoroughly believe in America and its opportunities for character development (was) encouraged to continue working in the Department of
Work with Foreign Born."[128]

The concern with education for citizenship
was, as previously pointed out, not limited to
immigrants. School officials were concerned
with motivation of proper behavior in all of
their pupils. Worthy character was seen as the
basis of good citizenship and it was seen that
the school was the State's means of training its
citizens. The Tennessee Plan reiterated the
fact that:

> The need of character education
> is being keenly felt by progressive
> educators. It is everywhere being
> recognized that educating for know-
> ledge and training for skills, such
> as is now being offered in our
> secondary schools, does not assure
> us that, in addition to other results,
> the outcome in the lives of our pu-
> pils will be worthy character, and
> the intelligent participation in
> citizenship activities. Yet the

fundamental purpose of the State
in educating its children is to
make them intelligent, productive,
and cooperating citizens. And
fundamental to worthy citizenship
is worthy character.[129]

The Tennessee Plan called for the creation
of the Association of American School Citizens
which would make use of the gang spirit of the
children along with emblems, scales or rank and
meaningful rituals to recognize and reward merit-
oritous conduct. It also proposed giving pupils
points for good deeds. Pupils winning the requi-
site number of conduct credit points, but failing
in scholarship, were to be given certificates of
citizenship. Pupils winning in scholarship but
failing to win in citizenship, were to be given
a certificate of scholarship. A diploma was to
be issued only to those who won both in scholarship and in conduct.[130]

From 1924 to 1936, a Character Development
Program was followed in the Birmingham Public
Schools. Each year a Character Development
slogan was used which guided the lessons during
that year. The slogans used in those years (and
then to be repeated again in order), were Health,
Sportsmanship, Work, Beauty, Thrift, Courtesy,
Love of Nature, Worthy Use of Leisure, Service,
Wonder, Cooperation, and Self-reliance.[131]

The emphasis on work was that it was to be
seen as a blessing and not as a doom; not
drudgery but as a means toward a desirable end.
Character educators in Birmingham wanted to avoid
the false sense of values and dignities between
white-collar jobs and skilled or manual labor.

Rather it is hoped they will
absorb the healthy view that what a
man or woman does is less important
than how it is done; that in work as
in sportsmanship the emphasis must
not be wholly based on win or lose,

147.

but on how the game is played
as well.[132]

Unfortunately, pride in one's work could
not be taken to the bank. True it was important,
but character education in Birmingham was more
concerned with how the game was played than the
rewards of success or the penalties of failure.
This work ethic was supplemented by the objective
of thrift and its ideal of delayed gratification.
The schools set up Banking Plans where the students could begin learning to save their money.
Children were encouraged to repair their old
clothing and toys, and it was noted that "negro
children (were) particularly commendable in
this."[133] Even the concept of the beautiful
included the notions of order, cleanliness,
accuracy, and efficiency. Students thus were to
become good, self-respecting citizens, no matter
what their job or status in society. Character
education was education for citizenship, but
it also was education for order, stability, and
harmony. It was no wonder that "interracial
relations in Birmingham have been among the
first to improve under such development among
the school children of the two races in greatest
majority here."[134]

Along with the goals of health, work and
thrift, the Birmingham schools stressed worthy
use of leisure time in clubs, libraries, and
scouting, love of country and a desire to serve
it, and self-reliance in terms of self-control,
promptness, orderliness, and thrift.[135]

Pittsburgh's character education program
involved both direct and indirect methods of
procedure. It made use of clubs, athletics,
the student council and the homeroom for
character guidance. The fundamental traits
in all ten areas of experience (same as in
Copeland Experiment), were ambition, loyalty
and perseverance.[136] The Elgin Plan stressed
a different character objective each day of the

week: Monday was morals (obedience, honesty, punctuality, reliability), Tuesday was manners (cleanliness, politeness, neatness, kindness), Wednesday was respect for property (law and order), Thursday was safety, and Friday was thrift and patriotism.[137] The State of Oklahoma was concerned with the changing conditions of home and Church which had left the school as the only institution in a position to play the leading role in America's most urgent and important enterprise, character education.[138] All in all, character education programs were instituted across the country with only a small sample discussed here.[139]

Numerous books were used as source material for character education programs, but several stood out as the most influential. The works of Heaton, Charters, Germane and Germane, Fishback, Starbuck and Hartshorne provided character educators both with the necessary philosophy of education and with examples of application and content as well.[140]

D.

The Department of Superintendence of the N.E.A. devoted its Tenth Yearbook in 1932 to the topic of character education.[141] This report was a comprehensive analysis of all aspects of character education and was frequently cited in character education programs and books.

One of the recommendations of the Department's Commission on Character Education was the necessity of forging new conceptions of right and wrong. In the new age of social change, "relativity must replace absolutism in the realm of morals as well as in the spheres of physics and biology."[142] This relativity of morality was best suited for the pragmatic actions of the State. As long as the State sanctioned moral behavior, it needed the freedom

149.

to change the sanctions depending upon the circumstances. The goal was progress.

	With a relativity in moral outlook, it is
not surprising that the Commission viewed the
family as an instrument not for improving society, but for reproducing the present with all
its follies and deficiencies, as well as its
wisdoms and excellences. Thus the family was
seen as the most powerful of all educational
agencies, but it scarcely could be regarded as
an agency of betterment.[143] The Church as well
was seen to have lost its authority with outworn
dogmas.[144]

	The objective seemed to be a utilitarian
ideal, where character education would facilitate
the way of life which conserved and produced as
many values as possible for as many persons as
possible over as long a time as possible.[145] This
definition fit very nicely with the previous reference to relativity of morals. As society's
needs changed (the needs of the majority), the
values most cherished would also change. The
values needed to maintain a stable, orderly society were the crucial values and were prag-
matically determined, depending upon the
circumstances.

	The Tenth Yearbook gave extensive illus-
trations of how social problems that demand
immediate attack were best handled by character
education procedures in the curriculum. Much
space was also given to the contributions of
individual counseling to character education.

	A good counseling program,
	regardless of the size of the school
	or city, provides for all phases of
	individual study and adjustment,
	including physical, mental, emotional,
	social, educational and vocational
	analysis and treatment.[146]

Also important to school guidance and counseling programs was the concept of the Dean of Boys and Girls. They were viewed to have the status and authority represented by the concept of "in loco parentis." Attendance officers, psychiatric social workers and psychologists, all were requested to use the case study method of analysis, diagnosis, and treatment. It was crucial to collate all necessary material on the student's scholarship, health, and personality, in order to make a correct diagnosis. Schools were gradually taking on the responsibility of not only sorting out students according to intellectual criteria, but also differentiating them on emotional and character criteria as well. Adjustment was the key phrase in many aspects of character education. The factory metaphor schooling had been replaced by the clinic metaphor.

The research division of the N.E.A. undertook a project to examine character education programs across the country. Questionnaires were sent to 645 superintendents of schools in 1930, and various character education bulletins and courses of study were also examined. Most cities relied largely upon regular class work and upon extracurricular activities to stimulate character growth. The number using regular class work was greater than the number using extracurricular activities in the elementary and junior highs, but not in the senior highs.[147] A smaller number of schools used separate class periods for character education with a seemingly greater frequency of such use in the larger cities.[148] Only a small percentage of students obtained character education instruction through classes conducted during school hours by church schools in local churches.[149] Finally, in terms of programs of guidance and counseling, 19% of junior high schools and 22% of senior high schools reported their utilization, with the larger cities actually reporting usage more than twice the overall mean.

151.

The questionnaire also sought to obtain information from the superintendents on the relationship that they felt should exist between the home and school in programs of character education. While the majority felt that there should be the hearty, intelligent and active cooperation of the parents, a number of superintendents felt, however, that the school can expect little or no assistance from the average home, and that it was profitable only to give parents enough information so that they would not oppose the school's program. The school had to expect to carry the major burden of character education unaided by the home.[150]

Special bulletins, or outlines, for character education were reported in fewer than half of the systems for any one type of school and in fewer than one-fifth were specific suggestions for character building included in courses of study, dealing with the regular school subjects. Both types of materials were provided somewhat more often for the elementary school than for either the junior or the senior high. The special bulletins were prepared more often by outside agencies than by officers and teachers within the school system.[151]

Table Five indicated that in most systems the teachers of regular school subjects were wholly responsible for character education, especially in the elementary grades. Only 5% of the cities employed specially-trained teachers to assist in this work in the junior and senior high school, and the proportion in the elementary school was even smaller. About ten percent of the schools used persons representing some agency or agencies outside the school who participated regularly in the character building program of each type of school. About the same proportion had a school committee or council composed of teachers and principals which devoted considerable time to problems in character education.[152]

The research bulletin also described the various examples of group guidance (clubs, assemblies, athletics, student government, homeroom), and individual guidance (visiting teachers, psychological clinics, special schools, vocational guidance), which would enable the pupil to best adjust in accordance with desirable standards. Character education goals were thus both preventative as well as curative. One had not only to produce good, well-adjusted citizens to prevent later crime, delinquency, and discontent, but one also had to help maladjusted character deviants to readjust to the established norms of society. William Kilpatrick wrote:

> General and public repudiation of the doctrine of laissez faire in behalf of the principle and practice of general social control is necessary. Education has a responsibility for training individuals to share in this social control instead of merely equipping them with the ability to make their private way in isolation and competition. The ability and the desire to think collectively, to engage in social planning, conceived and conducted experimentally for the good of all, is a requirement of good citizenship under existing conditions. Educators can ignore it only at the risk of evasion and futility.[153]

E.

Character education became a form of civic religion by which the State could generate a new planned society. A society where the control of the home and the Church was replaced by a new State-sanctioned morality. A morality which was described as not only utilitarian, but was also relative and tentative. Whenever needs changed

153.

of circumstances necessitated it, the values
most cherished by the society could also change.
This pragmatic approach was well suited to the
aims of progress and the ideal society.

Education for character justified itself
not only in terms of creating good patriotic
citizens, but also made use of socio-economic
and psychological justifications as well. One
had to adjust to the norms of society, both
psychologically as well as socially and economically. Character education was education for
values, not for skills or knowledge. These
values were measured in terms of behavioral objectives which included the pupil's school
behavior and reached into his everyday life and
leisure as well.

The structure and function of the school
also changed as the result of character education
concerns. The school gained more control over
the lives of its students; it also reached into
the homes of the parents in an effort to re-
educate them. Differentiated curriculums
necessitated a better understanding of each
child's needs; this manifested itself in the
creation of behavior and personality records
for each student. Guidance, both psychological,
vocational, and educational, also became a part
of the everyday working of the school. Even
report cards, in some cases, were changed to
account for character and behavior ratings as
well as or in place of intellectual grading.

Group guidance programs for character education also left their mark on the school. Home
rooms were stressed in schools with departmental
classes so that students could receive the
inspiration of proper teacher example and planning of character building activities. Student
governments were instituted to enable students
to get the feel of self-government and self-
control.

The role of the teacher also changed from one who merely imparted knowledge to that of social worker, counselor and psychologist. Teachers were supposed to build up the social and moral character of their pupils and the schools could best be described by a clinic metaphor.

When the situation was not controllable, the problem students were sent to special schools for character deviants. Some schools also brought psychologists and counselors into their schools to assist them in adjusting their students to the norms of the society.

Thus, character education programs, while diverse and seemingly conflicting in methodology and objectives, were still, nevertheless, a major influence on American education. They not only changed the structure and function of schooling but they also generated a pragmatic, utilitarian, relativistic morality which best served the State in justifying its actions and the control of its citizens.

The next chapter will examine the attempts to objectify, quantify, and standardize character traits. The character measurement area was closely allied with the entire movement for character education in that it attempted to validate both the character training needs for specific groups in society as well as the results of the specific character education programs.

[1]F. Neff Stroup, "Character Education in Newark," New York State Education, 18, February 1931, p. 571.

[2]Edwin Starbuck, Character Education Methods, The Iowa Plan $20,000 Award (Washington, D. C.: National Capital Press, 1922), pp.1-3.

[3]Ibid., p. 3.

[4]Ibid., p. 5.

[5]Ibid., p. 6.

[6]As pointed out in Chapter Two, the fear of anarchy in Russia as well as the "goose step" obedience witnessed in Germany during W.W.I. were both vital factors in the growth of character education in this country.

[7]Ibid., p. 11.

[8]Ibid. Starbuck's concept of child-centered education denied the laissez faire outlook, which is sometimes attributed to it, in favor of the deliberate shaping and moulding of the child's conduct and thought.

[9]Ibid., p. 25.

[10]Ibid., p. 15.

[11]Ibid., p. 34.

[12]See G. Stanley Hall, Educational Problems, V. 1 (New York: D. Appleton and Company, 1911), Chapter VII, "The Pedagogy of Sex," pp. 388-539. Hall wrote, "The better ethical consensus of man has long tabooed all this (pornography, sadism, sexual perversion and excess, etc.), and striven

to eliminate and purify the processes of reproduction by higher esoteric interpretation and by
spiritualizing the master passion of love,"
p. 395.

[13]Ibid., pp. 34-35. Starbuck was more concerned with positive eugenics (good breeding)
than he was in sterilization of the unfit. His
program stressed prevention of breeding with a
lower stock of person which would despoil the
human breed. See a similar warning in H. H.
Goddard, The Kallikak Family (New York: The
MacMillan Co., 1912).

[14]Jessie B. Davis, "The Iowa Plan of
Character Education Methods," Religious Education,
17, Dec. 1922, p. 435.

[15]Ibid., p. 439.

[16]Character Education Supplement to the
Utah State Course of Study for Elementary and
High Schools (Salt Lake City: Department of Pub-
lic Instruction, 1925).

[17]Ibid., p. 13.

[18]George A. Mirick, Progressive Education
(Cambridge: Riverside Press, 1923).

[19]Ibid., pp. 176-177.

[20]Ibid., p. 15.

[21]Frederick Bolton, Adolescent Education
(New York: The MacMillan Co., 1931), p. 475.

[22]Utah Plan, op. cit., p. 52.

[23]Character Education Supplement to the
Utah State Course of Study for Elementary and
High Schools (Revised Edition), (Salt Lake City:
Department of Public Instruction, 1929), p. 28.
For a fuller description of this significant

movement, see Chapter on "The Purpose and Scope of Visiting Teacher Work," by Howard W. Nudd in The Problem Child in School (New York: Commonwealth Fund, 1927).

[24] Ibid., p. 28.

[25] Ibid., p. 18.

[26] For more information on the influence of psychoanalysis on education, see G. H. Green, Psychoanalysis in the Classroom (New York: Putnam, 1922); W. A. White, Mechanisms of Character Formation (New York: MacMillan Co., 1916), and Mental Hygiene of Childhood (New York: Little, Brown and Co., 1917); O. R. Pfister, Psychoanalysis in Service of Education (New York: Moffat, 1922). For information on delinquency and the unstable child, see William Healy (Director of the Psychopathic Institute of the Juvenile Court in Chicago), Mental Conflicts and Misconduct (New York: Little, Brown & Co., 1916). Also see Florence Mateer, The Unstable Child: An Interpretation of Psychopathy as a Source of Unbalanced Behavior in Abnormal and Troublesome Children (New York: Appleton Co., 1924). She saw the "need for institutions, hospital schools for psychopaths, hospital schools where the young delinquent will be treated, educated, trained, made independent and self-directing and then sent out to redeem his delinquency," p. 459.

[27] Course of Study in Character Education, State of Nebraska (Lincoln: Department of Public Instruction, 1927).

[28] Ibid., p. 31.

[29] Paul Rankin, "The Training of Teachers for Character Education," NEA Proceedings, 68, 1930, p. 326.

[30] For information on the increase in crime see Louis Seibold, "Crime Increase Steady in

U.S. Since 1900, All Records Show," Evening
Star (Washington, D.C., Sept. 8, 1926), p. 3.
For the opposite conclusion see Phillip Parsons,
Crime and the Criminal (New York: Alfred A.
Knopf, 1926).   For the view that juvenile crime
was increasing see Hon. Ellen C. Potter,
"Spectacular Aspects of Crime in Relation to the
Crime Wave," Annals of the American Academy of
Political and Social Science, 125, May 1926,
p. 14. The view that juvenile crime had not
increased was put forth by the U.S. Dept. of
Labor Children's Bureau, Youth and Crime, Public
Document No. 196, U.S. Gov't Printing Office,
1930, p. 3. The view that crime among women was
increasing was expressed in "Trends of Modern
Education," The New York Times, Sunday, June 12,
1932, p. 8. For a discussion of crime among
children of immigrants, see Harry M. Shulman,
From Truancy to Crime: A Study of 251 Adolescents
(Albany: J. B. Lyon Co., 1928). Crime among
black youth was discussed in Virginia M. Murray,
A Study of Delinquency and Neglected Negro
Children Before the New York City Children's
Court (New York: Joint Commission on Negro Child
Study in New York City, 1925), p. 6.

[31]"Character Education," Chapter XIV,
Fourth Yearbook (Washington: Department of Superintendence of the N.E.A., 1926), pp. 379-450.

[32]Ibid., p. 381.

[33]Ibid., p. 383.

[34]Ibid., p. 384.

[35]Ibid., p. 385. The stress on guidance
and adjustment would come later.

[36]Ibid., Table 11, p. 387. See p. 389 for
elaboration of various activities.

[37]Ibid., Column 5, Table 12, p. 388, and
Column 11, Table 11, p. 387. Club activities,

while second to physical education activities and school control activities, as a suggested way of securing character education results, were ranked first overwhelmingly, in ways encouraged to secure character education results.

[38] Ibid., Table 13, p. 390.

[39] Milton Bennion, "Report of the Character Education Committee," NEA Proceedings, 61, 1923, p. 253.

[40] Department of Superintendence Fourth Yearbook, op. cit., p. 405.

[41] Ibid., Table 14, p. 422.

[42] Ibid., p. 421.

[43] Ibid., p. 446.

[44] Ibid., p. 447.

[45] Ibid., p. 448.

[46] Ibid., p. 449. Repentance was represented in the counselor's approach as reestablishment of diplomatic relations. Confession was represented as approval or disapproval of confession. Restitution was represented by the counselor's forgiveness. Finally, consecration was represented by restored fellowship.

[47] "The New York Committee on Character Education," School and Society, 21, April 1925, p. 465.

[48] Ibid., p. 466.

[49] Charles W. Taylor, "Nebraska's Character Plan," Journal of Education, Boston, 115, Jan. 1932, p. 84. Bill 79-2132 incorporated a course of study for the first twelve grades.

160.

[50]Knighthood of Youth Club Guide--National Child Welfare Association (Lincoln: State Department of Public Instruction--Nebraska, 1933), p. 16.

[51]J. H. Harris, "Character Education in Pontiac Schools," Journal of Education, 109, May 1929, p. 518. The Lab School experiment in character education at Pontiac was to be directed by Kenneth Heaton of the University of Chicago who was about to receive his Ph.D. in character education.

[52]Gordon Hendrickson, "Character Education in the Schools," Ohio Schools, 9, Sept. 1931, p. 256. Edwin Starbuck also disliked the factory metaphor of education.

[53]Adelaide Nichols, "Connecticut Bends the Twig," Survey, 66, Sept. 1931, p. 504. See also Ruth White Colton, "Character Education in Connecticut," School Executive's Magazine, 50, March 1931, pp. 313-315.

[54]Colton, op. cit., p. 314. The same sentiment was expressed by the State Superintendent of Public Instruction in Nebraska, 1932, when he wrote, "Any effort, however, to fix the responsibility (for breakdown of morality) might well result in endless argument between the home, the church, the school and various other agencies with which the child definitively comes in contact." Taylor, op. cit., p. 85.

[55]Ibid., p. 315.

[56]Ibid.

[57]Ibid., p. 314. Thus the factory metaphor that Hendrickson and Starbuck despised was still prominent in some educational circles.

[58]Nichols, op. cit., p. 535-536.

[59]James F. Hosic, "Character Education in the Elementary School," School Executive, 51, Nov. 1931, p. 112.

[60]Ibid.

[61]Earl K. Hillbrand, "Character Education in Seven City School Systems," Kansas Teacher, 31, May 1930, p. 7.

[62]Ibid. See also Character Education, State of Indiana Department of Public Instruction, Bulletin No. 134, 1942.

[63]Ibid., p. 8.

[64]Ibid., p. 7.

[65]Character Education in Denver Public Schools, Monograph No. 14 (Denver: Board of Education, 1929) also Arthur K. Loomis, A. Helen Anderson, et al., "A Survey of Character Education in Denver," Journal of N.E.A., 19, Oct. 1930, pp. 217-218; Nov. 1930, pp. 243-244; Dec. 1930, pp. 307-308; and V. 20, Jan. 1931, pp. 11-12; Feb. 1931, pp. 51-52; March 1931, pp. 79-80; April 1931, pp. 125-126; May 1931, pp. 149-150; June 1931, pp. 201-202.

[66]"Character Education," Report of the Character Education Committee to the Second Annaul Meeting of the Society for the Study of Education, Montana Education, 6, Feb. 1930, pp. 28-32.

[67]Character Education in Catholic parochial schools was remarkably compatible with the values and goals previously stated. The clergy agreed with the goals previously stated. The clergy agreed with the goals of good citizenship, vocational guidance, obedience to authority and conformity, while they also stressed knowledge of what conduct is demanded of the average Catholic

American and why it is demanded. They also put a great deal of emphasis on child psychology and personality and character tests. The bond between science and religion, while manifesting itself chiefly in the liberal Protestant clergy within the Social Gospel movement also seemed to pervade parts of the Catholic Establishment. See entire "Superintendents' Section," National Catholic Educational Association Bulletin, 26, 1929-1930, pp. 450-573.

[68] "Character Building: Principles and Suggested Procedures," Kansas City School Service Bulletin, Vol. 1, No. 2, April 1, 1929, pp. 7-8; see also George Melcher, "Character Building: Elementary School Procedures," Kansas City School Service Bulletin, 4, No. 3, Nov. 1931. In this bulletin, procedures and activities were suggested for development of character education objectives, such as use of grade cards, citizenship charts, homeroom civic club, nature club, good manners club, assemblies, scouting and even a thrift campaign. In this campaign students opened bank accounts and were encouraged to save and become real business folks, p. 100.

[69] Ibid., p. 11. This consensus was a result of a questionnaire which was sent out to 700 teachers and principals in the elementary schools.

[70] "Character Education in the Schools of the State of New York," Elementary School Journal, 32, Feb. 1932, p. 411.

[71] Ibid., p. 415.

[72] Ibid., p. 416. See also "Education for Citizenship," James E. West, (Chief Scout, Boy Scouts of America) New York State Education, 18, Feb. 1931, pp. 555-557, pp. 625-630; "Campfire and Character Achievement," C. Frances Loomis, New York State Education, 18, Feb. 1931,

pp. 561-563, p. 636. "Girl Scouts and Character Building," New York State Education, 18, Feb. 1931, pp. 566-569.

[73]Carrol B. Johnson, "Character Education," New York State Education, 18, Feb. 1931, p.564.

[74]O. Wendell Hogue, "Character Education in Lyons," New York State Education, 18, Feb. 1931, p. 573.

[75]Building Character Through Activities in the Elementary Schools, Superintendent's Council of the Oakland Public Schools, 1929.

[76]Ibid., p. 11.

[77]Character Education in Los Angeles, Los Angeles Board of Education School Publication #262, 1934, p. 7.

[78]Ibid., p. 9.

[79]Ibid., p. 12.

[80]Ibid., p. 29.

[81]Ibid., p. 53.

[82]P. M. Vincent, "A Study of Character Education in Wisconsin Schools," Bulletin of the Department of Elementary School Principals Eighth Yearbook (Washington: National Education Association, 1929), p. 278.

[83]Ibid., p. 279.

[84]Ibid.

[85]Beulah M. Charmley, "An Effectual Program for Character Building," Education, 53, Dec. 1932, pp. 240-243.

164.

[86]William Clark Trow, _Educational Psycho-logy_ (Boston: Houghton-Mifflin Company, 1937), p. 369.

[87]_Emphasizing Character in the Elementary School_ (Boston: The Commonwealth of Massachusetts Department of Education, 1937), p. 12.

[88]Ibid., p. 15.

[89]Ibid., p. 16.

[90]Ibid., p. 29.

[91]Ibid., p. 37.

[92]Ibid., p. 26.

[93]Ibid., p. 48.

[94]Ibid.

[95]_Report on Character Education in the Secondary Schools_ (Boston: The Commonwealth of Massachusetts Department of Education, 1935), p.5.

[96]Ibid., p. 28.

[97]Ibid., p. 33.

[98]Ibid., p. 58.

[99]Ibid., p. 60.

[100]_Preliminary Report on Character Education_, District of Columbia School Document No. 9 (Washington: U. S. Government Printing Office, 1931), p. iii.

[101]Ibid., p. 3.

[102]Ibid., pp. 4-6.

[103] Ibid., p. 18.

[104] W. W. Charters, "The Copeland Experiment in the District of Columbia," Educational Record, 15, 1934, p. 403. The average age of the prison population was 23 years, with the largest group found at 19 years, followed by 18 years.

[105] Ibid., p. 404.

[106] Ibid., p. 406.

[107] Ibid., pp. 409-410.

[108] Ibid., p. 412.

[109] Ibid., pp. 409-411.

[110] Ibid., pp. 413-414.

[111] Frank Ballou, "An Experiment in Character Education in the Washington Schools," Educational Record, 15, 1934, p. 288.

[112] Royal S. Copeland, "Education and the Prevention of Crime," Educational Record, 15, 1934, p. 123.

[113] Ibid., p. 132.

[114] Ibid., pp. 134-135.

[115] Ibid., p. 136. Senatore Copeland introduced his Bill (#2838), on February 21, 1934. See Congressional Record, V. 78, Part 3, 73rd Congress, Second session, p. 2946. It never got out of the Judiciary Committee. He introduced another bill, S.B. #16, on January 4, 1935, see Congressional Record, V. 79, Part 1, 74th Congress, 1st Session, p. 101. This bill also failed.

[116] Senator Copeland's address on "Education

and the Prevention of Crime," (see f.n.111) was placed in Congressional Record, V. 78, Part 4, 73rd Congress, 2nd Session, March 8, 1934, pp. 3963-3966. His address on "Education and Crime" given at the Citizens Conference on the crisis in education at Ohio State University, was placed in the Congressional Record, V. 78, Part 6, 73rd Congress, Second Session, April 14, 1934, pp. 6609-6612. Finally his address before the American Council on Education on May 18, 1934, entitled, "Crime and a Revised National Policy," was placed in the Congressional Record, V. 78, Part 10, 73rd Congress, 2nd Session, June 4, 1934, pp. 10350-10351.

[117]G. C. Phipps, "Some Selections and Outlines of Typical Elementary School Character Education Plans," The Chicago Principals Club Sixth Yearbook on Character Education, June, 1931, p. 72.

[118]Ibid., p. 95.

[119]Ibid., Edward H. Stullken, Chapter IX, "Character Education in Special Schools," p. 205.

[120]Ibid., p. 208.

[121]Montefiore Special School was established on September 1929, and Mosley Special School in September, 1930. For more information on special schools and classes for the delinquent and unstable child see Thomas Edison School in Cleveland, Ohio. "The Special Schools and the Curriculum Centers," Report of the Superintendent of Schools to the Board of Education, 1930 (Cleveland: Board of Education, 1931), pp. 71-85; Elsie Marteus, "Biennial Survey of Education in the U.S., 1928-1930," U.S. Department of Interior, Office of Education Bulletin, No. 20, 1931, p. 21; Arch. O. Heck, "Special Schools and Classes in Cities of 10,000 Population or More in the U.S.," U.S. Office of Education Bulletin, No. 7, 1930.

[122]Ibid., p. 210.

[123]Ibid., pp. 234-235. Table I Summary Description of Social Composition and Economic Status of the Pupils and Parents of Seven Chicago Schools.

[124]Ibid., p. 250.

[125]Ibid. It was determined that the children's characterization of their ideal should be well integrated with adult conceptions of desirable conduct. See also Flora J. Cooke, "Training for Character at Francis W. Parker School," Chicago Schools Journal, 13, Nov. 1930, pp. 98-104; Raymond W. Osborne, "Training for Character Through Cooperative Student Government," Chicago Schools Journal, 13, March 1931, pp. 314-319; Elsie Wygant, "The Morning Exercise as Character Training," Chicago Schools Journal, 13, Jan. 1931, pp. 221-228.

[126]Character Education in Detroit (Detroit: Board of Education, 1927).

[127]Ibid., p. 38.

[128]Ibid.

[129]Thomas J. Golightly, "The Tennessee Plan for the Motivation of Character and Citizenship Activities in Secondary Schools," Bulletin of the Middle Tennessee State Teachers College at Murfreesboro, Educational Series, No. 1, August 1927, p. 7.

[130]Ibid., p. 12.

[131]Something Better for Birmingham Children (Birmingham: Board of Education, 1936), p. iii.

[132]Ibid., pp. 17-18.

168.

[133]Ibid., p. 30.

[134]Ibid., p. 36.

[135]Ibid., p. 63; see also C. B. Glenn, "A Character Training Experiment and How it Has Succeeded," Nations Schools, 8, Oct. 1931, pp. 63-65.

[136]"Character Training," Pittsburgh Schools, 8, No. 5, May-June 1934, p. 216.

[137]Annual Report of the Public Schools of Elgin, Illinois for School Year, 1924-1925. Part III Special Study, "A Course in Character Education" by R. W. Fairchild and Mae T. Kilcullen, p. 70.

[138]Character Education Handbook for Teachers (State of Oklahoma: Department of Education Bulletin, No. 131, 1931), p. 5.

[139]Other plans not readily available were in Buffalo, N.Y.; LaCrosse, Wisconsin; Lewes, Delaware; Philadelphia, Penna.; Maryland; St. Louis, Mo.; Minneapolis, Minn.; Norfolk, Va.; New Hampshire and Oregon.

[140]See Kenneth Heaton, The Character Emphasis in Education (Chicago: University of Chicago Press, 1933). This book dealt with the importance of generating a social civic consciousness as well as the desirability of individual pupil guidance; Edwin Fishback, Character Education in Junior High Schools (New York: D. C. Heath and Co., 1928). Fishback wanted students to develop their moral judgment and obtain a knowledge of the accepted ideals of the better class of people; W. W. Charters, The Teaching of Ideals (New York: The MacMillan Co., 1927; Charles E. Germane, Edith E. Germane, Character Education New York: Silver, Burdett and Co., 1929). They stressed that the fundamental aim of education

was to fit the individual for successful adjustment to group life by the stimulus response way
of learning; Hugh Hartshorne, Character in
Human Relations (New York: Charles Scribner's
Sons, 1933). Hartshorne felt that the problem
was how to arrange the situations in which a
child grows up in such a way as to permit him to
function with increasing completeness in the
life of the world; Edwin Starbuck and Frank
Shuttleworth, A Guide to Literature for Character
Training, Vol. I, Fairy Tale, Myth and Legend
(New York: The MacMillan Co., 1928) and Vol. II,
Fiction (New York: The MacMillan Co., 1930).

[141]"Character Education," Tenth Yearbook
(Washington, D. C.: Dept. of Superintendence
of the N.E.A., 1932).

[142]Ibid., p. 11.

[143]Ibid., p. 20.

[144]Ibid., p. 23.

[145]Ibid., p. 59. A good Jesuit critique
of the utilitarian, relativistic, pragmatic
morality of character education can be found in
Irene McGrough, "A Critical Evaluation of the
Character Education Inquiry, Particularly of
the Underlying Philosophy," Unpublished Ph.D.
dissertation, Fordham University, 1933.

[146]Ibid., p. 247. See Goodwin Watson and
Ralph B. Spence, Educational Problems for
Psychological Study (New York: MacMillan Co.,
1930), pp. 333-343; Jane Culture, The Visiting
Teacher at Work (New York: Commonwealth Fund,
1929); George E. Myers, The Problem of Vocational
Guidance (New York: MacMillan Co., 1927).

[147]"Education for Character: Part II
Improving the School Program," Research Bulletin
of the N.E.A., 12, May 1934, Table 2, p. 90.
In terms of cities of all sizes, 82% of elementary

schools, 71% of junior highs and 76% of senior highs used out-of-class activities.

[148]Ibid., Table 2. Only 13% of elementary schools, 11% of junior high schools and 8% of senior high schools reported use of separate class periods for character education. The percentage in each almost doubled from cities under 2,500 population to those over 100,000.

[149]Ibid., Table 2. Ten percent of elementary school students, 5% of junior high students, and 3% of senior high students. The percentage was also much higher in the larger cities than in smaller cities (19% of elementary students in cities over 100,000 attended church schools).

[150]Ibid., Table 3, p. 91. Sixty-five percent of Superintendents sought active parent cooperation, while 26% expected little assistance from home. Nine percent combined aspects of both sides.

[151]Ibid., Table 4, p. 92.

[152]Ibid., Table 5, p. 95.

[153]William H. Kilpatrick, et al., The Educational Frontier (New York: D. Appleton-Century Co., 1933), p. 69.

IV. THE ATTEMPTS TO OBJECTIFY, QUANTIFY, AND STANDARDIZE CHARACTER AND CHARACTER TRAITS

A.

In order to understand the origins of the character testing movement in America, it will be necessary to examine its historical antecedents in Europe in the late nineteenth and early twentieth centuries as well as its main origin in America as an outgrowth of the Army Intelligence Tests during the First World War. The reasons for the necessity of such a development will be examined as well as the persons and institutions involved. The character tests will also be scrutinized to see if they reflected racial or ethnic differences similar to the intelligence test. Correlations between character measures and other variables such as intelligence, success in school, success in a vocation, and delinquency will also be examined. From these correlations certain vocational programs and schools for character deviates were instituted, and the rationale for these programs will be analyzed.

The beginnings of character analysis can be traced back to the English psychologist and founder of eugenics, Francis Galton, whose measurement and study of character began in the mid-part of the last century.[1] One of the early elaborate statistical studies of character traits, based on data from biographies, was published by Heymans and Wiersma in Holland in 1906.[2] Character testing in the United States was inaugurated in 1912 by Guy Fernald, who administered ethical discrimination tests to the defective-delinquent inmates of the Massachusetts Reformatory.[3] The growth in psychological methodology and status as a result of its success in the First World War gradually found its way into the field of character testing and measurement.

During World War I, the U. S. Army made unparalleled advances along the line of scientific selection. There were studies of occupational requirements, methods of interview, use of intelligence tests, special vocational tests, trade proficiency tests, ratings, and records of individual qualifications and progress. Most notable among the psychologists enlisted by the Army were E. L. Thorndike, L. M. Terman, W. V. Bingham and R. M. Yerkes.[4]

One million, seven hundred thousand men were given the Army Alpha test during W.W.I. Following the War, the committee of psychologists who had been with the development of the army tests formulated the National Intelligence Test. Within less than a year after the test was issued, over 575,000 copies were sold. During the year 1922-1923, 800,000 copies of this test alone were distributed. They were used primarily for vocational guidance and selection procedures, as well as for delinquency programs.[5]

While the mental test was launched in the United States in 1916 with Terman's publication of the Stanford Revision of the Binet-Simon Scale, the War provided a vast arena for the psychologists' pursuit of the measurement of intelligence. After the War, the psychologists returned to their respective centers of study with the pride of their success in measuring intelligence. The success in intelligence testing gave them added impetus to continue their quantification and measurement of human nature. As Percival Symonds of Teachers College wrote:

Elated with their success with the measurement of intelligence during the World War, psychologists turned their attention to the measurement of personality and character. In a symposium on Intelligence and its Measurement in 1921, many of the

174.

contributors stated that one of
the next steps in research was development of the measurement of
character.[6]

That symposium was a gathering place for
the leading psychologists in testing and
measurement. The call for the incorporation
of criteria of temperament and moral character
into the present scheme of tests was overwhelming. While some argued that the total concept
of intelligence should include these factors,
others saw matters of temperament and character
operating largely independent of intelligence.
The objective measure of so-called character
traits would supplement existing intelligence
examinations. Furthermore, these character
factors were often viewed as more educable than
intelligence traits.[7]

Character testing would not only enable
adjustment and control of individuals but
would also supplement general intelligence tests
in securing valid general ratings of personal
efficiency.[8] While a child's ability and intelligence were viewed as hereditary and fixed, his
attitude was seen as largely the result of
outside influences, particularly the school.[9]
Since character and conduct were believed to be
controllable and had the capacity to be modified,
tremendous effort was expended in measuring personality and character traits.

Harold Rugg worked with Terman and Yerkes
for the Psychological Division of the Army during
W.W.I. While he helped develop the Army Rating
for Character, he felt that, practically, the
rating of human character was not effective or
reliable. He stressed the need to measure
character objectively.

. . . For the advancement of
the science of education and the
better fitting of people for their

175.

lifework and play, we need to
analyze character in greater detail to measure it objectively.
The measurement of the dynamic
personal and social traits stands
today where the measurement of
intelligence did fifteen years
ago--on a purely subjective basis.[10]

The goal of character testing included
fitting people for work and play by objectifying
and analyzing their character. As a result of
such measurement, standards of human conduct
would be established and controls on behavior
instituted. Percival Symonds greeted this challenge with optimism and approval.

Progress in the control of
inanimate nature has been accomplished
in part by the development of more
exact methods of describing natural
phenomena. This control of nature has
been particularly facilitated by the
invention of instruments of measurement. Similarly, the control of human
conduct and education depends on the
development of more exact methods of
describing human conduct. The exact
description of human conduct can be
rendered more efficient when it is
reduced to a form of measurement, for
the then small differences are most
accurately portrayed and small changes
most accurately noted . . . The writer
believes that progress in the diagnosis of conduct inevitably leads towards
standardization and he has been at
pains to point out the possibility
and advantages of standardization
whenever possible.[11]

Thus, the result of the analysis and objective measurement of character would be the ability
to standardize and thereby control human conduct

and behavior. Symond viewed this end-product in terms of a planned society.

In a planned society, one would study individuals to help them make the best adjustments possible. Those discovered with criminal tendencies would be re-educated, so as to prevent these tendencies from finding overt expression. Vocational guidance would become interested in the best placement of each individual rather than in the selection of the most fit. Society would be looking for leaders rather than waiting until they forced themselves to the front. In a planned society, the needs of the individual and the demands of the society would become identical.[12]

Character testing would help single out those with criminal tendencies for re-education, enable better vocational guidance and assist the society in its search for leaders. The society would be planned across the board so that the demands of the society would dictate the needs of the individual.

This methodology, supplied by the psychologists, was given added impetus by its allegience with religious and moral educators. At Catholic University of America in Washington, D. C., there was much experimentation in character and moral testing. Paul Hanley Furfey wrote that the

Success of intelligence-testing movement has led many psychologists to hope that similar tests might be developed to measure other aspects of personality. The need of such quantitative techniques is constantly becoming more apparent.[13]

177.

Marie Cecilia McGrath, also at Catholic University, attempted to "standardize a series of moral information tests as perhaps a useful aid in study of delinquent children."[14]

The desacralization of religious dogma and morality by means of scientific test measurement was highly significant of the bond between science and religion in character testing as well as character education. The new social gospel united the old gospel of salvation with the new gospel of the planned society. The result was the systematic quantification, objectification, standardization and ultimate control of human conduct in the interests of the planned society on the road to perfection and a "heaven on Earth."

Paul Voelker studied the character traits of Boy Scouts in 1921. His studies were one of the earliest systematic investigations of moral conduct. As a result of Augusta Bronner's study of delinquent girls in 1913[15] and her conclusion that high moral discrimination did not necessarily insure high moral conduct, Voelker decided to confront the Scouts with real situations. His rationale for measuring the moral conduct of children was that he felt that education had to be social and active in nature. For Voelker the negative freedom of the nineteenth century, represented by the doctrine of the rights of the individual, was to be replaced in the twentieth century by the freedom of the state and community to ensure the efficiency and welfare of the society.

Education is becoming conscious of its social mission and purpose . . . It will need to sever connection with the point of view of the political philosophers of the nineteenth century, who preached the gospel of the rights of the individual, and to proclaim a twentieth century gospel of the rights of the

community and the duties of the
individual, even to the extent of
taking away from the individual
some of the liberties which in a
former generation would have been
considered inalienable.[16]

B.

Like I.Q. testing, Character testing was
often used to delineate differences in racial
and ethnic groups. In his Study of American
Intelligence, Carl Brigham spoke of the menace
of race deterioration and the detrimental influence of certain immigrant groups on national
progress and welfare. His findings supported
the intellectual superiority of the Nordic race,
while calling the Alpine and Mediterranean races
peasants and intellectually inferior. The
American Negro was considered below the Alpine
and Mediterranean races in intellectual level.
The Alpine and Mediterranean races, however, were
considered closer to the Negro than to the
Nordic in intelligence.[17]

The decline in American intelligence was
blamed on the change in races migrating to this
country from the intellectual superior Nordic,
to the intellectual inferior Southern and
Eastern European. Other problems included the
immigration of lower and lower socio-economic
representatives of each race and the attempt to
incorporate the Negro into America's racial
stock. Brigham's solution was both a restrictive
and highly selective immigration policy, as well
as "the prevention of the continued propagation
of defective strains in the present population."[18]

Charles Davenport, of the Department of
Genetics of the Carnegie Institute, set out, not
to study the intelligence differences between
races, but the differences in social traits.[19]

179.

He made use of a list of traits of defectives,
developed by S. D. Porteus, who was Director of
Research of the Vineland Training School in
Vineland, New Jersey. Since Porteus felt that
"good qualities do not compensate for bad,"[20]
his list of traits of defectives contained only
negative qualities.

Davenport examined 51 pupils of different
'races' from Washington Irving High School for
Girls in New York City. He found the German
students highest in leadership, pertinacity,
humor, frankness, sympathy, and loyalty (half the
traits and all the good traits). The Irish were
highest in suspiciousness and at the bottom of
all the other traits. The Jews were highest in
generosity and obtrusiveness, but also second-
highest in suspiciousness. It seems clear
that the need to legitimize racial and ethnic
prejudices and stereotypes made its way into the
measurement of character as well as intelligence.

The Downey Will Temperament Test was a
means of measuring the personality factors of
an individual. It is not surprising to note
that this test revealed racial differences between Whites and Blacks. John McFadden and
J. F. Dashiell undertook a project to compare
38 high school and 39 college students from
each race. In the introduction to their paper,
they reviewed the previous studies showing the
intellectual superiority of Whites,[21] the differences in work curves, and the finding that
Negro children showed further departure than
white children from the normal adult association
standard. Their findings revealed that:

> The average white student has
> greater speed of movement . . . that
> he tends to work on the weighing of
> evidence or less decisiveness; that
> he is slightly average more nearly
> at his greatest speed; that he has
> slightly greater flexibility and

ability to meet new conditions in
life; that he is slightly slower
in making decisions--which may
mean a better less liable to become explosive under distraction
from conflicting stimuli; that he
is less forceful when contradicted,
which may mean a greater degree of
social adjustment.[22]

While the list went on, certain points are
immediately significant. The Negro was reported
to have a higher tendency to motor impulsion,
finality of judgment and motor inhibition. This
meant that he was more impetuous and resistant
to contradiction. While the higher total score
of all traits was indicative of a stronger personality, it is ironic that in those areas
where Blacks were superior, it was explained as
negative. In reference to Blacks' tendency to
resist contradiction, the authors quoted Dr.
Bevis's findings that dementia praecox headed
the list of psychoses of Southern Negros, with
the catatonic form occurring about twice as
often as in the Whites.[23]

Northern Blacks were aggresive as a compensation for their inferiority complex. The
"tendency of Negro drivers to beat their mules
more mercilessly than do white drivers is a
matter of observation."[24] The high score of
Blacks in motor impulsion was seen as indicative
of their lack of restraint and consequent extreme expression of feelings.[25] But in the end,
the white college students were seen to surpass
the Negro college students in their totals
which was seen to indicate a greater force of
personality.

The Character Education Inquiry at
Teachers College, Columbia, was a center for
significant research in character testing and
measurement. It's findings, however, often
reflected racial and ethnic differences.

181.

Socio-economic background was found to be significantly related to honesty and moral knowledge
(as was IQ), but there was a low relationship to
cooperation, inhibition, or persistence. Children of Northern European parents were found to
be more honest, cooperative, and charitable,
while those of Irish or Italian parents were at
the bottom of the list.

Low intelligence and low socio-economic
status among Blacks and Southern Europeans were
associated with a corresponding high tendency
for deceit. The negative correlation between
intelligence and deception failed to materialize
in the case of the Jews, however, who were seen
to exhibit high intelligence and high occupational status with a similarly high deceptiveness.

C.

The new programs of character education
needed some form of scientific verification of
their programs. There was a decided move away
from subjective observation and towards objective measurement and analysis. Morality was
seen as more susceptible than intellect to new
environmental influence. Since educators were
concerned during this period with social
adjustment and they felt that the "development
of proper dispositions may in many instances be
far more imperative than the development of
more skill or more knowledge,"[27] it was necessary
to develop objective measures of moral character.
Character tests could validate character education programs, make possible homogeneous group-
ing of children, enable study of outstanding
types, and even be used in vocational guidance
and personnel work in industry.[28]

Edwin Starbuck's subcommittee on character
tests and measurements of the N.E.A. Committee
on Character Education reported in 1926:

We are clearly in the midst of
an era of determination to gain more
adequate insights into the elements
of character to determine definitely
what aspects of it are and which are
not capable of change through training, and to ascertain by tests and
measurements the relative value of
different methods of training the
moral impulses.[29]

Another reason that character and personality testing was deemed important was because
it was seen as an indication of school achievement. According to Hartshorne and May, "school-
men and psychologists have been realizing that
prediction of success in any vocation depends
upon other factors than intelligence and tal-
ent."[30] These factors, which included interest,
motive, persistence, social adjustment, temperament, and emotional balance, were considered very
important to the scrutinous students of human
nature. The psychologists wanted to predict, not
only success in school (intelligence measures)
but also "success in living."[31] Besides the need
to predict one's success in living, including
vocational affinities, the precise measurement
of personality traits was seen as crucial to the
study of causes and remedies of character deficiencies.

In most cases, the correlation between
intelligence and school marks (success), was
around +0.50. While W. W. Charters stated that
this meant merely that there was a slight tendency for bright students to make higher grades in
class and nothing more, he also stated that

As a matter of fact it has been
shown that the less bright students
make on the whole better grades than
would naturally be expected, while
bright students make lower grades than

they ought, judged by their intelligence sources.32

S. L. Pressey of Indiana University also
felt that factors other than intelligence were
important in determining a child's success in
school. These factors often included such elements as conscientiousness, deportment, interest,
and application. While a person's relative
standing in intelligence was seen as a matter
largely fixed and unchanging, his character
traits and attitudes were viewed as changeable
from year to year, or depending on the person
with whom he was interacting. Pressey concluded
that a child's intellectual abilities are

> Born in him and their flowering
> is a process over which the school
> has relatively little control. But
> the child's attitude toward his
> school work, his attitude toward
> things in general, perhaps this is
> a matter where the policy of the
> school and the personality of the
> teacher may most of all count.33

Charters also found an almost zero correlation between intelligence and success in the
vocational field of salesmanship. The bright
man was seen as no more likely to make a good
salesman than was one less bright. Charters
concluded that "in face of these facts, the
question regarding the existence of other possible factors which may influence success in
school life is naturally raised."34

A. T. Poffenberger also was concerned with
the low correlation between intelligence and
success in an occupation. He felt that other
conditions of success, like physical health,
interest, aggressiveness, and social qualities
were also very influential. Success in some
occupations seemed to be negated by an abundance
of intelligence. Poffenberger wondered, "Is

184.

intelligence really a detriment in such occupations (example, mill worker), or is it merely likely to have accompanying it certain character traits not suited to the task?"[35] Such an argument would no doubt justify the tracking and sorting of supposedly low I.Q. students into preparatory programs suited to their "ability." The differentiated curriculum would be justified by the fact that certain menial routine tasks were best done by those of lower intelligence. Also if the success and compatibility of the worker were seen as important concerns, and they often were to the orderly efficient running of an industrial society, then the placing of "low I.Q. persons" in routine factory situations was justified.

The correlation between intelligence and character was found to be around +0.50. Poffenberger thus felt that since the presence of one (could) not be taken as the sign of the presence of the other, then both must be measured.[36] He concluded:

> Such a combined measure of intelligence and character, if used for vocational purposes, would prevent the waste of high grades of intelligence in positions where it is not needed and enable low intelligences to be located where their character traits would make them successful . . . In the individual of low intelligence but stable character, qualities may be a partial remedy for restlessness induced by extreme specialization and automaticity of work.[37]

D.

As Gordon Allport wrote, "psychology is the application of science to vocation and conduct."[38] All the interest in personality

185.

measurement was an attempt to establish an adjustment between the individual and his fellows which would be a benefit to both. This testing for sociality was for the "guidance, understanding, control, and amelioration of other human beings."[39] For this reason, vocational guidance was not only an integral part of the rise in industrialization, mechanization, and the corporate industrial state, but also greatly influenced character testing and measurement, and vice versa. Character analysis was less viewed as being foretold by phrenology, physiognomy, palmistry or astrology, but was instead replaced by the science of vocational guidance and vocational selection. In vocational guidance, the character of the person was determined and a job which suited this character was sought, while in vocational selection the character of the job was stressed and the employer sought an individual to fit it.[40]

Arthur Kornhauser was a leader in the "Psychology of Vocational Selection."[41] He stressed the importance of a functionalized, centralized employment under scientific management and a specialized personnel department. It was his belief that the personnel involvement in America began its period of rapid growth about 1916, favored by unusual expansion of industry and the unprecedented mobility of labor during the following years.[42] After the Armistice, tests and testers invaded industry with the intelligence tests they developed for the Army. These tests were used by scientific management to increase efficiency and thus "eliminate lowgrade workers from industrial tasks, where they would be dangerous or incompetent, and to call to the attention of management men of exceptional alertness."[43]

As previously pointed out, however, the correlation between intelligence and success at a vocation was not high. The need for measures other than intellect slowly entered the vocational

scene. Hollingworth's supplement to his earlier
volume on Vocational Psychology (1916) was his
work on Judging Human Character (1922). In it he
stressed the importance of letters of application,
human character as revealed in photographs, and
personal interviews in vocational selection of
employees.[44] By 1929 Hollingsworth "saw clearly
that although the economic, humanitarian and
esthetic features of work are important, its
mental hygiene aspect also looms large."[45] It
was extremely important, not only to help the
worker choose a suitable vocation, but also to
help the employer choose the right worker. The
only way to accomplish this was by a thorough
character analysis of the workers, possibly including "objective scales of skill and subject
matter and even by tentative scales of conduct,
feeling and attitude."[46]

The notion of the measurement, quantification, and standardization of human nature for the
control of conduct was summed up by Hollingworth
in the following statement:

The nineteenth century witnessed
an extraordinary increase in our knowledge of the material world and in our
power to make it subservient to our
ends; the twentieth century will probably witness a corresponding increase
in our knowledge of human nature and
in our power to use it for our own
welfare.[47]

E.

A prevailing notion of this period was
that a principle of compensation of mental
traits existed, which meant that if a person was
deficient in one trait he would excel in another,
and vice versa. Psychologists, including E. L.
Thorndike at Columbia, set out to test this hypo-
thesis. In his article on "Individual Differences," published in 1918, Thorndike reported that:

187.

All trustworthy studies so far
made of the relations between the
amounts of desirable single traits
in the same individual, agree in
finding direct or positive relations
between such traits. Having a large
measure of one good quality increases
the probability that one will have
more than the average of another
good quality. Intellectual ability
and moral worth hang together. The
correlations are of course not perfect. A large degree of superiority
in one desirable trait may involve
only a slight superiority in many
others, and since the relations vary
enormously amongst individuals, a
person highly gifted in one respect
will often, though not usually, be
very inferior in others.[48]

Thorndike later reported a correlation coefficient of "+0.40 or more"[49] between intelligence and character. He felt that correlation
and not compensation was the rule and thus good
traits went together. There was no principle of
compensation whereby a weak intellect was offset
by a strong will. Thorndike found that every
pair of such supposed compensation qualities
that had been investigated had been found really
to show correspondence. He concluded that "to
him that hath a superior intellect is given also
on the average a superior character."[50]

Desirable qualities, according to Thorndike, were positively correlated. Intellect was
viewed as good in and of itself, and also for
what it implied about other traits. Thorndike
concluded from this that the abler persons in
the world in the long run were the most clean,
decent, just and kind. While Thorndike seemed
for an instant to realize that the correlation
between character and intellect was only +0.40 to
+0.50, and not +1.00, and that consequently many

men of great intelligence would of course be unjust and cruel tyrants, he concluded that in the
long run it has paid the masses to be ruled by
intelligence.[51]

> The argument for democracy is
> not that it gives power to all men
> without distinction, but that it
> gives greater freedom for ability
> and character to attain power.[52]

Clara Frances Chassell's study of the
"Relation Between Morality and Intellect," published in 1935, concluded that the correlation
between moral character and intelligence, as
found in the case of non-delinquent groups, was
clearly positive and tended to be low or marked
in degrees.[53] The relation between morality
and intellect in restricted groups was clearly
direct, extremely variable, but tended to be low.
Expressed in correlational terms, the obtained
relation may therefore be expected to fall between +0.10 and +0.39, and the true relation to
be under +0.50. While the relation between
morality and intellect in the general population
was considerably higher than that usually found
in restricted groups, nevertheless it was hardly
probable to Chassell that this relation was
high.[54]

Chassell wrote that the

> Compendium of evidence upon which
> this conclusion is based incorporates
> the findings of nearly 300 studies
> pursued by many investigators in this
> country and abroad, affording diverse
> types of evidence bearing upon the
> relation between morality and intellect,
> representing various types of groups
> and countries, and a mass of correla-
> tional results consisting of nearly
> 700 coefficients of different types
> calculated between measures of

morality and intellect for three
types of subjects, including more
than 11,000 feebleminded, approxi-
mately 300,000 delinquents, and
nearly 12,000 non-delinquents.[55]

While Chassell's findings agreed with the
majority of psychologists, including Thorndike,
that morality (character) and intellect were
positively correlated, she was quick to caution
that certain problems were left unanswered.
First of all, even if the two were correlated,
it did not establish which of the two qualities,
morality or intellect, was antecedent and which
was consequent.[56]

A. S. Otis sought to correct this current
misconception as to the meaning of correlation in
his Statistical Method in Educational Measurement,
as follows:

When two variables are correlated,
we tend to assume that one is the
cause of the other . . . All that is
proved when two variables are found to
be correlated, is that some cause or
causes (such as heredity) are operating to produce changes in both variables.[57]

Also, the fact of the correlation between
morality and intellect did not face the heredity-
environmental question, nor was the degree of
relationship in research scarcely sufficient for
predictive purposes. The coefficient of correlation between morality and character was found to
lie between .10 and .39 (obtained relation),
while the true relation was usually given as
.50. The figure representing the true, that is,
the theoretical relation obviously had to be
interpreted as a corrected coefficient. As such,
Chassell pointed out it had no function to serve
in prediction.[58]

190.

Chassell concluded that only the obtained correlations of 0.10 to 0.39 could be used for predictive purposes, but authorities disagreed on what constituted a marked relationship. Otis stated that a .50 correlation was very low indeed. Goring stated that at least a .60 correlation was needed for prediction. Garrett believed that the correlation coefficient had to be .866 before the standard error of estimate was reduced by one-half.[59] Chassell's own conservative conclusions were that there was a low but still positive correlation between morality and intellect. She agreed with Thorndike that correlation, not compensation, was the rule but was not as optimistic as he on the relationship between those of high intellect and their qualities of moral character.

F.

The fact that a child's success in school or in an occupation could no more be predicted from his intelligence score than could his character was a great boost to character education and testing. If a high intelligence would guarantee success and worthwhile behavior, then it would be enough to educate merely for intellect. But since it did not, and other factors than intelligence seemed to be necessary for the worthwhile citizen, it was necessary to educate the child both in social adjustment and worthwhile conduct and also to measure and quantify his traits of temperament and character.

There can be no question that the study of delinquency influenced the character education movement as well. Members of both fields of endeavor were more concerned with one's action and behavior than with one's intelligence. The capacity for thinking was seen as related to the degree of intelligence, not character. Quality of thought as manifested in action and behavior was seen as related to character. Guy Fernald of

191.

the Psychopathic Laboratory of the Massachusetts Reformatory, stated that what was needed
was not better thought but better action.

> . . . Sociologically and econo-
> mically inimical personalities are
> such because of their behavior, since
> it is action, essentially, not thought,
> except incidentally, which brings a
> personality into contact with others.
> At the very basis of all sociologic
> endeavor for the correction of perni-
> cious activities of the parasitic
> elements of the population is the
> identification of inimical personalities
> and the determination in each of the
> possibilities of restoration to eco-
> nomic usefulness.[60]

The delinquency movement did pioneering
work in classifying and studying defective, dependent, and delinquent classes. The qualities
of mind and the character traits observed were
often used by other institutions, including the
schools and industry, to determine the efficiency
of their pupils and workers. The bond between
psychology, criminology, and sociology was also
one which grew stronger with time. While formerly many cases of delinquency were attributed
to low intellect, studies later revealed that
this bond was not as strong and sure as once
thought. Dr. Edith Spaulding, President of the
Association of Clinical Criminology, stated in
her presidential address before the Prison Congress in Columbus, Ohio, on October 14, 1920,
that

> In consideration of mental de-
> fect we are now being told by experts
> in the field of the feebleminded that
> there are a great number of good
> feebleminded in the world, capable of
> filling fairly important positions in
> the industrial situations of the

present day, and of being good citizens. So that even though the factor of mental defect may make more unfavorable the prognosis of the delinquent individual, still mental defect in itself is considered of less significance than formerly as a primary cause of anti-social behavior; and again the personality of the individual and its possibilities of development appear in greater relief.[61]

M. E. Haggerty, President of the National Association of Directors of Educational Research, concurred with Spaulding in his review in 1921 of Dr. Mabel Fernald's six-year study of delinquent women in State reformatories in New York. The data, he stated, failed

Absolutely to justify the view expressed by certain propagandists that delinquency and defective intelligence are practically synonymous and that solving the problem of mental deficiency will solve the problem of delinquency.[62]

A great deal of impetus for such a high correlation between criminality and mental deficiency came from the work of C. Goring on English convicts.[63] He found a correlation of +0.66 between criminality and mental deficiency. Even if this correlation was correct and many questioned its validity, it still left much to be desired in equating criminality with mental deficiency. Curt Rosenow adequately pointed this out by revealing once again the mistaken interpretation of statistical analyses. What Goring's results did show was that very probably lack of intelligence was of less importance than all other factors combined in determining delinquency. Rosenow concluded:

He (Goring) is correct when he

193.

states that the Intelligence-
Delinquency relation is the most
important relation measured so far
statistically. He is absolutely
wrong when he claims that in the
absence of other data we must accept his own conclusions as the
nearest approach to the truth
attained thus far. For if the
coefficient of correlations between
intelligence and delinquency is
0.66, the correct conclusion to
be drawn is that it is exceedingly
probable that factors other than
intelligence are of greater importance as determinants of crime than
intelligence.[64]

Studies of delinquent children revealed
that not only were most of them of normal intelligence[65] but often the delinquencies of the
brighter children were much more serious than
those of the duller group.[66] The overwhelming
conclusion of those involved was that "the dull
pupil should not be looked upon as inevitably
headed for delinquency, nor should it be assumed
that the bright pupil needs no guidance in matters of conduct."[67]

Thus while intelligence measures failed to
account for all differences between delinquents
and non-delinquents, certain measures of temperament and character seemed more reliable.[68]
Character testing arose partly as a necessary
phase in predicting success and adjustment in
school and in a vocation, and partly as a means
of determining and classifying potential character
deviates to educate the whole child for his adjustment into a worthwhile citizen, character
testing set out to augment the narrow range of
intellectual measures with measures of character,
temperament, and personality.

Criminology made use of both the family

history and the case method approach of psychology and psychiatry, and also of mental testing and personality testing. The aim was to blame the delinquency of the child on some personality or character trait. A long list of such personality traits were available from such studies as the Hogh-Amsden Guide to the study of personality, the study of traits made by Charles Davenport at the Eugenics Laboratory at Cold Springs Harbor, the work of Dr. F. W. Wells at the McLean Hospital at Waverly, as well as from several other sources.[69] The study of character was not only the key to the problem of delinquency, but also would greatly influence the areas of vocational guidance, hygiene, and education. Dr. Spaulding stated that "the study of personality is not unworthy of the highest standards of scientific endeavor, and it is felt that there is no field of human inquiry that will yield more remunerative results."[70]

S. D. Porteus in his attempt to determine social efficiency, studied the groups of characteristics most frequently observed in the feebleminded. While he found that mental age could not be readily translated into terms of social efficiency, his tests were at least as reliable as the Stanford-Binet in the cases of males, and in the case of females, considerably more so. The average of Binet and Porteus Test ages were better than either alone.[71]

The list of traits assembled by Porteus contained only negative qualities because Porteus felt that good qualities did not compensate for bad. He was more concerned with assigning "causes of failure rather than reasons for success."[72] Inefficiency was seen by Porteus as more easily rated than efficiency, especially since he was studying only defectives in an institutional setting.

The traits most frequently observed in defectives were lack of planning, lack of volution,

impulsiveness, suggestibility, nervousness and
excitability, irresolution, moodiness, obtrusiveness, cunning and shyness, bad temper, and
disobedience. While the last three traits were
dropped because it was felt they had no relation
to social adaptability, the Porteus social rating
scale was seen as a better indicator of social
adjustment than the Stanford-Binet.

G.

While much has been written about the concept of character, it should not be misconstrued
that those involved were in total agreement about
what really constituted character. Psychologists,
theologians, educators, philosophers and psycho-
analysts differed on their definition of character,
depending upon their own theoretical framework.
Even within the psychological community, there
were differences between behaviorists, environ-
mentalists, hereditarians, and endocrinologists.
While most involved saw personality as the way
in which an individual reacted to his environment,
his tendencies to behavior, the distinctions between character, personality, temperament, intellect and will were not so easily drawn.

The N.E.A. Research Bulletin on character
education, published in 1934, stated:

> Both heredity and environment
> play a part in determining the per-
> sonality of the individual. Heredity
> provides basic potentialities from
> which character develops. Environ-
> ment furnishes stimuli which cause
> the individual to respond and con-
> sequently to change. The relative
> influence of these two groups of
> factors in the mature and highly de-
> veloped personality has not been
> completely determined . . . heredity
> determines individual basic capacities

and fundamental urges or desires,
while environment determines the application of his capacities and the
specific warp in which his desires
are satisfied.[73]

The report went on to state that while

Personality may be defined as
the composite of individual tendencies
to behavior, including mental as well
as physical activities, character on
the other hand implied the evaluation
of behavior tendencies with reference
to standards of right and wrong.[74]

This distinction was shared by Gordon and F. E.
Allport, when they stated that "character is the
interplay of the fundamental personality tendencies in the social and economic environment as
seen from the point of view of ethics and legal
right."[75]   Thus, while personality was seen as
constituting all a person's reactions against,
or adjustment to his surroundings in terms of
urges, tendencies or behavior (whether heredi-
tarily or environmentally induced), character
ratings entailed the evaluation of such inter-
action.[76]   J. B. Watson, the behaviorist,
probably recognized best the mistaken search for
a scientific view of character. For Watson, one's
personality was merely the total mass of his
organized habits, but one's character was his
personality evaluated according to prevailing
standards of conduct. He cautioned that character study did not belong in the province of
psychology, but in social ethics.[77]

Character measurement and definition was
heavily laden with moral criteria and social
ethics. Disagreements as to what really constituted character, what variables were involved,
what was the relative importance of the various
elements, and what constituted the desired
maximum, made the movement a constant hotbed of

argument. With the constantly changing standards
of society, how could the State sanction a uni-
form stable morality? How could the State
educate for a desired character type which may be
undesirable in the future? These problems continued to haunt character educators as well as
psychologists. Gordon Allport revealed the high
premium put on reliability in character measurement, over and above that of validity.

> In all probability, as has been
> the case with the study of intelli-
> gence, we shall be able to give
> reliable quantitative results before
> we understand the precise nature of
> that with which we are dealing.[78]

Percival Symond concurred with Allport
that progress in character measurement would be
more rapid if, instead of trying to construct
valid tests, we should try to construct reliable
tests. He saw much effort wasted in building
tests that measured something (valid tests),
but were so unrealiable as not to give the same
answer on a second trial. He felt that, once
having constructed a reliable test, it would be
comparatively easy to find out what it measured
and what would be gained.[79]

The concern with reliability over and
above validity was characteristic of parts of
the character testing movement. The emphasis was
on a better understanding and control of human
nature. It was not so vital to know exactly what
constituted character or even what was being
measured, as long as it gave reliable results.
Hartshorne, May and Maller concurred on the discovery of new avenues of control.

> The human body is the same as it
> was 1000 years ago. But what a TOTALLY
> different object it seems to us from
> what it did to our ancestors! . . .
> Science, by filling in the details of

the picture is providing us not
only with a new perspective, but also
with new avenues of control; so, with
those even more subtle aspects of human nature we call mind and character,
we move toward more perfect understanding and control by the process
of analysis and experiment.[80]

H.

In their 1925 summary of the work to date
on the "Objective Methods of Measuring Character,"
Hartshorne and May reported that there were about
one hundred tests, either standardized or in the
form of definite proposals and pertaining mostly
to character traits, attitudes, interests, ethical discrimination, moral judgment, instincts,
emotions and certain motor skills.[81] They set
forth an outline of the types of tests to date
and the differing testing techniques that they
employed.[82]

Goodwin Watson reported that there were
167 references on character testing published in
1926. In an attempt to break down the types of
tests and show their individual emphasis, he
calculated the percentage of contributions in
each area (some were repeated so that the total
exceeds 100%). His study showed that in 1926,
7% of references were public summaries of the
work done by others, 16% were ratings, 8% were
tests of social attitude, 5% were on moral attitudes, 4% were on other related attitudes and
information, 4% were on introvert-extrovert indi-
ces, 11% were the result of further work on older
tests, 8% were on occupational interest, 11%
were on the case-study approach, 10% were questionnaires, 12% were on physical or physiological
indications, 6% were moral conduct tests, 12%
were on interpretations of conduct in light of
data other than test scores, 3% were objective
observations of behavior in natural situations,

and 4% were analyses and criticisms of the
methods of character measurement.[83]

May and Hartshorne found 130 researches
reported in the journals and books for 1926, but
that was "half as many for the preceding five
years, and before 1920, rarely was a study
found in print."[84] According to Paul Hanley
Furfey, during 1927 alone, eighteen separate
summaries of the literature on personality
traits were published.[85] The most comprehensive
were Grace Manson's bibliography for the National
Research Council (1364 titles) and A. A. Roback's
bibliography (3341 titles).[86]

While Lentz saw the necessity of character
measurement because "character education without
character measurement would appear to be as
logical as target practice in the dark, good
shots and poor ones being equally gratifying,"[87]
it was not so simple as it seemed. Many differing types of tests were developed for very practical matters like vocational guidance and
behavior control. In the early days those involved were very optimistic about the potential in
character measurement for use in working with
maladjusted individuals, especially delinquents.

Brotemarkle devised a test whereby:

Under a closer examination the
individual problem of faulty adjustment might be discovered, presenting
a better opportunity to the social
worker, psychiatrist, criminologist,
or kindred worker to correct the
underlying motivating behavior of
morals, personality, or character.[88]

Other tests, such as the Downey Will
Temperament Test,[89] the Ethical Discrimination
Test,[90] and the Pressey X-O Test,[91] were developed to rate personality types, emotions and moral
character. The results in the long run, however,
proved to be far from conclusive. While

reviewing these and other tests, Paul Hanley
Furfey wrote:

> This brief summary of standard
> tests for personality traits will
> show that such tests are markedly
> inferior to our best intelligence
> and achievement tests. They are so
> far inferior indeed, that few if
> any of them are perfect enough to
> be of practical use except to re-
> search workers. But this review
> should show something more as well.
> It should show that in spite of their
> defects, these tests are being con-
> stantly improved and that the day is
> not far distant when they can bear
> comparison with standardized tests
> of other types.[92]

Watson and Biddle published a review of
the research which took place in 1927, which bore
upon the programs of religious, educational and
social agencies. In it they also expressed
their concern with the unreliability of the personality tests already developed. They reported
that several of the studies in the field were
directed at "correcting an undue optimism about
some previously developed tests."[93] While they
showed the critical work being done on the Downey
Will Temperament Test (low correlations and
little reliability), and the Pressey X-O Tests
(little reliability), they were optimistic about
the many new ideas introduced. These included
testing sociability by recognition of photographs
and testing social perception by having children
match stories with photographs (facial expressions).

The criticism of the validity of character
testing was very aptly expressed by Witty and
Lehman in 1927.[94] They felt that hypothetical
tests did not really measure character. For them
the precise relationship between knowing and

doing had not yet been determined, since it was
obvious that in many instances the mere knowledge
of right and wrong was per se little safeguard
against wrong doing. Also traits manifested
themselves in different ways, depending on the
circumstances and individuals involved. A man
might be very trustworthy in terms of money, but
it may be a different matter when it concerned
his feelings towards his wife. Witty and Lehman
saw the human being as a constantly changing
organism who "reacts very differently from time
to time, depending upon his physiological condition and his past and immediate background of
experience."[95]

Character traits were not viewed as unitary entities as exemplified by many of the
early character studies. Morality was seen as
something acquired in terms of habit formation.
Morality posited the sum total of specific habit
reactions which facilitated adjustment in society,
and which society approved. For Witty and Lehman,
morality (character) was considered as a process
of habit acquisition and never as a specific
entity or static quality.[96] They concluded:

> This means that instead of at-
> tempting to develop a few specific
> traits with the expectation that
> these traits will transfer to situa-
> tions outside the classroom, we should
> seek out diligently those specific
> habits which we call good in life and
> make provision for their acquisition.
> If one accepts the point of view that
> character is acquired in terms of
> habits of action (and who has any evi-
> dence to the contrary), the attempts
> at character measurement spurious and
> unnecessary.[97]

Gladys Schwesinger, in her study in 1933
of social eugenics for the Eugenic Research Association at Cold Spring Harbor, concurred with

Witty and Lehman. She found that while intelligence could be viewed as cumulative and additive, personality could not. She concluded:

> Thus it will be seen that
> while intelligence may be roughly
> held as an accumulation of abili-
> ties or a certain point on a scale
> from 'very little to very much,'
> personality can not be considered
> from any such additive point of
> view; nor can its value be expres-
> sed by any numerical concept
> comparable with I Q, the index
> of brightness.[98]

R. Bain concurred that since ". . . all measurement and hence all exact science (depended) upon the relative stability and uniformity in the behavior of defined units"[99] testing and measurement did not belong in the realm of personality. All of these people saw character or personality as too fluid, too unpredictable, to accurately test and standardize. While a person's intelligence remained fairly stable day to day, his character might change drastically; he may be honest one day and dishonest the next.

This notion of describing character in terms of habits of conduct was expressed in 1924 by Percival Symonds. He was most interested in the traits of character which were most general, and called them confacts or conduct responses to common elements of various situations. Symonds stated that "we need to come down out of the sky and think less in terms of kinds of personality, or of traits of character, and more in terms of habits of conduct; or specific reactions to well-defined situations."[100]

The Character Education Inquiry at Teacher's College, Columbia University, under the leadership of Mark May and Hugh Hartshorne, developed a whole battery of tests.

To summarize now the conduct
tests, we have taken twenty-three
samples of situations involving deception or dishonesty, five samples
of situations involving service,
four samples of situations involving inhibition and five samples of
situations involving persistence.
Add to this sampling of conduct,
some 500 samples of imaginary situations in which children are required
to make some kind of intellectual
decision and some 350 situations in
which they are required to express
a preference or desire, and you have
a fairly good picture of the scope
of the tests of the Character Education Inquiry which have been brought
to the point of actual use.[101]

The Character Education Inquiry provided
the teacher with a whole battery of tests to
determine not only the personality traits but
also the attitudes of the children as well. As
time progressed, however, they found that children tested from day to day differed on their
responses to various tests. Thus, character
was seen not a unified trait but was viewed as
due to specificity of conduct. They stated,
"results of these studies show that neither deceit nor its opposite, honesty, are unified
character traits, but rather specific functions
of life situations."[102]

Later they concluded that

Although recognizing the importance of attitude and motive for both
social welfare and individual character, as ordinarily understood, we
realized that in any objective approach
to ethical conduct, we must begin with

the facts of conduct. We must know
what the specific behavior tendencies are before we can talk
intelligently about their causes
and consequences.[103]

Since a person's conduct was thought to be
controlled by external stimuli and not his inner
nature, the goal of the Character Education Inquiry was a controlled environment which in turn
looked toward a "24-hour school. Experience
with such an environment would lead naturally
to a corresponding unity of character, if we
conceive of unity as external consistency."[104]

Not all those concerned went along with
this stimulus-response methodology. Literally
hundreds of reports were published every year.
Some were for use in preschool and elementary
school, while others were for use in high school,
college, and business. In the field of young
children, behavior observation was very important in lieu of the lack of reading and writing
ability in consideration of character study.

Goodenough created an observation scheme
so that teachers could chart the movements of
each child in each of twenty-five, one-minute
observations.[105] The Lehman Play Quiz studied
the adjustment of children according to their
play.[106] Herbert Woodrow even devised a picture
preference test for children aged seven to nine.
The children were shown 44 pictures, four at a
time, which presented things in a life-like manner, involving situations of either a kind
gesture or unkind behavior. The children were
asked to rank the pictures in terms of which they
liked best. In view of Woodrow, the pictures
had a better chance of taking the child off his
guard than did questions.[107] Other character
tests used on children included Furfey's Developmental Age Test which was a questionnaire consisting of a measure of reading preferences,
play interests, attitudes, and activity preferences.[108] There was also the "Telling What I Do

205.

Tests," developed by Harry Baker, which obtained
statements from children concerning their attitude toward a variety of situations which children
commonly face.[109]

This concern with attitudes of children as
well as adults gradually found its way into the
measurement of personality and character. A tremendous number of tests, including Vetter's
Test of Social and Political Attitudes, which
measured the social and political attitudes of
high school and college students and related them
to personality factors, were utilized to gauge
prejudices and attitudes of pupils, constituen-
cies, congregations and to record shifts in
opinion.[110]

In the U.S. Office of Education Circular
of 1932, David Segel reported on a "Selected
List of Tests and Ratings for Social Adaptation."[111] He discussed the importance of social
adaptation and how tests and ratings schemes
could be used to measure the effectiveness of the
new character education programs. While he also
recognized the limitations of the tests, in terms
of reliability and uniformity, he still saw the
need to know more of the child's interests and
attitudes so as to help him to adapt to society
more easily. The report contained a list of
twenty-one examples of preschool, kindergarten,
elementary, junior high, high school, college and
adult measurements, including the major tests discussed previously.

J. B. Maller later pointed out the two
basic inadequacies inherent in the nature of
tests of attitude and opinion tests. First of
all, the overt expression of an individual opinion and attitude may not at all correspond to his
true opinion and attitude, thus giving no sign of
validity. A person may give a dishonest answer
consistently. Also, individual differences in
degree of constancy and stability of attitude are
possible.[112] The important thing to realize here,

however, is not the faults of attitude measurement, but its existence altogether. In the desire to know and control the whole child, scientific measurement had attempted to quantify, objectify, and standardize the intelligence, character, personality, emotions, attitudes and beliefs of the child.

While more and more character tests were being developed, the debate over their validity and reliability continued. In the N.E.A.'s Department of Superintendence Tenth Yearbook on "Character Education," published in 1932, character testing was once again chastized.

There is no good reason for expecting tests of persons to yield the constant results found in physical measures. Exactly the same situation can never recur and never be presented to two different persons. We deal in human life with a series of events having common elements but always distinguished by unique features and having thus unique totalities. The attempt to measure one trait after another, eventually to be summed up into a total character, is doomed for two reasons. One is the very simple fact that before we can get to the last traits in the series, the individual will have changed in some of the aspects in earlier tests. We cannot act fast enough. Even our measuring does something to change the person we would measure. Moreover, if we could bid the sun and all events in time to stand still for our interests, we still could have the impossible task of combining a series of rigid abstractions into an integrated whole, the parts of which interact, supplement, and compensate.

Even our carefully tested measurements for character education
will be found relative to a particular group and time. With another
group, another time, in a changed
community, the relative effect is
apt to change. We deal, even in
measurement and research, with
evanescent approximations.[113]

I.

Beginning with Fernald's character testing
of defective delinquents in 1912, and Voelker's
testing of Boy Scouts' honesty in 1921, coupled
with the tremendous rise in mental testing during
the First World War, personality and character
testing and measurement gained in popularity
in the decade following the War. Measures of
intellect were seen to be inconclusive in predicting one's success in school or in a vocation,
one's potentiality for delinquency, or one's
day-to-day behavior.

While the character measurement movement
began by attempting to isolate specific character
traits, which often reflected racial and ethnic
differences, and integrate them into a unified
whole, the emphasis later changed to measuring
general character. Tests repeated over time revealed an inconsistency and unreliability which
took much of the impetus out of the movement.
Personality "traits" were seen to change from
day to day, and from person to person, depending
upon external circumstances. Human personality
was viewed by the psychologist as more complex
than previously thought. While the debates
raged, the educator seemed to make full use of
the tests available.

As described previously, there was a wide
range of tests, questionnaires, and rating scales
which were used by the schools, both to examine

the personality, character and temperament of the child and to determine their attitudes, beliefs and opinions. While the psychologists had originally called for the analysis and objectification of character and the standardization of conduct, this eventually led to the measurement of the children's thoughts as well. The distinction between thought (intellect) and action (character) was thus not as clear as previously anticipated. While character education attempted to generate an ideal planned society by emphasizing development of good habits of conduct, it also seemed concerned with the thoughts and attitudes of the child. The goal was to make the student's desires and needs mesh with those of society's demands. In order to accomplish this, it was very important to determine the student's attitudes, beliefs, and opinions on a wide range of issues. Thus, while it became increasingly more difficult to rationalize testing of such an evanescent approximation as personality, the whole area of questioning the student's attitudes and beliefs opened up.

In the next chapter, I shall attempt to analyze some of the character and personality tests in terms of the value assumptions maintained, as well as those implicit in the questions and answers which were given.

NOTES

[1]See Frances Galton Address "Nature," 6, Aug. 23, 1877, pp. 344-347 and "Measurement of Character," Fortnight Review, 1844, p. 42. See also his book, Hereditary Genius (New York: MacMillan, 1869).

[2]G. D. Haymans and E. Wiersma, "Beitrage zur Speciellen Psychologie and Grund einer Massen-unter-suchung," Zsch.f.Psychol, 42, 1906, pp. 81-127, 258-301.

[3]Guy Fernald, "The Defective-Delinquent Class Differentiating Tests," American Journal of Insanity, 68, April 1912, pp. 530-531.

[4]See E. L. Thorndike, "Scientific Personnel Work in the Army," Science, 49, Jan. 1919, pp. 53-61; L. M. Terman, "The Use of Intelligence Tests in the Army," Psychological Bulletin, 14, June 1918, pp. 177-186; W. V. Bingham, "Army Personnel Work," Journal of Applied Psychology, 3, March 1919, pp. 1-12; R. M. Yerkes, "Report of the Psychology Committee of the National Research Council," Psychological Review, 26, March 1919, pp. 83-149.

[5]Frank Freeman, Mental Tests: Their History, Principles and Applications (Cambridge: Riverside Press, 1926), p. 3.

[6]Percival Symonds, Diagnosing Personality and Conduct (New York: D. Appleton Century Co., 1931), p. v.

[7]"Intelligence and Its Measurement: A Symposium," Journal of Educational Psychology, 12, March & April 1921, pp. 123-147 and pp. 195-216. See especially the statements of S. S. Colvin of Brown University, p. 139; Rudolf Pinter of Ohio State University, p. 142; Frank Freeman of the University of California, p. 123; S. L.

Pressey of Indiana University, p. 147; L. L.
Thurstone of Carnegie Tech, p. 206; and Herbert
Woodrow of the University of Minnesota, p. 216.

[8]Vernon Cady, "The Psychology and Pathology of Personality," Journal of Delinquency, 7, Sept. 1922, p. 226. Cady later made use of a $10,000 grant to Stanford from the U.S. Interdepartment Social Hygiene Board to study incorrigibility. See his "The Estimation of Juvenile Incorrigibility: A Report of Experiments in the Measurement of Juvenile Incorrigibility by means of Certain Non-Intelligence Tests," Journal of Delinquency Monograph, #2, 1923.

[9]S. L. Pressey, "At Attempt to Measure the Comparative Importance of General Intelligence and Certain Character Traits in Contributions to School Success," Elementary School Journal, 21, Nov. 1920, pp. 220-229.

[10]Harold Rugg, "Is the Rating of Human Character Practicable," Journal of Educational Psychology, 12, 1921, p. 386.

[11]Symonds, op. cit., pp. v-vi.

[12]Percival Symonds, Psychological Diagnosis in Social Adjustment (New York: American Book Co., 1934), p. vii.

[13]Paul Hanley Furfey, "Tests for Measurement on Non-Intellectual Traits," Educational Research Bulletin, Catholic University of America Studies in Psychology, Psychological Monographs, 32, 1922-1923, p. 1.

[14]Marie Cecelia McGrath, "A Study of the Moral Development of Children," Catholic University of America Studies in Psychology, Psychological Monographs, 32, No. 2, 1923, p. 1.

[15]Augusta F. Bronner, "Comparative Study of the Intelligence of Delinquent Girls," Columbia

University Contributions to Education, Teachers College Series No. 68, 1914.

[16]Paul Voelker, "The Function of Ideals in Social Education," Columbia University Contributions to Education, Teacher's College Series No. 112, 1921, p. 3. For a complete discussion of the concepts of negative and positive freedom see Isaiah Berlin, Four Essays on Liberty (New York: Oxford University Press, 1971).

[17]Carl Brigham, A Study of American Intelligence (Princeton: Princeton University Press, 1923), p. 197.

[18]Ibid., p. 210. For a complete discussion of the racial implications of intelligence testing, see Russell Marks, "Testers, Trackers, and Trustees: The Ideology of the Intelligence Testing Movement in America, 1900-1954," Unpublished Ph.D. Thesis, University of Illinois, 1972.

[19]Charles Davenport, "Comparative Social Traits of Various Races," School and Society, 14, Oct. 1921, pp. 344-348. See also R. S. Woodworth, "Comparative Psychology of Races," Psychological Bulletin, 13, 1916, pp. 388-397.

[20]S. D. Porteus, "Social Rating Scale," Training School Bulletin, 18, May 1921, p. 35.

[21]See M. J. Mayo, "The Mental Capacity of the Negro," Archives of Psychology Monograph, No. 28, 1913; other related works on the intellectual inferiority of Blacks included Dagney Sunne, "A Comparative Study of White and Negro Children," Journal of Applied Psychology, 1, 1917, pp. 71-83; S. L. Pressey and G. F. Teter, "A Comparison of Colored and White Children By Means of a Group Scale of Intelligence," Journal of Applied Psychology, 3, Sept. 1919, pp. 277-282; and A. C. Strong, "Three Hundred and Fifty White and Colored Children Measured by Binet-Stanford Measurement Scale of Intelligence," Pedagogical Seminary, 20, 1913, pp. 485-515.

[22] John McFadden and J. F. Dashiell, "Racial Differences as Measured by the Downey Will Temperament Test," Journal of Applied Psychology, 7, March 1923, pp. 38-39.

[23] W. M. Bevis, "Psychological Traits of the Southern Negro with Observations as to Some of his Psychoses," American Journal of Psychiatry, 1, July 1921, pp. 69-78.

[24] McFadden, op. cit., p. 40.

[25] See H. W. Odum, "Special and Mental Traits of the Negro," Columbia University Studies in History, Economics, and Public Law, V. 37, No. 3, Whole No. 99, 1910.

[26] Hugh Hartshorne and Mark May, "Studies in Deceit," Studies in the Nature of Character, V. I (New York: MacMillan Co., 1928), p. 252.

[27] Theodore Lentz, "An Experimental Method for Discovery and Development of Tests of Character," Columbia University Contributions to Education, Teachers College Series No. 180, 1925, p. 1.

[28] Ibid., pp. 3-4.

[29] "Character Tests and Measurement," Report of Subcommittee on Character Tests and Measurement, Chapter V, "Character Education," U. S. Office of Education Bulletin, No. 7, 1926, p. 3.

[30] Hugh Hartshorne and Mark May, "Research in Character Education, Phi Delta Kappa, 9, April 1927, p. 129.

[31] Ibid

[32] W. W. Charters, "Success, Personality and Intelligence," Journal of Educational Research, 11, March 1925, p. 170.

[33]S. L. Pressey, "An Attempt to Measure the Comparative Importance of General Intelligence and Certain Character Traits, in Contributing to Success in School," Elementary School Journal, 21, Nov. 1920, p. 227.

[34]Ibid., This opinion was shared by Walter Bingham, Director of the Personnel Research Foundation. He agreed that in many occupations there was no clear relationship between success and intelligence. He wrote, "Given necessary minimum of intelligence, it would seem that one's relative success in business is determined more by certain other factors than by mental alertness as measured by these intelligence tests." See "Intelligence and Personality in Vocational Success," Vocational Guidance Magazine, 3, Jan. 1925, p. 124.

[35]A. T. Poffenberger, "Measures of Intelligence and Character," Journal of Philosophy, 19, 1922, p. 263.

[36]Ibid.

[37]Ibid., pp. 265-266.

[38]Gordon Allport, "Personality and Character," Psychological Bulletin, 18, 1921, p. 441.

[39]F. H. Allport and G. W. Allport, "Personality Traits: Their Classification and Measurement," Journal of Abnormal Psychology, 16, 1921, pp. 21-22.

[40]Henry F. Adams, "Mythology and Science of Character Analysis," Scribner's Magazine, 69, 1921, p. 569.

[41]Arthur Kornhauser, "Psychology of Vocational Selection," Psychological Bulletin, 19, 1922, pp. 192-229.

[42] Ibid., p. 195.

[43] Ibid., p. 207. For more information on the pioneering works in the field of the industrial use of psychological methods of selection, see works of Hugo Munsterberg, Psychology and Industrial Efficiency (Boston: Houghton Mifflin, 1913); H. C. Link, Employment Psychology (New York: MacMillan Co., 1919); H. L. Hollingworth, Vocational Psychology (New York: D. Appleton & Co., 1916); National Association of Corporation Schools Reports--"Committee on Application of Psychological Tests and Rating Scales to Industry," and Committee on Job Analysis, 8th Annual Proceedings, New York, 1920, pp. 115-139, pp. 163-184; "Committee on Job Analysis," 9th Annual Proceedings, Niagara Falls, 1921, pp. 511-540, pp. 211-236.

[44] H. L. Hollingworth, Judging Human Character (New York: Harcourt Brace, 1925). Hollingworth's use of photographs seems to show the influence of Kretschmer's study on the relationship of physical form and psychic nature. See E. Kretschmer, Physique and Character (New York: Harcourt Brace, 1921).

[45] H. L. Hollingworth, Vocational Psychology and Character Analysis (New York: D. Appleton & Co., 1929), p. 351.

[46] Ibid., p. 353.

[47] Ibid., p. 358.

[48] E. L. Thorndike, "Individual Differences," Psychological Bulletin, 15, 1918, pp. 158-159.

[49] E. L. Thorndike, "Intelligence and Its Uses," Harpers, 140, Jan. 1920, p. 233.

[50] Ibid.

[51] Ibid., p. 235.

[52] Ibid.

[53] Clara Frances Chassell, "The Relation Between Morality and Intellect," Columbia University Contributions to Education, Teachers College Series No. 607, 1935, p. 196. The correlation between delinquency and mental inferiority as found in the case of feebleminded groups, was clearly positive and tended to be marked in degree.

[54] Ibid., p. 470.

[55] Ibid., pp. 470-471. Feebleminded subjects were from f-m at large in the community, f-m in institutions and f-m in schools. Delinquent sample came from adult criminals, juvenile delinquents, sex offenders, and alcoholics. Non-delinquent sample included members of general population, royalty, aviation cadets, college grads, college students, school children, and Boy Scouts. The areas contributing to data base included the United States, Canada, Great Britain, France, Belgium, Puerto Rico, Europe, Sweden, Central Europe, and Australia.

[56] Ibid., p. 488.

[57] A. S. Otis, Statistical Method in Educational Measurement (Yonkers-on-Hudson: World Book Co., 1925), pp. 230-231.

[58] Chassell, op. cit., p. 489. See T. L. Kelley, Statistical Method (New York: MacMillan 1924), p. 208. "The coefficient of correlation obtained by the use of the Spearman formula for correction for attenuation should never be used for the estimation of one actual measure from a second."

[59] Ibid., p. 490.

[60] Guy Fernald, "Character vs. Intelligence in Personality Studies," Journal of Abnormal

Psychology, 15, 1920, p. 9.

[61]Edith Spaulding, "The Role of Personality Development in the Reconstruction of the
Delinquent," Journal of Abnormal Psychology, 16,
1921, p. 98.

[62]M. E. Haggerty, "Recent Developments in
Measuring Human Capacities," Journal of Educational Research, 3, 1921, p. 249; The finding that
prison inmates were of average intelligence can
be found in E. A. Doll, "The Comparative Intelligence of Prisoners," Journal of Criminal Law and
and Criminology, 2, 1920, pp. 191-197.

[63]C. Goring, Abridged Edition of the
English Convict (London: H. M. Stationery Office,
1919).

[64]Curt Rosenow, "Is Lack of Intelligence
the Chief Cause of Delinquency?" Psychological
Bulletin, 27, 1930, p. 148.

[65]See William Healy and Augusta Bronner,
Delinquents and Criminals: Their Making and
Unmaking (New York: MacMillan Co., 1928). They
found that of the 4,000 juvenile delinquents
they studied in Chicago, 72% were of normal
intelligence and only 23% were mentally subnormal
or feebleminded; Anna Spiesman Starr, "A Problem
in Social Adjustment," Psychological Clinic, 17,
May 1928, pp. 88-96. She found that of the
7,664 juvenile delinquents studied at the Neuro-
Psychiatric Clinic of Municipal Court of Philadelphia, 41% were of normal intelligence and
only 25% were morons.

[66]C. H. Calhoon, "A Follow-Up Study of 100
Normal and 100 Subnormal Delinquent Boys,"
Journal of Juvenile Research, 12, Sept.-Dec.
1928, pp. 236-240.

[67]"Education for Character: Part I--The
Social and Psychological Background," National

Education Association Research Bulletin, 12, March 1934, p. 54. The lack of a close relationship between intelligence and mental stability can be found in F. L. Wells, "Intelligence and Psychosis," American Journal of Insanity, 77, July 1920, pp. 245.

[68]See Edythe Bryant, "Delinquents and Non-delinquents on the Will Temperament Test," Journal of Delinquency, 8, 1973, pp. 46-63. She found an appreciable difference between two groups in emotional maturity (speed of decision) and coordination of impulses; Franklin B. Fearing, "Some Extra-Intellectual Factors in Delinquency," Journal of Delinquency, 8, 1923, pp. 145-153. While none of 157 juvenile delinquents passing through Juvenile Court were classified as feebleminded by I.Q. tests, 31% were classified as psychopathic personalities. Of 200 cases of adult delinquency studied, 28.5% were feebleminded, 25.5% normal, and 18.8% were psychopathic.

[69]In Spaulding, op. cit., p. 100.

[70]Ibid., p. 106.

[71]Porteus, op. cit., p. 38.

[72]S. D. Porteus, "Personality in Relation to Social Maladjustment," Training School Bulletin, 18, Oct. and Nov. 1921, p. 82.

[73]N.E.A. Research Bulletin, 1934, op. cit., pp. 50-51.

[74]Ibid., p. 49.

[75]F. H. Allport and Gordon W. Allport, "Personality Traits: Their Classification and Measurement," Journal of Abnormal Psychology, 16, 1921, p. 8. They viewed personality on the other hand as the adjustment tendencies of an individual to his social environment.

[76]See also the works of George Brandenburg, "Analyzing Personality, Parts I and II," Journal of Applied Psychology, 9, 1926, pp. 134-155 and pp. 281-292. Brandenburg saw personality as a composite of an individual's typical reactions; physical, intellectual, emotional, to his environment, together with his various physical characteristics which constituted what we call his general appearance. While personality depended upon both inherited qualities and environment, character was more hereditary, dealing with innate qualities, pp. 140-141. W. McDougall, Social Psychology (Boston: Luce, 1921). McDougall considered character to be the organization of sentiments, which were innate, into a system of hierarchy, within the individual, and thus not measurable as a unitary function, p. 418. Guy Fernald, "Character vs. Intelligence in Personality Studies," Journal of Abnormal Psychology, 15, 1920, p. 170. Fernald saw personality as made up of a blending of character and intellect. Character provided the quality of action, while intellect provided capacity for thought, p. 7. H. I. Gosline, "Personality from the Introspective Viewpoint," Journal of Abnormal Psychology, 15, 1920, pp. 36-44. Gosline considered character, along with intelligence and temperament, to be inborn, though susceptible to alteration by the environment. Raymond Filter, "A Practical Definition of Character," Psychological Review, 29, 1922, pp. 319-324. Filter defined character as persistence of morals. He wanted to rule our moral values as criteria for a definition of character; Morton Prince, The Unconscious (New York: MacMillan Co., 1915). Prince defined personality as the sum total of all biological innate dispositions, impulses, tendencies, appetites and instincts, and all acquired dispositions, p. 549.

[77]J. B. Watson, Psychology from the Standpoint of a Behaviorist (Philadelphia: Lippincott, 1919), p. 420.

[78]Gordon W. Allport, "Personality and Character," Psychological Bulletin, 18, 1921, p. 447. This article contains a rather extensive discussion and bibliography of competing theories of character.

[79]Percival Symonds, "The Present Status of Character Measurement," Journal of Educational Psychology, 15, Nov. 1924, pp. 492-493.

[80]Hugh Hartshorne, Mark A. May and Julius B. Maller, Studies in Service and Self-Control (New York: MacMillan Co., 1929), p. 3.

[81]Mark A. May and Hugh Hartshorne, "Objective Methods of Measuring Character," Journal of Genetic Psychology, 32, 1925, p. 45.

[82]Ibid., pp. 46-49.

[83]Goodwin Watson, "Character Tests of 1926," Vocational Guidance Magazine, 5, 1927, pp. 289-290.

[84]Hartshorne and May (Phi Delta Kappa, 1927), op. cit., p. 129.

[85]Furfey, op. cit., p. 3.

[86]Grace Manson, "A Bibliography of the Analysis and Measurement of Human Personality up to 1926," National Research Council Reprint and Circular Series, No. 72 (Washington: National Research Council, 1926); A. A. Roback, A Bibliography of Character and Personality (Cambridge: Sci-Art Publishers, 1927). Other useful bibliographies are those of Mark May and Hugh Hartshorne, "Personality and Character Tests," Psychological Bulletin, 25, July 1928, pp. 442-443; A. A. Froemming, "Bibliography of Character Tests and Measurements," Journal of Educational Research, 16, 1927, pp. 223-226; J. M. Pangburn, "The Psychology of Personality," Social Science,

2, Aug.-Oct. 1927, pp. 370-381; E. Faris, "Topical Summaries of Current Literature; Social Psychology in America," American Journal of Sociology, 32, Jan. 1927, pp. 623-630; K. Shuttleworth, "The Social Relations of Children," Psychological Bulletin, 24, Dec. 1927, pp. 708-716; "Tests of Personality and Character," Review of Educational Research, 2, June 1932, pp. 183-270; J. B. Maller, Character and Personality Tests (New York: Bureau of Publications Teachers College, Columbia University, 1937).

[87] Lentz, op. cit., p. 2.

[88] R. E. Brotemarkle, "Comparison Test for Investigating the Ideational Content of the Moral Concepts," Journal of Applied Psychology, 6, Sept. 1922, p. 242.

[89] Downey Individual Will-Temperament Test (Yonkers-on-Hudson: World Book Co., 1921). Dr. June Downey of the University of Wyoming developed this test. See also, June Downey, The Will Temperament and Its Testing (Yonkers-on-Hudson: World Book Co., 1923). The reliability of the test varied and the correlation between test scores, ratings, intelligence and school grades were low or negative. See Richard Stephen Uhrbrock, "An Analysis of the Downey Will-Temperament Tests," Columbia University Contribution to Education, Teachers College Series No. 296, 1928.

[90] S. C. Kohs, "Ethical Discrimination Test," Journal of Delinquency, 7, Jan. 1922, pp. 1-15. Kohs was a member of the Psychological Court of Domestic Relations of Portland, Oregon.

[91] S. L. Pressey, Pressey X-O Test (Chicago: C. B. Stoelting).

[92] Furfey, op. cit., p. 23.

[93]Goodwin Watson and Delia Biddle, "A Year of Research--1927--Some Investigations published between Jan. 1, 1927 and Jan. 1, 1928, Bearing Upon the Programs of Religious, Educational and Social Agencies," Religious Education Association Monograph, No. 4, July 1929.

[94]Paul A. Witty and Harvey Lehman, "The So-Called General Character Test," Psychological Review, 34, Nov. 1927, pp. 401-414.

[95]Ibid., p. 403.

[96]Ibid., p. 412.

[97]Ibid., p. 413.

[98]Gladys Schwesinger, Heredity and Environment (New York: MacMillan Co., 1933), p. 96.

[99]R. Bain, "Theory and Measurement of Attitudes and Opinions," Psychological Bulletin, 27, May 1930, p. 362.

[100]Symonds, "The Present Status of Character Measurement," op. cit., p. 493.

[101]Mark May and Hugh Hartshorne, "A Summary of the Work of the Character Education Inquiry," Religious Education, 25, Sept. 1930, p. 615.

[102]May and Hartshorne, Studies in Nature of Character, Vol. 1, "Studies in Deceit," op cit., p. 411.

[103]May, Hartshorne, and Shuttleworth, Studies in the Organization of Character, V. 3, op. cit., p. 362.

[104]May and Hartshorne, "A Summary of the Work of the Character Education Inquiry," op. cit., p. 762.

[105]F. L. Goodenough, "Inter-relationships in Behavior of Young Children," Child Development, 1, March 1930, pp. 29-48.

[106]H. C. Lehman and P. A. Witty, Psychology of Play Activities (New York: A. S. Barnes, 1927).

[107]Herbert Woodrow, "Picture Preference Test," Journal of Educational Psychology, 17, Nov. 1926, pp. 519-531.

[108]Paul Hanley Furfey, "A Scale for Measuring Developmental Age," Mental Hygiene, 14, 1930, pp. 129-136. Also P. H. Furfey, "A Revised Scale for Measuring Development Age in Boys," Child Development, 2, June 1931, pp. 102-114.

[109]Harry J. Baker, "The Analysis of Behavior Problems," Ohio State Educational Conference Proceedings of the Eleventh Annual Session: Ohio State University Bulletin, V. 36, No. 3, 1931, pp. 125-152.

[110]See also Watson's Test of Public Opinion (fairmindedness), Hart's Social Attitudes Test, Moss's Social Intelligence Test, The Personal Attitude Test, the Student Opinion Test, the Social Distance Scale, the Liberal Attitudes Test, and the Test of Student Opinion on the War (W.W.I.). For complete listings and references, see Percival Symonds, Appendix to Psychological Diagnosis in Social Adjustment (New York: American Book Co., 1934) pp. 284-312.

[111]David Segel, "A Selected List of Tests and Ratings for Social Adaptation," U.S. Office of Education Circular, No. 52, Washington, 1932.

[112]Maller, op. cit., p. 1.

[113]"Character Education," Tenth Yearbook (Washington: Department of Superintendence of the N.E.A., 1932), p. 404.

223.

V. AN ANALYSIS OF SEVERAL CHARACTER TESTS AND MEASURES

A.

The early attempts at character measurement were often crude, besides being questionable in terms of their reliability and validity. Voelker, in trying to answer the question, "Will the boy cheat on a test?" inserted a waxed paper between the leaves of a test booklet and then had the student grade his own paper. Discrepancies between the answers on the test and those on the waxed paper would reveal erasures, which would indicate deceit.[1] Inhibition was measured by the Character Education Inquiry by putting an unpleasant substance in the child's mouth and seeing how long he would keep it there without spitting it out, or by seeing how long he would keep a straight face with an obnoxious odor under his nose, or finally by seeing how long he could keep from smiling when being tickled by a feather.[2] The measures also revealed the basic value assumptions of those involved in the creation of the tests, questionnaires, and rating schemes. If one looks closely at the test questions and supposed correct responses, much can be learned about the values that the testers thought to be important. It can be determined not only if the questions or answers reflected any racial, cultural, or ethnic biases but also what was the accepted conception of character as revealed by the choice of questions and answers.

The National Research Council's Committee on Emotional Fitness for Warfare was headed by Prof. R. S. Woodworth of Columbia University.[3] In 1918, Woodworth designed a personal data sheet of over two hundred questions to help identify psychotic tendencies in soldiers. The list was later reduced to one hundred and sixteen questions and was given to 2,000 drafted men. Ellen Mathews lamented that "extensive use

225.

of the final list was prevented by the signing of
the armistice."[4] She later revised the list for
use on school children. Louis Terman made use of
this revised questionnaire in his Genetic Studies
of Genius.[5] In his study, pupils were asked to
answer a long list of questions either yes or no.
It is clear from the questions and the correct
answers that any child who was worried about his
health, afraid of the dark, anxious to get away
from school and get a job, enjoyed being idle,
felt that he (she) was being treated unfairly by
his teachers, or felt that he (she) was often
punished unjustly and was not getting a square
deal in life, was paranoid and exhibited psychotic tendencies.[6] Apparently no attempt was made
to corroborate any of the possible affirmative
responses to the above. The scenario of a child
being unjustly treated or punished and then
classified as paranoid is a frightening nightmare.

       As a result of a rigorous intelligence
testing and selection program, Terman's main
gifted group was finally composed of 30.7%
English, 15.7% German, 11.3% Scotch, 10.5% combined Jewish, and only 1.4% Italian, 0.1% Negro,
0.1% Mexican and 0.1% Indian.[7] He concluded that
that gifted group, in comparison with the general
population of the cities concerned, (Los Angeles,
San Francisco, Oakland, Calif.), showed a 100
percent excess of Jewish blood; a 25% excess of
parents who are of native parentage; a probable
excess of Scotch ancestry; and a very great
deficiency of Latin and Negro ancestry.[8] Thus,
while these figures reflect the standard conceptions of the intellectual inferiority of
Blacks, Southern Europeans, and Latins, it also
possibly showed why the controls scored higher
than the gifted group on the revised Woodworth
Questionnaire which was seen as indicative of
psychotic tendencies. These controls attended
the same schools as the gifted attended, and
usually but not always the same class. But,
while Blacks represented 2% of the total combined population of the cities studied, only two
Blacks made the gifted group and both of them

were "part white." The total Latin population
of the cities concerned was not exactly known
but was considered high while the porportion of
Latins in the gifted group was low. Thus many
more Blacks and Latins, living under adverse
environmental and psychological conditions were
in the control group.

Mathews had concluded at an earlier time
that Italians had definitely larger scores than
others on the revised Woodworth Questionnaire,
and Jewish children as a group had a slightly
larger score than did children of Saxon, Celtic,
and Teutonic stock.[9] This follows exactly the
results from the work of the Character Education
Inquiry. They, too, saw Jews as having high
intelligence as well as high deceptiveness, opposed to the Southern Europeans and Blacks, who
had low intelligence and high deceptiveness.
While Terman's gifted group (determined by I.Q.
scores) was filled with twice the percentage of
Jews in the general population, no mention was
made how the Jewish gifted scored on the Woodworth Questionnaire as compared to other gifted
or to the Jewish controls.

It seems clear, however, that children
of Southern European immigrants, Blacks and
Latins, who were struggling to survive in a
hostile, often overcrowded, dirty urban area,
were often classified as having psychotic tendencies, merely because they saw the world treating them unfairly. To classify these children
as paranoid or anti-social was to beg the question of their real predicament.

B.

Another leader in the area of character
measurement was S. L. Pressey of the Psychological
Laboratory at Indiana University who developed a
cross out test which was to be used to measure
emotions. It consisted of four parts which aimed

to uncover particular kinds of unpleasant feeling and anxiety tendencies by the use of an ethical discrimination test. Originally called the Mental Survey Scales Schedule E,[10] it was later known simply as the Pressey X-O Test. It was intended as "A Group Scale for Investigating the Emotions,"[11] and the participant was given rows of words and asked to cross out the disagreeable words.

The right answers were those chosen most often, making the dominant values the right values. There were four tests. In the first, the student was asked to cross out all unpleasant words from a list of words, such as: naked, snicker, wonder, spit, and fight. In the second the student was told to cross out all words in small letters which were connected or associated with the initial word in capital: for example, King: father, baseball, queen, rights, and razor. The third test required that the subjects cross out everything that they considered wrong from a list of words, such as: dullness, weakness, ignorance, innocence, and meekness. In the fourth test, the subjects were told to cross out all the things in the list that they have ever worried about. This list contained words such as: clothes, conscience, heart-failure, poison, and sleep.

In the first test, the selection of words was made in the first place on the basis of extended experience in work with the insane and with delinquents. The words were grouped as unpleasant because of their relation to emotions of disgust, fear, sex-feeling and suspicion. There was also a joker (pleasant, or at least not unpleasant word) in each list, to check, in order to see if the directions were understood.

The second test once again used words which were chosen very carefully with reference to pathological conditions and criminology. It was an attempt to present a free association test

in a group test form.[12] The third test was an
attempt to put in a convenient group test form,
an ethical discrimination test. A person's
anxiety tendency (total number crossed out), and
his emotional idiosyncrasy (choice in words cir-
cled), were supposedly revealed by the fourth
test. The words were divided into categories of
"hypochondriacal" words, melancholic and self-
accusatory words, paranoid or suspicion words,
self-conscious or shut-in personality words, and
neurotic words. Once again it is amazing to see
that anyone who worried about heart-failure or
religion was melancholic; or one who worried
about injustice or enemies was a paranoid; or one
who worried about money was a neurotic.[13]

The actual living conditions of life experiences of the individual being examined were
seldom taken into account. Instead the individual tests were summarized and the total number
of words crossed out on all four tests were first
summed up and then was considered an indication
of total affectivity or emotionality. The
deviations were then added together and the
total use as an expression of "total idiosyn-
cracy."[14]

Pressey also felt his scale was important
because he had condensed a great deal of matter
on one blank. Each word in each list was actually a separate question, and thus with 125
questions in each of four tests, this gave a
total of five hundred questions. In addition,
each test asked the subject to go back and circle
the worst word in each list. This added another
hundred questions, giving a total of 600 items.
Pressey stressed the value of the little reading
time necessary to take the test and the fact that
the entire test was on two sides of a 9 x 12
sheet. Furthermore, the average adult required
less than thirty minutes to cover the 600 items,
and the blank could be scored in less than three
minutes.[15]

The strong factors for Pressey were not the reliability or validity of the test (which later came under attack), but its ease in giving. Pressey felt that he could foretell a person's emotional peculiarities or anxiety without a cross reference to the person's actual life. Many of the words chosen were taken from studies on delinquency, insanity, pathological conditions and criminology.

This tendency to determine the moral or ethical character of delinquents or defectives in order to form a basis of opinion about the everyday populace was begun by Guy Fernald in 1912, when he administered ethical discrimination tests to the defective-delinquent inmates of the Massachusetts Reformatory.[16] His tests, however, were more reflective of ethical knowledge and reading ability than they were predictive of conduct. A typical test question asked if a man who has stolen money and hidden it is caught and serves his sentence, has he a right to the money? Many of the so-called character tests were more tests of knowledge than of aptitude, and were hardly predicative of behavior.

The Brotemarkle Comparison Test,[17] which was very influential and popular during this period, also seemed to reflect one's ability with words rather than one's moral concepts. The subject was given a list of words indicative of a certain principle, attitude, or response, and the extremes of such a list, (example, good . . . . . evil). The subject had then to fill the given words (bad, fair, mean, kind, pure, wicked, considerate), into the appropriate spaces. Then a deviation score was obtained which indicated the number of spaces each word was misplaced from the standard. Brotemarkle then asked his subjects to state if they felt that the test revealed their own individuality and personal character. If their answer was negative they were asked to list which words in or out of the test were indicative of their

individuality. They were subsequently asked
if their response would coincide with the general
opinion of their family, friends, and acquaintan-
ces, and if not, why. The reason for all this
examination for Brotemarkle was that

> Under a closer examination, the
> individual problem of faulty adjust-
> ment might be discovered; presenting
> a better opportunity to the social
> worker, psychiatrist, criminologist
> (sic), or kindred worker, to correct
> the underlying motivating background
> of morals, personality, or character.[18]

S. C. Kohs of the Psychological Court of
Domestic Relations in Portland, Oregon also
created an Ethical Discrimination Test in 1922,
making use of the common sense questions of the
Army Alpha Test, Pressey's Moral Judgment Test
in its entirety, some of the proverbs of the
Otis Tests, and some of the problems on Fernald's
Ethical Discrimination Test. He supplemented
these with two new tests of definitions of moral
terms and evaluation of different kinds of
acts.[19] From the subjects' ability to choose
the correct response to a social relations question such as: Parents should be made to send
their children to school because

    a) it prepares them for later life

    b) it keeps them out of mischief

    c) they are too young to work

plus their ability to explain proverbs like: A
penny saved is a penny earned; plus their ability
to rate the reactions that should be given certain acts on a scale from praise, to nothing, to
scold, to jail, to prison, to kill, they were
scored as average, sub-average, inadequate,
morally deficient, or moral imbecile.

Once again the need to classify and categorize personality or character types was prevalent. The stress was on knowledge of moral principles and proverbs and the accepted standards of dealing with various actions. There was no attempt to show a correlation between moral knowledge and action nor was there an adequate understanding of the language skills and cultural environment necessary for subjects to do well on this test. A lack of knowledge of proverbs is hardly an indication of a morally deficient character, anymore than a lack of understanding of English is an indication of low intelligence as revealed by an I.Q. test.

C.

In 1935, Goodwin Watson and George Forlano of Teacher's College set out to determine the validity of some of the existing character tests.[20] They selected 629 sample items from 31 tests and submitted these to a panel of judges. The judges were 150 graduate students who had nearly completed a course in psychology of character and who had read both the Tenth Yearbook of the Department of Superintendence on "Character Education," as well as Hugh Hartshorne's Character in Human Relations. The judges found that the values which best indicated good character were those of reliability, trustworthiness, and dependability, with those of cooperation, acceptability in the group, and kindness next in line.[21] Items rated low in validity included the neurotic symptom questions popularized by Woodworth et al. These were seen as irrelevant for character. Some of the typical tests of inhibition and self-control were similarly regarded as having little bearing upon character. Home background or religious training were also found to have little effect on character. Many of the school virtues which were greatly emphasized on report cards at that time were said by these judges to tell us little about character. Thus promotion, thrift, sitting still, keeping quiet, reciting well, taking part, sitting up straight, having a life goal, showing interest in class, concentration, effort, punctuality, and careful preparation of assignments, while stressed by many teachers, were not considered as having any general or widely recognized character significance.[22]

According to the judges, less emphasis should be given to measures of neurotic symptoms, inhibition, self-control, home background and academic deportment, and more stress was to be given to developing better tests and better teaching methods which would aid in developing

    a) trustworthiness despite strong temptation,

    b) creative cooperation as contrasted with mere conformity to the group,

    c) popularity, and

    d) consideration for the feeling of others.[23]

It is interesting how the character education movement began stressing these social values but gradually moved into the area of psychological adjustment while character testing seemed to go the opposite way. While Watson criticized the personality tests developed by the Character Education Inquiry, he saw their Coordination test, Guess Who reports, Opinion Ballots, and Good Citizenship Tests as the most obviously valid and acceptable battery of existing character measures for children.

The Character Education Inquiry at Teacher's College, headed by Hugh Hartshorne and Mark May, was quick to point out that the single tests or groups of tests that they developed were not measures of character, but of the particular abilities exhibited in the test. Written in the test manual were the following statements:

> Caution in use of results of character tests cannot be too frequently emphasized. Indiscriminate testing of children is to be deplored and treatment of results in any but the most confidential manner involves grave injustice to the individual concerned--recommendation for honesty or dishonesty, based on a single test, would not only be a gross violation of confidence but also a contradiction of facts of previous tests. The time may come when we can treat the facts of social behavior with as much objectivity as we treat behavior of physical objects. But unlike physical objects, persons have a stake in the measurements which are made of them. Let us take warning, therefore, from the misuse of I.Q. and achievement scores and make haste slowly.[24]

Hartshorne and May recognized the misuse of I.Q. tests at an early date but failed to take the responsibility in terms of their own work. Their findings on the high deceptiveness in Blacks, Southern Europeans, and Jews can hardly be seen as noncontroversial or not affecting the future of those involved. True, they pushed for personal anonymity, but group or racial injustices were not considered. They felt that where educational procedures could be guided by objective consideration, without prejudice to individuals, the use of the results was seen as surely justifiable and necessary.

The question of C E I's responsibility for the use of its tests was also never considered. If they felt that indiscriminate testing was going on and children were being unjustly labeled by the results, what responsibility should they have taken to control its use or regulate its

implementation? It is not enough to merely state
the limitations or narrow objectives of the test,
knowing full well that it is being used for other
reasons. The test creator has a moral responsibility to control the use of his measures.

While the conduct tests (manuals 6-19)
developed by C E I revealed differences between
ethnic and racial groups, the moral knowledge
tests seemed to acknowledge controversial issues.
Tests like the Good Citizenship Test, the
Information Test, and Opinion Ballots, A and B,
were very informative in revealing the concerns
of the testers in terms of the pressing social
problems of the day. The tests were seen as
merely a means of giving the teacher an idea of
the views of the students on a variety of issues.
They were to be helpful in pointing out weak
spots in the children's concepts of morality and
ethical knowledge. Some of the questions and
answers on the Information Test revealed that the
testers felt that it was harder for a poor man
to get justice in a law case than a rich man;
success does not always come from hard work;
no one can "earn" a million dollars; if people
are poor it is not usually their own fault;
people are not good or bad according to the way
God made them.[25]

The Opinion Ballots asked the student to
vote (yes, no, or sometimes) if he thought that
it was his duty to do certain listed things.
As in the Information Test, the correct answers
revealed some interesting things about the testers. They felt that obedience was not of
greater importance than honor; clean speech was
not a sign of being a "goody-goody;" the best way
to treat any enemy was to be kind to him; one
should not do what one's own people or one's
own crowd or set do if one knows his own people
or crowd or set are wrong; and finally, they
felt that it was not better for a country to
save itself at the expense of a world war than
to sacrifice itself for the sake of world peace.[26]

235.

While it was not stated why the various questions and answers were selected and what types of programs needed to be implemented as a result of the findings, it is evident that the testers had a foothold on some of the controversial social issues of the day. The concepts of obedience, war, poverty, success, and justice seemed to be appreciated in all their complexity. The Christian notion of love thy enemy and the moralistic concern with cleanliness of speech were also present.

The Character Education Inquiry also developed an Attitudes Test, a Coordination Test (which measured honesty by the participant's ability to negotiate corners in squares, circles and mazes with his eyes shut), a Puzzles Test, an Athletic Contest Test (to measure cheating in sporting events), a Stunt Parties Test (to measure the tendency to deception under play conditions), and a Kits, Envelopes and Money Vote Test. While their main concern was to test children under real life conditions, their results were far more conclusive.

Another series of tests which revealed the values promulgated, were the Social Intelligence Tests, developed in 1925 by F. A. Moss, T. Hunt, and K. T. Omwake at George Washington University. While the tests included sections on judgment in social situations; recognition of mental states from facial expressions, memory for names and faces, and recognition of the mental state of the speaker, the section on observation of human behavior was enlightening. The authors felt that all men were not created equal in mental ability; good conduct was not a reliable indication of high intelligence; all people who became wealthy or famous were not necessarily either bright or hard-working; and finally, they believed that the patriotism exhibited by the Americans in the War (W.W.I.) was not an example of the carefully thought-out judgment of the masses to stand up for the right.[27]

The Social Intelligence Tests were influenced by the study of the correlations of
facial expression with intelligence and emotions.[28]   A great deal was made of both the
ability to memorize names and faces and the ability of matching up facial expressions with the
correct mental state. Once again this entailed
that the testee had a broad understanding of the
vocabulary used. The 1925 and 1927 editions of
the Test revealed that employees in Executive
and Administrative positions scored highest on
the Social Intelligence Tests, followed by college graduates, upper-class college students,
college freshmen, high school students and industrial groups. By the 1930 Second Edition, a
more complete breakdown of employees had been
undertaken; administrators and executives out-
ranked teachers who were followed by high-grade
secretaries, salesmen, engineering employees,
clerical and stenographic employees, low-grade
office workers, sales clerks, nurses and lower-
grade industrial workers.

In the revised form of the Second Edition,
developed in 1949, new photographs were added
and a new easier scoring format was utilized.
Hunt, et al. was now working out of the Center
for Psychological Services at George Washington
University. The authors also stated various
usage of the Tests, as a supplement to the usual
types of tests for identifying students' social
abilities and deficiencies in adjustment, in
industry and business testing programs, in selection and placement of employees in jobs involving
human relationships as in sales and supervisory
work, and finally it was thought to have possibilities in vocational guidance testing.

The Social Intelligence Tests were measures
of how well a person could handle social situations and how observant he was of facial expressions and their corresponding emotional states.
One part of the test even asked the testee to
choose the best punch line for a given joke.

The stress on social relations and adjustment made it quite applicable to business and sales work, as well as to the program of selection and placement of employees. While some of the questions revealed interesting value orientations, all in all, the test was a rather crude measure of social intelligence.

The Y.M.C.A. administered a series of what they called Character Growth Tests, beginning in 1926. These tests were in the form of questionnaires which recorded the personal attitudes of boys, ages 12-14, on a variety of issues. The topics polled included the boys' attitudes toward smoking, keeping one's hair slick, making Negroes, Mexicans and Jews keep their place, getting a square deal for foreigners, and finding out God's will for oneself. Next the boys were asked about their feelings concerning group relationships with Jewish boys, poor boys, sissies, rich boys, non-Christian boys, Negro boys, foreigners, Mexican boys, boys who cheat on exams, boys who study hard, and sneaks. Finally, the boys were asked to state if they would be willing to have the previously named boys in the same school, the same class, on the same team, as an acquaintance, as a friend or as a guest in their homes.[29]

Another measure developed by the General Board of the Y.M.C.A. was HOW DO YOU FEEL ABOUT IT?[30] questionnaire. Once again this measure was intended to aid leaders in discovering major appreciations and problems in groups of adolescent boys and girls. It was to be used to start discussions of the best programs for the coming year or to indicate differences in interest between groups, and even to show whether candidates for participation in a group had enough in common with the rest of the group to form a basis of cooperation. The testee was to indicate his response to a variety of issues by either a zero for no interest, a check if he was interested, or a double check if he felt that the issue was tremendously valuable and necessary. The norms were decided by the answers given most often. The issues receiving the most attention were as follows: 58% of those tested were interested in socialism; 50% were interested in getting acquainted with people of different races or countries; 52% were interested in thinking through the puzzling questions in sex relations; 62% were interested in evolution; 79% were interested in getting rid of poverty and getting a square deal for workers; and 54% were interested in understanding birth control.

L. L. Thurstone of the University of Chicago developed a series of Social Attitude Scales. These scales measured one's attitude toward such topics as War, the Negro, Prohibition, Communism, Treatment of Criminals, Patriotism, the Constitution, Birth Control, God, the Chinese, the Germans, Law, Censorship, and Evolution. No intended attempt was made to acknowledge the right or wrong of any opinion but merely to point out the specific ideological tendencies in each case.[31]

For example, in the case of Attitude toward War, Thurstone stated that he was only looking for militaristic or pacificist tendencies and that he had no intention of putting any value judgment on the results. Unfortunately, it is virtually impossible to set up a test or questionnaire of such a sort and not involve value judgments. The case of the scale for measuring one's attitude toward the Negro is a prime example. In separating out liberal, neutral, and conservative tendencies toward the Negro, an answer of "yes" to the statement, "The difference between the Black and White race is not one of mere degree but of kind," was marked as a neutral answer. If one answered, "yes" to the statement, "After you have educated the Negro to the level of the White man, there will still be an impossible gulf between them," it was also considered a neutral response. Liberal responses included the feeling that, "The Negro should have the advantages of all the social benefits of the White man but be limited to his own race in the practice thereof."[32] The values toward the Negro which were prevalent at the time Thurstone developed his scales were reflected on his indications of attitude. It was not the case that he was objectively determining attitude preferences because the tendencies themselves were defined by the social milieu of the time. The concepts of liberal or conservative, militarist or pacificist, change over time and are subsequently redefined by each societal period involved. Thurstone's attempt to objectively measure social attitude was doomed from the start by the subjectivity of the values inherent in each question.

D.

Many character tests and measures were also developed for younger children. Children in the primary grades often times did not have the general reading ability necessary to take the previously mentioned character measures, so new techniques had to be developed.

Herbert Woodrow of the University of Minnesota developed "A Picture Preference Character Test," for use with children, ages 7-9. The test was composed of eleven pages, each with four pictures on them. Each page was devoted to a specific trait, (example: orderliness, disorderliness), and the child was to rank the four pictures from the one liked best to the one liked least. Woodrow decided to ask the children which situations they liked, rather than which were good or bad, because that method

> (Stood) a better change of taking him 'off his guard' than (did) direct questions about goodness or badness of acts portrayed and unless this unsuspecting attitude on the part of the child

be secured, there (was) little chance
of arriving at any valid estimate of
his true character.[33]

Woodrow saw nothing unethical or immoral in
trying to measure the child's true character by
"taking him off his guard." The technique involved was probably a better indication of his
character than that of the children tested. The
pictures were ambiguous and hard to rank within
the categories of like and dislike. Values
stressed included not only notions of cleanliness,
industry, initiative, obedience, thrift, manners,
and honesty, but also those of opposition to
thumb-sucking, boxing as opposed to fighting,
studying with lamp behind instead of in front
of the person, and the necessity of girls helping their mothers.[34] Tests were scored in terms
of errors or deviations from the norm. The norm
was established by the nine-year old age group
which had the highest median score. Thus, once
again, the social values of the majority were
considered to be the best indication of the
highest values in society. One sought after the
norm. Anyone who deviated significantly from
such a norm was by definition defective in character and social adjustment.

Another character test for young children
was developed by Harry J. Baker, a clinical psychologist for the Detroit Public Schools. The
character test was prepared for both primary
grades, 4-6, and advanced grades, 7-9. In his
"Telling What I Do Test," he also stressed the
idea that no mention should be made to the
pupils that character (was) being tested.[35] It
was his belief that "behavior tendencies (were)
much more firmly embedded in the fundamental
nature of human beings than (was) originally supposed."[36] Baker agreed with most of his
contemporaries in the scientific tradition that
the most certain way to learn about the nature of
character and its susceptibility to change was
by scientific measurement. The behavioral

241.

tendencies of the children were examined in school, at home, at play, in a social setting, and in ethical, moral situations. Norms were determined by pooling the judgment of fifty adults among the supervisors and staff of the Psychological Clinic of the Detroit Public Schools. Since there appeared to be no gain in scores with age, all pupils were compared with a general norm.

While the reliability and validity coefficients of the test were low to moderate,[37] and there seemed very little correlation with general intelligence, the tests were still seen as useful in detecting extreme cases of behavior and enabling the teacher to better understand his pupils. The values promulgated in this test were obedience, honesty, patriotism, social acceptance, politeness, neatness and respect for parents. A good child never slammed doors, ate fast, talked too loud, wiggled in his seat, swore, kept a messy desk, ran in the hall, used his hands in talking, played unfair, hurt animals, was noisy at home, whispered in school, had bad habits, lied, or was bad when his parents went away.

The test asked the children what they did in specific situations. For instance, they were asked what they did after school. The choices were:

a) I always play alone,

b) I play with just one playmate,

c) I want many playmates.

The correct response was c. When asked what they did when they saw our Flag, the children had to choose from:

a) I like it a little,

242.

b) I always love it, or

c) I don't care for it.

The correct answer was b. When asked about their behavior at home, the children had to choose from:

a) I make much noise,

b) I am noisy sometimes, or

c) I keep very quiet.

The correct answer was c. Finally an example from the advanced form was the question once more about behavior at home. The choices include:

a) I obey but don't like it,

b) I have my own way, or

c) I like to obey.

The correct answer was c. Once more it is clear how the values of socialization and adjustment to society were intermingled with the moralistic tones of cleanliness, manners, and neatness in the name of character. A person was viewed as having high character not only if he was obedient, quiet, patriotic and had many friends, but also if he ate slowly, kept neat and didn't slam doors.

In the same tradition of testing non-cognitive traits of children, Paul Hanley Furfey of Catholic University devised a Developmental Age Test to study the changing volitional life of the growing child. He defined developmental age as:

The progressively increasing
and non-intellectual maturity of
general behavior which shows itself

243.

in the growing child's play preferences, in his fantasy life, in
his choice of books and movies, in
his ambitions, and in general, in
his whole behavior type.[38]

It was presupposed that developmental age was
the same as mental age, and certain evidence actually showed that there was little or no
correlation between mental age and developmental
age if the effect of chronological age was eliminated.

The final scale (there were several re-
visions) was composed of six tests dealing,
respectively, with play preferences, vocational
ambitions, reading preferences, and things the
child would like to have, to see, and to think
about. The child was to pick from a pair of
alternatives. While some items were obviously
geared to show emotional development (example,
would you rather play the saxophone or play tag),
others were not so clear, (example, would you
rather fly kites or bowl). Childhood games and
activities included playing Puss in the Corner,
Follow the Leader, I Spy, Cowboys, playing with
electric trains, bows and arrows, stilts, tops,
while emotional development was revealed by the
child's desire to dance, shoot baskets, play
golf, read magazines, work with tools, go to
parties, play basketball, repair cars, do puzzles,
or the desire to take a walk with a girl.

The second test, dealing with "Things to
Be When You Grow Up," had the supposedly childish desires to be a blacksmith, cowboy, pirate,
fireman, knight, king, soldier, Indian, policeman, circus performer, and the mature desires to
be a stockbroker, banker, astronomer, congressman,
builder, or civil engineer. Besides the obvious
cultural definitions and preferences exhibited by
this classification, certain pairs seemed very
difficult to choose from. For example, would you
rather be a mail carrier or a dentist: a

244.

cartoonist or a judge; a wireless operator or a
truck driver; a jeweler or a scientist. Occupations such as fireman, policeman, soldier, or
truck driver seemed to indicate a low level of
emotional development.

The same was true of Test 3, "Books to
Read," where all fantasy or romantic literature
was classified as juvenile, while all realism,
mystery, or non-fiction was indicative of maturity. "Things to Have" was the fourth test and
it showed that to have a punching bag or a
sweater was more fun than to have a pet rabbit,
or to have a Scout suit was more fun than to
have a watch or a pet dog, and a raincoat was
more fun to have than a pet canary. Once again
certain items were indistinguishable by this
author, such as the choices between a fountain
pen and a pair of rubber gloves, and a baseball
glove and a pair of rubber boots. The same problem of identifying certain simple, enjoyable
acts as juvenile came up in Test 5. When asked
what one would rather see, the right items were
an auto race, as opposed to animals in the zoo,
a chemist working as opposed to a bakery window,
banquet as opposed to a lot of Indians, and a
riot as opposed to a fairy castle.[39]

The tendency to think of anything to do
with pets, Indians, and fantasy as indicative of
a lack of emotional development was as ludicrous
as classifying anything to do with sports, scouting or the "real" world as indicative of emotional
maturity. Children were stereotyped in developmental stages from a fantasy-oriented child to
pragmatic, rational stage in adulthood. That
classification was not only unfair and inaccurate
to the child's complex development, but it also
negated a great deal of adult experiences as
childish and indicative of escapism and withdrawal
from society. The attempt to cut off the creative
imagination and sense of play in growing children
structures our concept of adulthood into a logical, rational, positivist straitjacket.

Finally, there were character measures
where the student rated themselves. An example
of this was the Character Inventory Chart.[40] In
this procedure, the children were to rate themselves on the positive qualities of health, loyalty, honesty, cheerfulness, courtesy, cooperation, moral courage, industry, self-control, and
leadership. The negative qualities to be avoided
were delicateness, illness, unfairness, deceit-
fulness, suspiciousness, sadness, unsocialable-
ness, wavering, depression, rudeness, vulgarity,
unwillingness, hindering, doubtfulness, coward-
ness, hopelessness, laziness, idleness and
recklessness. Once again, anti-social factors
were intermixed with psychological problems. A
person was of less than perfect character if he
were sad, depressed, or felt hopeless or doubtful.
Even illness was viewed as a sign of character
deficiency.

The authors of this chart stressed that
the primary aim of the chart was to stimulate the
pupil to examine or analyze his own character
without reference to any fixed standard, and
from this resulting introspection he was to produce or define his character development. When
one looks, however, at the motivational ideas
suggested, like biographies of Great Men, or sayings of Great Men (example, Emerson's, "Obedience
alone gives the right to command," or Ovid's
"Cheerfulness makes labor light,") it is clear
that a fixed standard was called for. The Handbook to the Chart even stated:

Since the primary concern of
education is to enable the youth to
become a desirable member of society,
and since his desirableness to society
is determined by his character, it is
only logical that moral training should
be considered as basic to the very core
and substance of the entire school
program.[41]

246.

Thus the selection of desirable traits was
done with reference to a standard, the standard
values of society. Dougherty also suggested that
diplomas should acknowledge both that a person
has obtained a required amount of knowledge, and
should certify that the holder had acquired and
applied those principles of character which made
for real success all through life.[42] The Human
Inventory Chart would enable the student to de-
clare his right intentions to develop a worthy
standard of conduct. The responsibility would be
on the student's shoulders. From this stance it
was felt that delinquent tendencies, inhibition,
anti-social attitudes, and self-repressions would
all vanish.

E.

Character tests, especially in the early
days of their development, were very concerned
with psychological problems. They set out to
weed out the neurotics, paranoids, melancholics,
and hypochondriacs, without ever attempting to
substantiate the responses. Anyone who might
have been persecuted or felt that he was getting
an unfair deal in life was automatically seen
as exhibiting psychotic tendencies. Children
were also told that sadness and depression were
examples of negative character traits which had
to be eliminated. Thus Character Tests often
classified children according to their symptoms
without really ever looking into the nature or
cause of their predicament.

Many character tests were also more indicative of the language skills, cultural environment, and ethical knowledge of the pupils
involved than they were of their moral worth or
possible behavior. Complex proverbs, analogies,
and synonym-antonym delineations were common.
To score highly on many of these tests, the
pupils had not only to know the language but
they also had to be familiar with the law and the
moral sanctions of the majority in the society.
Thus many non-English speaking minorities

(Mexicans, Latins, Indians), Blacks and immigrant groups scored poorly.

While character education programs seemed to move from promoting social values to identifying and correcting psychological adjustment problems, the character testing group seemed to move in the opposite direction. Many of the earlier tests of inhibition, self-control and neurotic tendencies were discouraged in lieu of tests of sociability. According to the C E I, individual anonymity was to be upheld at all costs, so as not to adversely classify or prejudice the record of the student. Unfortunately, most character education programs advocated instituting behavior records for children which would accompany them throughout their career. The Character Education Inquiry seemed to be aware of this, but did not feel that their responsibility went any further than a strong warning in the test manuals.

Also, while the C E I strove to maintain individual anonymity, it obviously did not feel that this applied in the case of racial or ethnic groups. The adverse effects of classifying Jews, Blacks and Southern Europeans as more deceptive than the other members of the population never seemed to occur to them. The fires of racial and ethnic hatred must have been intensified by such "scientific" proclamations.

Many character tests were also developed for younger children, and these measures reveal more about the testers than they do about the pupils tested. In many cases the children were to be caught off guard, so as to get an accurate measure of character. As stated previously, this appears to more accurately reveal the character of the tester than that of the child. Norms for the right answers for these tests were either decided by experts or by the answers chosen most frequently. The majority value was taken as the right value. Any student that deviated significantly from the norm was classified as a character defective. It is clear how the stress on the group, conformity, and obedience significantly effected the establishment of such norms and sanctions.

There was even an attempt to objectify, quantify and standardize the children's emotional development by a series of tests which asked the children about their vocational preferences, play preferences, reading preferences, and things the child would like to have, to see, or to think about. This measure set up a shallow concept of fantasy which misrepresented not only children, but also adults; it also put a negative connotation on certain occupations, hobbies, and interests by classifying them as not indicative of emotional development.

Thus the character tests and measures of this period were heavily laden with handicaps for minority and immigrant groups in terms of reading language skills as well as familiarity with cultural mores and ethical knowledge; they also sought psychotic and neurotic explanations for the feelings of alienated children. No attempt was made to corroborate the fears of the oppressed. They were just classified as paranoid. More often than not the burden of blame for character deficiencies was placed squarely on the shoulders of the child. Society took the responsibility for the cure but not the blame for the disease.

NOTES

[1]Paul Voelker, "The Function of Ideals and Attitudes in Social Education," Columbia University Contributions to Education, Teachers College Series No. 112, 1921.

[2]Mark May and Hugh Hartshorne, "A Summary of the Work of the Character Education Inquiry," Religious Education, 25, Sept. 1930, pp. 613-615.

[3]See J. T. MacCurdy, War Neuroses (Cambridge: University Press, 1918).

[4]Ellen Mathews, "A Study of Emotional Stability in Children," Journal of Delinquency, 8, Jan. 1923, p. 3.

[5]Louis Terman, Genetic Studies of Genius, Vol. 1 (Stanford: University Press, 1926). Terman found gifted girls to score significantly superior to gifted boys in all measures but trustworthiness. Gifted children scored higher than controls (score was number of answers scored correctly), pp. 516-517.

[6]Ibid., pp. 502-505. See questions Nos. 2, 4, 37, 61, 62, and 85.

[7]Ibid., Table 8, p. 55.

[8]Ibid., p. 82.

[9]Mathews, op. cit., p. 20, 32.

[10]See S. L. and L. W. Pressey, "Cross-out Tests with Suggestions as a Group Scale of the Emotion," Journal of Applied Psychology, 3, June 1919, pp. 138-150. These scales consisted of a Verbal Ingenuity Test, a Logical Judgment Test, an Arithmetical Ingenuity Test, and a Moral Judgment Test. While each test was seen to be of independent interest, the combined result

was seen to give something of a "Rating of
General Ability," p. 143.

[11]S. L. Pressey, "A Group Scale for Investigating the Emotions," Journal of Abnormal
Psychology and Social Psychology, 16, April 1921,
pp. 55-64.

[12]See Carl Jung, "The Association Method,"
American Journal of Psychology, 21, April 1910,
pp. 219-269, and Grace Helen Kent and A. J.
Rosanoff, "A Study of Association in Insanity,"
American Journal of Insanity, 67, Part I, Associa-
tion in Normal Subjects, July 1910, pp. 37-96;
Part II, Association in Insane Subjects, Oct.
1910, pp. 317-390. The words for this part of
the Pressey X-O Scale were taken from the Kent-
Rosanoff Study.

[13]S. L. Pressey, 1921, op. cit., p. 59.

[14]Ibid.

[15]Ibid., p. 63.

[16]Guy Fernald, "The Defective-Delinquent
Class Differentiating Tests," American Journal
of Insanity, 68, 1912, pp. 530-531.

[17]R. A. Brotemarkle, "A Comparison Test for
Investigating the Ideational Content of the Moral
Concepts," Journal of Applied Psychology, 6, 1922,
pp. 235-242.

[18]Ibid., p. 242.

[19]S. C. Kohs, "Ethical Discrimination
Test," Journal of Delinquency, 7, Jan. 1922,
pp. 1-15.

[20]Goodwin Watson and George Forlano,
"Prima Facie Validity in Character Tests,"
Journal of Educational Psychology, 26, Jan. 1935,
pp. 1-16.

[21] Ibid., p. 13.

[22] Ibid., p. 15.

[23] Ibid., pp. 15-16.

[24] Character Education Inquiry Test Manual No. 1 (New York: Association Press, 1930). This test found in the Odell Test Collection at the Education and Social Science Library of the University of Illinois, Urbana, Illinois.

[25] Information Test of Character Education Inquiry, Form I, Manual No. 3 (New York: Association Press, 1930), Odell Test Collection, University of Illinois, see questions Nos. 4, 8, 12, 17 and 24.

[26] Ibid., Opinion Ballot A. See questions Nos. 2, 8, 10 and No. 9 (A2).

[27] F. A. Moss, T. Hunt, and K. T. Omwake, Social Intelligence Tests (Washington: George Washington University Series, 1925-1949), see Odell Test Collection, University of Illinois, see questions in Test 4, Nos. 5, 12, 14 and 50.

[28] See Katherine T. Omwake, "The Value of Photographs and Handwriting in Estimating Intelligence," Public Personnel Studies, 3, No. 1, Jan. 1925, pp. 2-16; D. E. Buzby, "The Interpretation of Facial Expression," American Journal of Psychology, 35, Oct. 1924, pp. 602-604; G. S. Gates, "A Test for Ability to Interpret Facial Expression," Psychological Bulletin, 22, Feb. 1925, p. 120; L. R. Feissler, "Descriptive Responses to the Human Face," Psychological Bulletin, 22, Feb. 1925, pp. 119-120; H. S. Langfeld, "The Judgment of Emotions from Facial Expression," Journal of Abnormal Psychology, 13, Aug. 1918, pp. 172-184; D. V. Pope, "The Interpretation of the Human Face from Photographs," Bulletin of Randolph Macon Woman's College, 8, 1922, pp. 1-17.

[29]Character Growth Tests, Series 1926, Home Division of National Council of Y.M.C.A.'s. See Odell Test Collection, University of Illinois. Other tests developed in this series included a Religious Concept Test and an Immediate Life Situations Test.

[30]How Do You Feel About It? General Board of Y.M.C.A. (New York: Association Press), see Odell Test Collection, University of Illinois.

[31]L. L. Thurstone, Social Attitude Scale (Chicago: University Press, 1930), see Odell Test Collection, University of Illinois.

[32]Ibid., see E. D. Hinckley, Attitude Toward the Negro Scale, Questions Nos. 1, 11 and 16.

[33]Herbert Woodrow, "A Picture Preference Character Test," Journal of Educational Psychology, 17, Nov. 1926, p. 522.

[34]A Picture Preference Character Test, 1926, see Odell Test Collection, University of Illinois.

[35]Harry J. Baker, Telling What I Do Test, 1930, p. 2, Odell Test Collection, University of Illinois.

[36]Ibid., p. 5.

[37]Ibid., Reliabilities of Specific Activities were as follows: School, .632; Home, .620; play, .550; social, .558; ethical-moral, .733. The validity was determined by correlating scores with the Chassell-Upton Scale for Measuring Habits of Good Citizenship. Correlation was .420 with initial testing and .483 with final testing.

[38]Paul Hanly Furfey, "A Revised Scale for

Measuring Developmental Age in Boys," Child
Development, 2, June 1931, p. 102. See also
P. H. Furfey, "The Measurement of Developmental
Age," Catholic University of America Educational
Research Bulletin, Vol. II, No. 10, Dec. 1927.

[39]Ibid., pp. 104-109.

[40]Bruce Lee Dougherty, F. L. O'Reilly,
and Mary Mannix, Character Inventory Chart
(Public School Publishing Co., 1931), see Odell
Test Collection, University of Illinois.

[41]Ibid., pp. 3-4.

[42]Ibid., p. 7.

VI. CONCLUSION: THE SEARCH FOR A STATE-SANCTIONED MORALITY

The growth of the Character Education Movement in America represented the response of the State, via the educational system, to the declining status and power of the Church and the Family. These institutions, which had previously held significant power in the sanctioning of morality and ethical behavior, were victimized by the secularization of a growing urban, industrial, scientific society. The schools assumed the responsibility for sanctioning moral behavior.

In the late nineteenth century many clergy, feeling a loss of power and prestige, made an attempt to secularize their dogma into a social gospel. The old dream of salvation was replaced with the Utopian ideal of a perfect civilization, a Kingdom of God on Earth. Religious values were stripped of their dogma and symbolism and were presented merely as ethical precepts. In order to generate a common ethical base, the State became the new bearer of morality and its dominant values became the basis of a new civic religion.

This new civic religion received its scientific justification from the work of a number of German philosophers including Johann Herbart and G. W. F. Hegel. Herbart's psychological theory, while stressing the importance of moral education, was built upon a framework based on the value of authority, obedience, and supremacy of law. G. W. F. Hegal, whose concept of the State as a divine institution also influenced many moral educators. The value of habit formation and internalization of the values of the society were crucial to the establishment of a concept of the State as the true bearer of morality. The values promulgated not only reflected the concern with unity and purity, but they also reflected the semi-mechanical virtues (regularity, punctuality, order, neatness, etc.)

dictated by the growing industrial order. The
concept of the good person was gradually redefined from that of a virtuous, just, kind, moral
connotation to that of being synonymous with the
concept of the good citizen or good workers. To
be a good person in society meant that one was
socially efficient, patriotic, and obedient to
authority.

The First World War convinced Americans
that intellect without a moral ideal was poten-
tially evil, since many believed Germany to be
a case in point. The war also represented a
period of extreme nationalistic jingoism in this
country. As one critic put it, while "Prussia
lost the War, Prussianism won it."[1] Out of this
concern with education for character, American
educators undertook a full-fledged program of
character education. The program advocated a
State-sanctioned morality which relied heavily
upon the values of loyalty, patriotism and obedience to law.

Those concerned with Character Education
objectives failed, however, to recognize the
potential drawbacks of generating a political
conscience. In a situation where the conscience
of the people was dictated by the State, free
criticism of the actions of such a body was not
possible. Whatever the State sanctioned as
moral regarding its own actions was, by definition, the just and the good. People were
considered primarily as citizens. Thus, their
first loyalty was to the State with little re-
course to any other or higher moral authority.

As the character education programs spread
across the country, their crucial ethical stance
became clearly evident. The concern with creating a new planned society in the midst of socio-
economic, industrial and political change
mandated the need for a pragmatic moral stance.
It was agreed upon by the educators involved
that the values to be promulgated by character

education programs had not only to be utilitarian but they also had to be relative and tentative as well. In order for the society to work most efficiently and progress towards the ideal of the perfect society, there had to be this pragmatic approach to values. The relativity of values would enable the State to change or justify its moral stance in order to fit the situation.

Character Education was a program for education for values, not for skills or knowledge. The acceptance of these values was to be evident by desirable behavioral objectives. The conduct and behavior of the students was to be shaped and controlled in order to produce the good citizen. Continuing in the footsteps of its predecessors, namely, moral and ethical education, character education seemed to equate the concept of the good person with that of the good citizen. With the State sanctioning moral behavior, the distinctions between morality and citizenship became necessarily blurred.

The structure and function of the school also changed as a result of character education programs. Homerooms and homeroom teachers were added to secondary schools to provide the students with a moral example to follow as well as to set aside a daily period for character education. Behavior grades or ratings were put on to report cards to reflect the concern with character as well as intellect. Even behavior records were set up for each child which followed him throughout his educational career. Finally, student governments were instituted which were to provide the students with an opportunity to understand the workings of government (seldom, if ever, however, did they actually govern themselves).

Since children were to be selected and classified according to character traits or personality profiles, character education programs also mandated the creation of a differentiated curriculum. The teacher's role became more and more like that of a social worker, psychologist, and guidance counselor. While many persons have described education during this period by the factory metaphor, character education seemed more clearly represented by a clinic metaphor. Programs were more concerned with adjustment of children to the existing social order and the diagnosis and remedial treatment of character deviates than they were with acquisition of knowledge or skills.

Measurement of character and personality traits was a natural outgrowth of the intelligence testing developed during the First World War. Intelligence tests were found to be inconclusive in predicting one's success in school or in a vocation, one's potential for delinquency, or one's day-to-day behavior. Gradually many psychologists turned to the classification, quantification, and standardization of non-cognitive character traits as a means of predicting an individual's success in life and possible adjustment to society as well as determining the occupation best suited to his character.

These character and personality tests reflected the same racial and ethnic biases as did the I.Q. tests. Those persons of Northern European, Nordic-type racial stock were found to be more honest and moral than those of Southern European, Black, Mexican, or Indian racial stocks. Reflecting similar prejudices, while Jews tested highly on many I.Q. measures, they were also found to have a high tendency towards deceit. A careful examination of the tests involved indicated that they were more indicative of language skill abilities, cultural environment, and knowledge of the law and ethical mores than they were indicative of moral worth or possible moral conduct. It was no small wonder that many non-English speaking immigrants and minorities as well as many Blacks who were outside the mainstream of American life scored poorly on these character tests. The tests reflected deviations from the accepted cultural norm rather indicated moral character. Correct responses for the tests were most often determined either by "experts" or by the answer chosen most frequently.

The standardization of the tests, according to the most frequent responses, once again reflected the maxim that the majority value was the right value. This notion of the relativity of values was as previously pointed out, crucial to the Character Education rationale. Any person who significantly deviated from the norm was classified as a character defective and was earmarked for remedial treatment. Some test designers acknowledged that this was taking place and recognized the potential harmful effects of stigmatizing an individual. They made a plea for individual anonymity (race or ethnic group anonymity was never even considered, as evidenced by the results showing racial and ethnic differences) of test results. While they pointed out the misuse of the I.Q. test and their concern with unfair stigmatizing of individuals, they failed on the one hand to realize the stigmatizing of racial ethnic groups that they were fostering, and on the other hand even though they knew that individual anonymity was not being maintained, they felt that their responsibility stopped at the printed warning on the test blank. The tests continued to be used by educators as a means of obtaining data on individual students.

As an example, children were classified as exhibiting psychotic tendencies if they felt that they were being treated unfairly or were not getting a square deal in life. There was no attempt to corroborate the fears of the oppressed. Persons who might have had to live in a hostile, alien environment were often classified as paranoid or neurotic if they could not accept or adjust to their situation in life.

The Character Education Movement epitomized the growing power of the State via the

259.

educational system over the weakening institutions of the Church and the Family. Morality became increasingly a State-sanctioned concept, and thus the individual developed a political conscience rather than a moral conscience. There was no viable way to criticize the moral authority of the State. If the State sanctioned the morality, then whatever actions it undertook were by definition moral.

The good person became the good citizen, and the values of patriotism, loyalty, obedience, and adjustment became the dictates of a new civic religion--a secularized, nationalistic religion, based upon a utilitarian, relativistic, pragmatic value orientation. The educational system saw its primary function to generate good citizens who were both socially and economically adjusted to society, as well as loyal and obedient to its authority. William Irwin Thompson captured the fate of the education system when he wrote, "The public school system, which had been created to put muscle into democracy, ended by becoming the closing fingers of the long arm of the State."[2]

NOTES

[1]J. Montgomery Gambrill, "Nationalism and Civic Education," <u>Teachers College Record</u>, 23, 1922, p. 120.

[2]William Irwin Thompson, <u>Passages About Earth</u> (New York: Perennial Library, 1973), p. 16.

BIBLIOGRAPHY

BOOKS AND ESSAYS

Abbott, Jacob. The Teacher, Moral Influences Employed in the Instruction and Governance of the Young. New York: Harper and Brothers, 1856.

Adler, Felix. The Moral Instruction of Children. New York: D. Appleton and Co., 1892.

Bagley, William. Education, Crime and Social Progress. New York: Macmillan Co., 1931.

Beer, Sidney J. Crime . . . Character . . . Education. Los Angeles: The United Printing Co., 1935.

Berlin, Isaiah. Four Essays on Liberty. New York: Oxford University Press, 1971.

Berman, Louis. The Glands Regulating Personality. New York: Macmillan Co., 1921.

Bolton, Frederick. Adolescent Education. New York: Macmillan Co., 1931.

Bourne, Randolph. War and the Intellectuals. New York: Harper's, 1964.

Brigham, Carl. A Study of American Intelligence. Princeton: Princeton University Press, 1923.

Charters, W. W. The Teaching of Ideals. New York: Macmillan Co., 1927.

Coe, George A. Educating for Citizenship. New York: Charles Scribner's Sons, 1932.

Cubberley, Ellwood P. Public Education in the United States. Boston: Houghton Mifflin, 1919.

Culbert, Jane. The Visiting Teacher at Work.
      New York: The Commonwealth Fund, 1929.

Curti, Merle. Social Ideas of American Educators.
      Patterson: Littlefield, Adams and Co.,
      1959.

Dean, Arthur D. Our Schools in Wartime and After.
      Boston: Ginn and Co., 1918.

DeGarmo, Charles. Herbart and the Herbartians.
      New York: Charles Scribner's Sons, 1896.

      _____, Principles of Secondary Education--
      Ethical Training. New York: Macmillan
      Co., 1910.

Dewey, John. Moral Principles in Education.
      Boston: Houghton Mifflin Co., 1909.

Dickson, Thomas. Critique on American School
      Histories. New York: Military Order of
      the World War, 1926.

Downey, June. The Will Temperament and Its
      Testing. Yonkers-on-Hudson: World Book
      Co., 1923.

Education and National Character. Chicago: R. R.
      Donnelley and Sons, 1908.

Edman, Irwin. Human Traits and Their Social
      Significance. Cambridge: The Riverside
      Press, 1920.

Felkin, Henry. An Introduction to Herbart's
      Science and Practice of Education. Boston:
      Heath and Co., 1898.

Fishback, Edwin. Character Education and Junior
      High Schools. New York: D. C. Heath and
      Co., 1928.

Freeman, Frank. Mental Tests: Their History, Principles and Applications. Cambridge: Riverside Press, 1926.

Galloway, Thomas. Parenthood and the Character Training of Children. New York: Methodist Book Concern, 1927.

_____. Sex and Social Health. New York: American Social Hygiene Association, 1924.

Galton, Frances. Hereditary Genius. New York: Macmillan Co., 1869.

Germane, Charles E. and Germane, Edith E. Character Education. New York: Silver, Burdett and Co., 1929.

Goddard, H. H. The Kallikak Family. New York: Macmillan Co., 1912.

Goring, C. Abridged Edition of the English Convict. London: H. M. Stationery Office, 1919.

Green, G. H. Psychoanalysis in the Classroom. New York: Macmillan and Co., 1916.

Hall, G. Stanley. Educational Problems V. I and II. New York: D. Appleton and Co., 1911.

Haller, Marc. Eugenics. New Brunswick: Rutgers University Press, 1963.

Hart, Joseph Kinmont. A Critical Study of Current Theories of Moral Education. Chicago: University of Chicago Press, 1910.

_____. Mental Conflicts and Misconduct. New York: Little, Brown and Co., 1917.

Hartshorne, Hugh. Character in Human Relations. New York: Charles Scribner's Sons, 1933.

_____ and May, Mark. _Studies in the Nature of Character Vol. I._ "Studies in Deceit." New York: Macmillan Co., 1928.

_____, May, Mark and Maller, Julius B. _Studies in Service and Self-Control._ New York: Macmillan Co., 1929.

Harvey, William. _The Remedy._ Chicago: Mundus Publishing Co., 1915.

Hays, Carlton. _Essays on Nationalism._ New York: Macmillan Co., 1926.

Healy, William and Bronner, Augusta. _Delinquents and Criminals: Their Making and Unmaking._ New York: Macmillan Co., 1928.

Heaton, Kenneth. _The Character Emphasis in Education._ Chicago: University of Chicago Press, 1933.

Herbart, Johann F. _The Science of Education and the Aesthetic Relevation of the World._ Boston: D. C. Heath and Co., 1893.

Hofstadter, Richard. _Age of Reform._ New York: Vintage Press, 1955.

_____. _Social Darwinism in American Thought._ New York: Beacon Press, 1955.

Hollingsworth, H. L. _Judging Human Character._ New York: Harcourt Brace, 1925.

_____. _Vocational Psychology._ New York: D. Appleton Co., 1916.

_____. _Vocation Psychology and Character Analysis._ New York: D. Appleton & Co., 1929.

Hopkins, Charles. _The Rise of the Social Gospel in American Protestantism 1865-1915._ New Haven: Yale University Press, 1967.

Kelley, T. L. Statistical Method. New York: Macmillan Co., 1924.

Kretschmer, E. Physique and Character. New York: Harcourt Brace Co., 1921.

Kilpatrick, William, et al. The Educational Frontier. New York: D. Appleton-Century Co., 1933.

Lehman, H. C. and Witty, P. A. Psychology of Play Activities. New York: A. S. Barnes, 1927.

Link, H. C. Employment Psychology. New York: Macmillan Co., 1919.

MacCurdy, J. T. War Neuroses. Cambridge: Cambridge University Press, 1918.

Maller, Julius B. Character and Personality Tests. New York: Bureau of Publications, Teachers College, Columbia University, 1937.

Mateer, Florence. The Unstable Child: An Interpretation of Psychology as a Source of Unbalanced Behavior in Abnormal and Troublesome Children. New York: D. Appleton Co., 1924.

May, Henry. Protestant Churches and Industrial America. New York: Harper and Row, 1967.

McDougall, William. Introduction to Social Psychology. Boston: John W. Luce and Co., 1912.

Mead, George H. Mind, Self and Society. Chicago: University of Chicago Press, 1934.

Merriam, C. E. The Making of Citizens. Chicago: University of Chicago Press, 1931.

Mirick, George A. Progressive Education. Cambridge: Riverside Press, 1923.

Moral Training in the Public Schools - The California Prize Essays. Boston: Ginn and Co., 1907.

Munsterberg, Hugo. Psychology and Industrial Efficiency. Boston: Houghton Mifflin Co., 1913.

Myers, George E. The Problem of Vocational Guidance. New York: Macmillan Co., 1927.

Otis, A. S. Statistical Method in Educational Measurement. Yonkers-on-Hudson: World Book Co., 1925.

Parsons, Philip. Crime and the Criminal. New York: Alfred A. Knopf, 1926.

Pfister, O. R. Psychoanalysis in the Service of Education. New York: Moffat, 1922.

Pierce, Bessie. Civic Attitudes in American School Textbooks. Chicago: University of Chicago Press, 1930.

Prince, Morton. The Unconscious. New York: Macmillan, 1915.

Radest, Howard. Toward Common Ground. New York: Ungar, 1969.

Rauschenbusch, Walter. Christianity and the Social Crisis. New York: The Macmillan Co., 1908.

Roback, A. A. A Bibliography of Character and Personality. Cambridge: Sci-Art Publishers, 1927.

Roberts, John S. William T. Harris, A Critical Study of His Educational and Related Philosophic Views. Washington, D. C.: National Education Association, 1924.

Ross, Edward A. Changing America. New York: The Century Co., 1912.

_____. Social Control. New York: Macmillan Co., 1901.

Sadler, Michael Ernest. Moral Instruction and Training in Schools. London: Longmans, Green and Co., 1908.

Schwesinger, Gladys. Heredity and Environment. New York: Macmillan Co., 1933.

Shulman, Harry M. From Truancy to Crime: A Study of 251 Adolescents. Albany: J. B. Lyon Co., 1928.

Starbuck, Edwin and Shuttleworth, Frank. A Guide to Literature from Character Training Vol. I. "Fairy Tales, Myth and Legend," New York: Macmillan Co., 1928; Vol. II, "Fiction," New York: Macmillan Co., 1930.

Symonds, Percival. Diagnosing Personality and Conduct. New York: D. Appleton-Century Co., 1931.

_____. Psychological Diagnosis in Social Adjustment. New York: American Book Co., 1934.

Terman, Louis. Genetic Studies of Genius. Vol. I. Stanford: Stanford University Press, 1926.

The Problem Child in School. New York: Commonwealth Fund, 1927.

Thompson, William Irwin. Passages About Earth. New York: Perennial Library, 1973.

Thorndike, Edward. Educational Psychology. New
York: Teachers College Press, Columbia
University, 1914.

Trotter, William. Instincts of the Hero in Peace
and War. London: T. Fischer, Unwin
Ltd., 1916.

Trow, William Clark. Educational Psychology.
Boston: Houghton Mifflin, 1937.

Ward, Lester Frank. Pure Sociology. New York:
Macmillan Co., 1903.

Watson, J. B. Psychology From the Standpoint of
a Behaviorist. Philadelphia: Lippincott,
1919.

White, W. A. Mechanisms of Character Formation.
New York: Macmillan Co., 1916.

_____. Mental Hygiene of Childhood. New York:
Macmillan Co., 1917.

Wiebe, Robert. The Search for Order. New York:
Hill and Wang, 1967.

HANDBOOKS, PAMPHLETS, SURVEYS, CONGRESSES, STUDIES

An Eleven-Year Survey of Activities of the Ameri-
can School Peace League from 1908-1919.
Boston: American School Citizenship
League, 1919.

Cope, Henry F. Ten Year Progress in Religious
Education. Chicago: The Religious Education Association, 1913.

Dewey, John. My Pedagogic Creed. Chicago:
A Flanagan Co., 1897.

Ethical Culture Fact Book 1876-1966. New York:
American Ethical Union, 1966.

Handbook. Chicago: The Religious Education Association 1903-1904.

McMurray, Virginia M. A Study of Delinquency and Neglected Negro Children Before the New York City Children's Court. New York: The Joint Commission on Negro Child Study in New York City, 1925.

Proceedings of Second International Moral Education Congress. The Hague: The American Committee of the International Congress, 1912.

ARTICLES

Adams, Henry F. "The Mythology and Science of Character Analysis." Scribner's Magazine, 69, May 1921, pp. 569-575.

Allport, Gordon. "Personality and Character." Psychological Bulletin, 18, September 1921, pp. 441-445.

Allport, F. H. and Allport, G. W. "Personality Traits: Their Classification and Measurement." Journal of Abnormal Psychology, 16, April 1921, pp. 6-40.

Bagley, William. "The Place of Duty and Discipline in a Democratic Scheme." Teachers College Record, 19, November 1918, pp. 419-430.

Bain, E. "Theory and Measurement of Attitudes and Opinions." Psychological Bulletin, 27, May 1930, pp. 357-379.

Baker, Harry J. "The Analysis of Behavior Problems." Ohio State Educational Conference Proceedings of the Eleventh Annual Session. Ohio State University Bulletin, 36, No. 3, 1931, pp. 125-152.

271.

Baldwin, Joseph. "Report of the Committee on Moral Education." N.E.A. Proceedings, 31, 1892, pp. 759-763.

Ballou, Frank. "An Experiment in Character Education in the Washington Schools." Educational Record, 15, 1934, pp. 284-288.

Barnes, Clifford. "The Status of Moral Training in the Public Schools." N.E.A. Proceedings, 49, 1911, pp. 400-413.

Bennion, Milton. "History of the Movement for Character and Citizenship Training in the Schools." Historical Outlook, May 1924, pp. 204-206.

_____. "Preliminary Report of the Committee on Citizenship and Character Education." N.E.A. Proceedings, 59, 1921, pp. 344-346.

_____. "Report of the Committee on Character Education." N.E.A. Proceedings, 61, 1923, pp. 250-253.

_____. "Report of the Committee on Character Education." N.E.A. Proceedings, 62, 1924, pp. 278-284.

_____. "Report of the Committee on Character Education." N.E.A. Proceedings, 63, 1925, pp. 182-183.

_____. "Report of the Committee on Citizenship and Character Education." School and Society, 14, September 1921, pp. 190-192.

Bevis, W. M. "Psychological Traits of the Southern Negro with Observations as to Some of His Psychoses." American Journal of Psychiatry, July 1921, pp. 69-78.

"Bibliography of Topics from 1857-1907." Topic No. 44 Religious and Moral Education

272.

Fiftieth Anniversary Volume. N.E.A. Proceedings, 1906, pp. 715-716.

Bingham, Walter. "Army Personnel Work." Journal of Applied Psychology, 3, March 1919, pp. 1-12.

_____. "Intelligence and Personality in Vocational Success." Vocational Guidance Magazine, 3, January 1925, pp. 122-126.

Branderburg, George. "Analyzing Personality." Parts I and II. Journal of Applied Psychology, 9, June 1926, pp. 139-155 and pp. 281-292.

Brotemarkle, R. A. "Comparison Test for Investigating the Ideational Content of the Moral Concepts." Journal of Applied Psychology, 6, September 1922, pp. 235-242.

Brown, Elmer Ellsworth. "Some Relations of Religious Education and Secular Education." Religious Education, 2, October, 1907, pp. 121-126.

Brumbaugh, M. C. "Moral Education: The Problem Stated." N.E.A. Proceedings, 49, 1911, pp. 347-350.

Bryant, Edith. "Delinquents and Non-Delinquents on the Will Temperament Test." Journal of Delinquency, 8, January 1923, pp. 46-63.

Butler, Nathaniel. "The Moral and the Religious Element in Education." Religious Education, 1, August 1906, pp. 89-93.

Butler, Nicholas Murray. "Education After the War." Educational Review, 57, January 1919, pp. 64-79.

Buzby, D. E. "The Interpretation of Facial Expression." American Journal of Psychology,

35, October 1924, pp. 602-604.

Cady, Vernon. "The Psychology and Pathology of Personality." Journal of Delinquency, 7, September 1922, pp. 226-248.

Calhoun, C. H. "A Follow-up Study of 100 Normal and 100 Subnormal Delinquent Boys." Journal of Juvenile Research, 12, September-December 1928, pp. 236-240.

Carney, Chester S. "National Conference on Americanization in Industries." Journal of Applied Psychology, 3, September 1919, pp. 269-276.

"Character Education in the Schools of the State of New York." Elementary School Journal, 32, February 1932, pp. 411-416.

"Character Training." Pittsburgh Schools, 8, No. 5, May-June 1937, pp. 207-245.

Charmley, Beulah M. "An Effectual Program for Character Building." Education, 53, December 1932, pp. 240-243.

Charters, W. W. "The Copeland Experiment in the District of Columbia." Educational Record, 15, 1934, pp. 403-418.

_____. "Success, Personality and Intelligence." Journal of Educational Research, 11, March 1925, pp. 169-176.

Coe, George A. "Religious Education and Political Conscience." Teachers College Record, 23, September 1922, pp. 297-304.

_____. "Shifting the National Mind-Set." Religioud Education, 19, October 1924, pp. 318-321.

Colton, Ruth White. "Character Education in
    Connecticut." School Executives Magazine,
    50, March 1931, pp. 313-315.

Committee on Character Education. "Thesis on
    Character Education." Journal of Educa-
    tional Method, 3, October 1923, pp. 84-86.

Cooke, Flora J. "Training for Character at
    Francis W. Parker School." Chicago
    Schools Journal, 13, November 1930, pp.
    98-104.

Copeland, Royal S. "Education and the Prevention
    of Crime." Educational Record, 15, 1934,
    pp. 123-137.

_____. "Education and the Prevention of Crime."
    Congressional Record, V. 78 Part 4, 73rd
    Congress, 2nd Session, March 8, 1934,
    pp. 3963-3966.

_____. "Crime and a Revised National Policy in
    Education." Congressional Record, V. 78,
    Part 10, 73rd Congress, 2nd Session,
    June 4, 1934, pp. 16350-16351.

_____. Introduction of Senate Bill #2838 on
    February 21, 1934. Congressional Record,
    V. 78, Part 3, 73rd Congress, 2nd Session,
    p. 2946.

Davenport, Charles. "Comparative Social Traits
    of Various Races." School and Society,
    14, October 1921, pp. 344-348.

Davis, Jessie B. "The Iowa Plan of Character
    Education Methods." Religious Education,
    December 1922, pp. 435-439.

"Declaration of Principles," N.E.A. Proceedings,
    45, 1905, pp. 42-45.

DeGarmo, Charles. "A Basis for Ethical Training in Elementary Schools." N.E.A. Proceedings, 30, 1891, pp. 170-177.

_____. "Ethical Training in the Public Schools." Annals of the American Academy of Political and Social Science, 12, 1891-1892, pp. 577-579,

_____. "Social Aspects of Moral Education." National Herbart Society Yearbook, 3, 1897, pp. 35-36.

Dewey, John. "Ethical Principles Underlying Education." National Herbart Society Yearbook, 3, 1897, pp. 7-33.

_____. "Interest as Related to Will." Second Supplement to National Herbart Society, 1895, pp. 5-39.

Doll, E. A. "The Comparative Intelligence of Prisoners." Journal of Criminal Law and Criminology, 2, 1920, pp. 191-197.

Dutton, Samuel. "Religious and Ethical Influences of Public Schools." Religious Education, 1, 1906, pp. 47-51.

Fairchild, Milton. "Character Education," N.E.A. Proceedings, 64, 1926, pp. 402-403.

_____. "Important Centers of Character." School and Society, 9, May 1919, pp. 566-568.

Faris, E. "Topical Summaries of Current Literature: Social Psychology in America." American Journal of Sociology, 32, January 1927, pp. 623-630.

Fearing, Franklin. "Some Extra Intellectual Factors in Delinquency." Journal of Delinquency, 8, May-June 1923, pp. 145-153.

Fernald, Guy. "Character vs. Intelligence in Personality Studies." *Journal of Abnormal Psychology*, 15, April 1920, pp. 1-10.

_____. "The Defective Delinquent Class Differentiating Tests." *American Journal of Insanity*, 68, 1912, pp. 523-594.

Filter, Raymond. "A Practical Definition of Character." *Psychological Review*, 29, July 1922, pp. 319-324.

Folsom, Joseph. "The Social Psychology of Morality and Its Bearing Upon Moral Education." *American Journal of Sociology*, 23, January 1918, pp. 433-490.

Froemming, A. A. "Bibliography of Character Tests and Measurements." *Journal of Educational Research*, 16, 1927, pp. 223-236.

Furfey, P. H. "A Revised Scale for Measuring Developmental Age." *Mental Hygiene*, 14, 1930, pp. 129-136.

_____. "A Revised Scale for Measuring Developmental Age." *Child Development*, 2, June 1931, pp. 102-114.

Galloway, Thomas. "Chemistry and Character." *Journal of Educational Psychology*, 13, 1922, pp. 303-306.

_____. "The Bearing of Sex Education Upon Character." *N.E.A. Proceedings*, 60, 1922, pp. 416-421.

Galton, Frances. "Address." *Nature*, 16, August 1877, pp. 344-347.

_____. "Measurement of Character." *Fortnight Review*, 1844, p. 42.

Gambrill, J. Montgomery. "Nationalism and Civic
    Education." Teachers College Record, 23,
    February 1922, pp. 109-120.

Gates, G. S. "A Test for Ability to Interpret
    Facial Expression." Psychological Bul-
    letin, 22, February 1925, p. 120.

Geissler, L. B. "Descriptive Responses to the
    Human Face." Psychological Bulletin, 22,
    February 1925, pp. 119-120.

"Girl Scouts and Character Building." New York
    State Education, 18, February 1931, pp.
    566-569.

Glenn, L. B. "A Character Training Experiment
    and How it Succeeded." Nations Schools,
    8, October 1931, pp. 63-65.

Goodenough, F. L. "Inter-relationships in Be-
    havior of Young Children." Child Develop-
    ment, 1, March 1930, pp. 29-48.

Gosline, H. I. "Personality from the Introspec-
    tive Viewpoint." Journal of Abnormal
    Psychology, 15, 1920, pp. 36-44.

Greenwood, James W. "The Home and School Life."
    N.E.A. Proceedings, 49, 1911, pp. 377-397.

Hall, G. Stanley. "Eugenics." Religious Educa-
    tion, 6, 1911, pp. 152-166.

Hamilton, W. J. "Character Education." Religious
    Education, August 1925, pp. 263-267.

Harris, J. H. "Character Education in Pontiac
    Schools." Journal of Education, 109, May
    1929, pp. 518-519.

Harris, William T. "Social Culture in the Form
    of Education and Religion." Educational
    Review, 31, 1892, pp. 759-763.

_____. "The Relation of School Discipline to Moral Education." National Herbart Society Yearbook, 3, 1897, pp. 58-72.

Hartshorne, Hugh and May, Mark. "A Summary of the Work of the Character Education Inquiry.: Religious Education, 25, September 1930, pp. 607-619 and October 1930, pp. 754-762.

_____. "Personality and Character Tests." Psychological Bulletin, 25, July 1928, pp. 422-443.

_____. "Research in Character Education." Phi Delta Kappan, 9, April 1927, pp. 129-131.

Hendrickson, Gordon. "Character Education in the Schools." Ohio Schools, 9, September 1931, pp. 256-258.

Hervey, Walter. "Moral Education in the Public Schools." Religious Education, 2, August 1907, pp. 81-85.

Heymans, G. D. and Wiersma, E. "Beitrage zur speciellen Psychologie au P. Grund einer Massenuntersuchung." Zsch. f. Psychol. 42, 1906, pp. 81-127 and pp. 258-301.

Hillbrand, Earl K. "Character Education in Seven City School Systems." Kansas Teacher, 31, May 1930, pp. 7-8.

Hogue, O. Wendell. "Character Education in Lyons." New York State Education, 18, February 1931, pp. 573-575.

Hosic, James. "Character Education in the Elementary School." School Executives Magazine, 51, November 1931, pp. 112 and 138.

Hughes, James L. "A Comparison of the Educational Theories of Froebel and Herbart,"

N.E.A. Proceedings, 34, 1895, pp. 538-545.

Hulbert, Albert. "The Habit of Going to the
    Devil." Atlantic Monthly, 138, December
    1926, pp. 804-806.

"Intelligence and Its Measurement: A Symposium."
    Journal of Educational Psychology, April
    1921, pp. 123-147, and pp. 195-216.

Johnson, Carrol B. "Character Education." New
    York State Education, 18, February 1931,
    pp. 564-565.

Jung, Carl. "The Association Method." American
    Journal of Psychology, 21, April 1910,
    pp. 219-269.

Kohs, S. C. "Ethical Discrimination Test."
    Journal of Delinquency, 7, January 1922,
    pp. 1-15.

Kornhauser, Arthur. "Psychology of Vocational
    Selection." Psychological Bulletin, 19,
    April 1922, pp. 192-229.

Langfeld, H. S. "The Judgment of Emotions from
    Facial Expression." Journal of Abnormal
    Psychology, 13, August 1918, pp. 172-184.

Loomis, Arthur K., Anderson, A. Helen, et al.
    "A Survey of Character Education in
    Denver." Journal of the N.E.A., 19,
    October 1930, pp. 217-218; November 1930,
    pp. 234-244; December 1930, pp. 307-308.

_____. "A Survey of Character Education in
    Denver." Journal of the N.E.A., 20,
    January 1931, pp. 11-12; February 1931,
    pp. 51-52; March 1931, pp. 78-80; April
    1931, pp. 125-126; May 1931, pp. 149-150;
    and June 1931, pp. 201-202.

Loomis, C. Frances. "Campfire and Character Achievement." New York State Education, 18, February 1931, pp. 561-563, and p. 636.

MacCurdy, T. "Synthesis: Symposium on the Relative Roles in Psychopathy of the Ego, Herd, and Sex Instincts." Journal of Abnormal and Social Psychology, 16, 1921, pp. 249-268.

Mathews, Ellen. "A Study of Emotional Stability in Children." Journal of Delinquency, 8, January 1923, pp. 1-40.

McFadden, John and Dashiell, J. F. "Racial Differences as Measured by the Downey Will Temperament Test." Journal of Applied Psychology, 7, March 1923, pp. 30-53.

McMurray, Charles. "Round Table Report to the National Council of the Influence of Herbart's Doctrine on the Course of Study in the Common Schools." N.E.A. Proceedings, 34, 1895, pp. 475-478.

Meyerhardt, M. W. "The Movement for Ethical Culture at Home and Abroad." American Journal of Religious Psychology, 3, May 1908, pp. 71-153.

Mott, Thomas. "The Means Afforded by the Public Schools for Moral and Religious Training." N.E.A. Proceedings, 1906, pp. 35-42.

Nichola, Adelaide. "Connecticut Bends the Twig." Survey, 66, September 1931, pp. 504-505, and pp. 535-536.

Omwake, Katherine. "The Value of Photographs and Handwriting in Estimating Intelligence." Public Personnel Studies, 3, No. 1, January 1925, pp. 2-16.

281.

Osborne, Raymond W. "Training for Character Through Cooperative Student Government." Chicago Schools Journal, 13, March 1931, pp. 314-319.

Pangburn, J. M. "The Psychology of Personality." Social Science, 2, August-October 1927, pp. 370-381.

Poffenberger, A. T. "Measures of Intelligence and Character." Journal of Philosophy, 19, May 1922, pp. 261-266.

Pope, D. W. "The Interpretation of the Human Face from Photographs." Bulletin of Randolph Macon Woman's College, 8, 1922, pp. 1-17.

Porteus, S. D. "Personality in Relation to Social Maladjustment." Training School Bulletin, 18, October and November 1921, pp. 81-90.

_____. "Social Rating Scale." Training School Bulletin, 18, May 1921, pp. 33-39.

Potter, Hon. Ellen C. "Spectacular Aspects of Crime in Relation to the Crime Wave." The Annals of the American Academy of Political and Social Science, 125, May 1926, p. 14.

Pressey, S. L. and Teter, G. F. "A Comparison of Colored and White Children by Means of a Group Scale of Intelligence." Journal of Applied Psychology, 3, September 1919, pp. 277-282.

_____. "A Group Scale for Investigating the Emotions." Journal of Abnormal Psychology and Social Psychology, 16, April 1921, pp. 55-64.

_____. "An Attempt to Measure the Comparative Importance of General Intelligence and

Certain Character Traits in Contributions to School Success." Elementary School Journal, 21, 1920, pp. 220-229.

_____, and Pressey, L. W. "Cross-out Tests with Suggestions as a Group Scale of the Emotions." Journal of Applied Psychology, 2, June 1919, pp. 138-150.

Rankin, Paul. "The Training of Teachers for Character Education." N.E.A. Proceedings, 68, 1930, pp. 319-326.

"Report of the Character Education Committee to the Second Annual Meeting of the Society for the Study of Education." Montana Education, 6, February 1930, pp. 28-32.

Resolutions of the American Historical Association." The American Historical Review, 29, April 1924, p. 428.

"Resolutions." N.E.A. Proceedings, 53, 1915, pp. 25-28.

"Resolutions." N.E.A. Proceedings, 54, 1916, pp. 27-28.

"Resolutions." N.E.A. Proceedings, 55, 1917, pp. 26-27.

"Resolutions." N.E.A. Proceedings, 56, 1918, pp. 23-26.

"Resolutions on the Moral Phases of Public Education." Religious Education, 6, 1911, pp. 117-119.

Rosanoff, A. J. and Kent, Grace Helen. "A Study of Association in Insanity." American Journal of Insanity, 67, Part I, Association in Normal Subjects, July 1910, pp. 37-96; Part II Association in Insane Subjects, October 1910, pp. 317-390.

Rosenow, Curt. "Is Lack of Intelligence the Chief
        Cause of Delinquency." Psychological
        Review, 27, March 1920, pp. 147-157.

Rugg, Harold. "Is the Rating of Human Character
        Practicable." Journal of Educational
        Psychology, 12, November 1921, pp. 425-536
        and December 1921, pp. 485-501.

Russell, James E. "The Relation of Industrial
        and Commercial Training to the Development
        of Character." Religious Education, 3,
        October 1908, pp. 133-134.

Seibold, Louis. "Crime Increase Steady in U.S.
        since 1900, all Records Show." Evening
        Star, Washington, D.C., September 8, 1926,
        p. 3.

Sherwood, Henry Noble. "The Morals of Modern
        Youth." N.E.A. Proceedings, 63, 1925,
        pp. 133-134.

Shiels, Albert. "The Coordination of the Commun-
        ity Agencies in Effecting Character
        Education." N.E.A. Proceedings, 60, 1922,
        pp. 409-416.

Shuttleworth, F. K. "The Social Relations of
        Children." Psychological Bulletin, 24,
        December 1927, pp. 708-716.

Sisson, Edward O. "Moral Education Again to the
        Front." School and Society, 21, May 1925,
        pp. 543-548.

Smith, Ernest. "Compulsory Character Education."
        N.E.A. Proceedings, 58, 1920, pp. 471-474.

Snedden, David. "Education Toward Formation of
        a Moral Character." Educational Review,
        57, 1919, pp. 286-297.

_____. "The Improvements of Character Educa-
tion." Journal of Education, 88, 1919,
pp. 144-145.

Spaulding, Edith. "The Role of Personality
Development in the Reconstruction of the
Delinquent." Journal of Abnormal Psy-
chology, 16, 1921, pp. 97-114.

Starbuck, Edwin. "Fundamentals of Character
Training." N.E.A. Proceedings, 62, 1924,
pp. 159-160.

_____. "Moral and Religious Education--Sociolo-
gical Aspect." Religious Education, 3,
February 1909, pp. 203-217.

_____. "Studies in Character at the University
of Iowa." Religious Education, 22, 1927,
pp. 48-49.

_____. "Tests and Measurements of Character."
N.E.A. Proceedings, 62, 1924, pp. 357-361.

Starr, Anna Spiesman. "A Problem in Social Adjustment." Psychological Clinic, 17, May
1928, pp. 85-96.

Stoops, John Dashiel. "Psychological Bases of
Religious Nature." Religious Education,
1, October 1906, pp. 123-128.

_____. "The Emotional Element in Religious
Education." Religious Education, 2,
August 1907, pp. 91-96.

Strong, A. C. "Three Hundred and Fifty White and
Colored Children Measured by Binet-
Stanford Measurement Scale of Intelligence."
Pedagogical Seminary, 20, 1913, pp. 485-
515.

Stroup, F. Neff. "Character Education in Newark."
New York State Education, 18, February

285.

1931, pp. 571-573.

Sunne, Dagney. "A Comparative Study of White and Negro Children." Journal of Applied Psychology, 1, 1917, pp. 71-83.

"Superintendent's Section." National Catholic Educational Association Bulletin, 26, 1929-1930, pp. 450-473.

Suzzallo, Henry. "The Training of the Child's Emotional Life." N.E.A. Proceedings, 45, 1907, pp. 905-909.

Symonds, Percival. "The Present Status of Character Measurement." Journal of Educational Psychology, 15, November 1924, pp. 484-498.

Taylor, Charles W. "Nebraska's Character Plan." Journal of Education, 115, January 1932, pp. 84-86.

"Tentative Report of the Committee on a System of Teaching Morals in the Public Schools." N.E.A. Proceedings, 49, 1911, pp. 342-347.

Terman, L. M. "The Use of Intelligence Tests in the Army." Psychological Bulletin, 15, June 1918, pp. 177-186.

"The New York Committee on Character Education." School and Society, 21, April 1925, pp. 465-466.

Thompson, W. O. "Effect of Moral Education in Public Schools upon the Civic Life of the Community." N.E.A. Proceedings, Fiftieth Anniversary, 1906, pp. 42-49.

Thorndike, E. L. "Individual Differences." Psychological Bulletin, 15, May 1918, pp. 148-159.

_____. "Intelligence and Its Uses." Harpers,

140, January 1920, pp. 225-235.

_____. "Scientific Personnel Work in the Army."
Science, 49, January 1919, pp. 53-61.

"Trends of Modern Education." The Sunday New
York Times, June 12, 1932, p. 8.

Watson, Goodwin. "Character Tests of 1926."
Vocational Guidance Magazine, 5, 1927,
pp. 289-309.

_____ and Forlano, George. "Prima Facie Validity in Character Tests." Journal of
Educational Psychology, 26, January 1935,
pp. 1-16.

Wells, F. L. "Intelligence and Psychosis."
American Journal of Insanity, 77, July
1920, p. 245.

West, James E. "Education for Citizenship."
New York State Education, 18, February
1931, pp. 555-557, and pp. 625-630.

White, Emerson E. "Moral Instruction in Elementary Schools." N.E.A. Proceedings, 35,
1896, pp. 407-410.

White, Hayden V. "The Burden of History."
History and Theory, 5, No. 2, 1966, pp.
111-134.

Williams, Charles. "Patriotism as an Instrument
for Moral Instruction in the Public
Schools." Religious Education, 2, June
1907, p. 58.

Witty, Paul and Lehman, Harvey. "The So-Called
General Character Test." Psychological
Review, 34, November 1927, pp. 401-414.

Woodrow, Herbart. "The Picture Preference Test."
Journal of Educational Psychology, 17,

November 1926, pp. 519-531.

Wygant, Elsie. "The Morning Exercise as Character Training." Chicago Schools Journal,
13, January 1931, pp. 221-228.

Yerkes, R. M. "Report of the Psychology Committee of the National Research Council."
Psychological Review, 26, March 1919,
pp. 83-149.

Yocum, A. Duncan. "Report of the Subcommittee on
Curriculum of the Committee on Superintendent's Problems." N.E.A. Proceedings, 58,
1920, pp. 174-176.

_____. "Resolution." N.E.A. Proceedings, 58,
1921, p. 270.

_____. "Three Reports on Character Education
Objectives." N.E.A. Proceedings, 61,
1923, pp. 253-255.

_____. "What Democracy Should Compel Through
Religion." Religious Education, 14, 1919,
pp. 180-189.

Zeublin, Charles. "The Relation of Commercial
and Industrial Training to the Development
of Character." Religious Education, 3,
October 1908, pp. 135-137.

MONOGRAPHS

Bronner, Augusta F. "Comparative Study of the
Intelligence of Delinquent 'Girls.'"
Columbia University Contributions to
Education, Teacher's College Series, No.
68, 1914.

Cady, Vernon. "The Estimation of Juvenile Incor-
rigibility." Journal of Delinquency
Monograph No. 2, 1923.

Chassell, Clara Frances. "The Relation Between
    Morality and Intellect." Columbia Univer-
    sity Contributions to Education, Teacher's
    College Series, No. 607, 1935.

Golightly, Thomas J. "The Present Status of the
    Teaching of Morals in the Public Schools."
    George Peabody College for Teachers
    Contributions to Education, 38, 1926.

Lentz, Theodore. "An Experimental Method for
    Discovery and Development of Tests of
    Character." Columbia University Contribu-
    tions to Education, Teacher's College
    Series, No. 180, 1925.

Mayo, M. J. "The Mental Capacity of the Negro."
    Archives of Psychology Monograph, No. 28,
    1913.

McGrath, Maria Cecilia. "A Study of the Moral
    Development of Children." Catholic Uni-
    versity of America Studies in Psychology,
    Psychological Monographs, 32, No. 2, 1923.

Odum, H. W. "Social and Mental Traits of the
    Negro." Columbia University Studies in
    History, Economics, and Public Law, 37,
    No. 3, 1910.

Selle, Erwin Stevenson. "The Organization and
    Activities of the National Education
    Association." Columbia University Contri-
    butions to Education, Teacher's College
    Series, No. 513, 1932.

Uhrbrock, Richards. "An Analysis of the Downey
    Will Temperament Tests." Columbia
    University Contributions to Education,
    Teacher's College Series, No. 296, 1928.

Voelker, Paul. "The Function of Ideals in Social
    Education." Columbia University Contribu-
    tion to Education, Teacher's College

Series, No. 112, 1921.

Watson, Goodwin and Biddle, Delia. "A Year of Research-1927: Some Investigations Published between January 1, 1927 and January 1, 1928, Bearing upon the Programs of Religious, Education, and Social Agencies." Religious Education Association Monograph, No. 4, July 1929.

REPORTS, BULLETINS

"Character Building: Elementary School Procedures." Kansas City School Service Bulletin, 4, No. 3, November 1931.

"Character Building: Principles and Suggested Procedures." Kansas City School Service Bulletin, 1, No. 2, April 1929.

"Character Education." Report of the Committee on Character Education of the National Education Association, U. S. Bureau of Education Bulletin, No. 7, 1926.

"Crime Prevention Through Education." Research Bulletin of the N.E.A., 10, No. 4, September 1932, pp. 133-201.

"Education for Character, Part II, Improving the School Program." Research Bulletin of the N.E.A., 12, No. 3, May 1934, pp. 83-141.

Furfey, Paul H. "Tests for Measurement of Non-Intellectual Traits." Catholic University of America, Educational Research Bulletin, 3, No. 8, October 1928.

_____. "The Measurement of Developmental Age." Catholic University of America Educational Research Bulletin, 2, No. 10, December 1927.

Heck, Arch. O. "Special Schools and Classes
in Cities of 10,000 Population and More
in the U.S." U.S. Office of Education
Bulletin, No. 7, 1930.

Larrabee, W. C. Second Annual Report of the
Superintendent of Public Instruction.
Indiana, 1853.

Manson, Grace. "A Bibliography of the Analysis
and Measurement of Human Personality Up to
1926." National Research Council Reprint
and Circular Series, No. 72, 1926.

Marteus, Elsie. "Biennial Survey of Education in
the U.S., 1928-1930." U.S. Office of
Education Bulletin, No. 20, 1931.

National Association of Corporation Schools Report. "Committee on Application of
Psychological Tests and Rating Scales to
Industry," and "The Committee on Job Analysis." 8th Annual Proceedings, 1920, pp.
115-139 and pp. 163-184; "Committee on Job
Analysis," 9th Annual Proceedings, 1921,
pp. 511-540 and pp. 211-236.

Neumann, Henry. "Moral Values in Secondary Education." U.S. Bureau of Education Bulletin, No. 7, 1926.

Report of the United States Commission of Education, 1, 1917, pp. 1-16.

"Report on the Causes of Crime." National
Commission on Law Observance and Enforcement, 1, No. 13, June 1931.

Segel, David. "A Selected List of Tests and
Ratings for Social Adaptation." U.S.
Office of Education Circular Series,
No. 52, 1932.

"Youth and Crime." U.S. Department of Labor Children's Bureau Public Document, No. 196, 1930.

UNPUBLISHED MATERIALS

Letter from Milton Fairchild to Edward Ross, dated September 19, 1916, Edward A. Ross Papers, Division of Archives and Manuscripts, the State Historical Society of Wisconsin.

Marks, Russell. "Testers, Trackers and Trustees: The Ideology of the Intelligence Testing Movement in America, 1900-1954." Unpublished Ph.D. Dissertation, University of Illinois, 1972.

McGeough, Irene. "A Critical Evaluation of the Character Education Inquiry, Particularly of the Underlying Philosophy." Unpublished Ph.D. dissertation, Fordham University, 1933.

COURSES OF STUDY, PLANS, CODES, YEARBOOKS

"A Course in Character Education." Annual Report of the Public Schools of Elgin, Illinois for the School Year, 1924-1925, Part III.

Building Character Through Activities in the Elementary Schools. Oakland: Superintendent's Council of the Oakland Public Schools, 1929.

"Character Education." Fourth Yearbook, Washington: Department of Superintendence of the N.E.A., Chapter 14, 1926.

"Character Education." Tenth Yearbook. Washington: Department of Superintendence of the N.E.A., 1932.

292.

"Character Education Handbook for Teachers."
    State of Oklahoma: Department of Educa-
    tion Bulletin, No. 131, 1931.

Character Education in Denver Public Schools.
    Denver: Board of Education, 1929.

Character Education in Detroit. Detroit: Board
    of Education, 1927.

Character Education in Los Angeles. Los Angeles:
    Board of Education School Publication,
    No. 262, 1934.

Character Education Methods, The Iowa Plan.
    Chevy Chase: Character Education Insti-
    tution, 1922.

Character Education. State of Indiana: Depart-
    ment of Public Instruction Bulletin, No.
    134, 1942.

Character Education: Supplement to the Utah
    State Course of Study. Salt Lake City:
    Department of Public Instruction, 1929.

Character Education Supplement to the Utah State
    Course of Study for Elementary and High
    Schools (Revised Edition). Salt Lake City:
    Department of Public Instruction, 1929.

Course of Study in Character Education. State of
    Nebraska. Lincoln: Department of Public
    Instruction, 1927.

Emphasizing Character in the Elementary School.
    Boston: The Commonwealth of Massachusetts
    Department of Education, 1937.

Golightly, Thomas J. "The Tennessee Plan for
    the Motivation of Character and Citizen-
    ship Activities in Secondary Schools."
    Bulletin of the Middle Tennessee State
    Teachers College at Murfeesboro Educational

Series No. 1, August 1927.

Hutchins, William. Children's Code of Morals for
    Schools. Washington: National Capital
    Press, 1917.

Knighthood of Youth Club Guide. National Child
    Welfare Association. Nebraska: State
    Department of Public Instruction, 1933.

Preliminary Report on Character Education in the
    Secondary Schools: District of Columbia
    School Document No. 9, U. S. Government
    Printing Office, 1931.

Report on Character Education in the Secondary
    Schools. Boston: The Commonwealth of
    Massachusetts, Department of Education,
    1935.

Something Better for Birmingham Children. Bir-
    mingham: Board of Education, 1936.

Vincent, P. M. "A Study of Character Education
    in Wisconsin Schools," Bulletin of the
    Department of Elementary School Principals'
    Eighth Yearbook. 1929.

INDEX

Herbartians, 8, 10, 12
Herd instinct, 58-61
Hofstadter, Richard, 1, 2
Hogh-Amsden Guide, 195
Hollingworth, H. L, 187
Housekeeping classes, 6
Hutchins Morality Code, 63-64, 66

Immigrants, 2, 3, 4, 22, 53, 145, 159, 179, 258
    Eastern European, 179
    German, 180
    Irish, 180, 182
    Italian, 182, 227
    Jewish, 180, 227, 234, 238, 248, 258
    Southern European, 179, 234, 258
    Northern European, 179, 182
    See also Character of; Intelligence of
Intellectual training. See Training
Intelligence
    correlation with character, 182, 185, 188,
        189-90, 191
    correlation with facial expression, 236-37
    correlation with grades, 183-84
    correlation with success in school, 184, 191,
        208, 258
    correlation with success in vocation, 184, 186,
        191, 208, 214, 258
    decline of American, 179
    of Blacks, 179, 212, 226
    of delinquents, 192, 193, 194, 208, 217, 258
    of immigrants, 4, 179, 227
    superiority of Nordics in, 179
    superiority of Whites in, 180
    tests, 173-75, 186, 226, 232, 234
International Committee on Moral Training, 33
International Conference on Moral Education, 45
International Conference of Religious Educators,
    76
International Union of Ethical Societies, 45
Iowa Plan, 65, 66, 69, 106-11, 115

Jensen, C. N., 54
Jordan, David Starr, 19

Kaiser Wilhelm, 52, 84
Kantian ethics, 4
Kilpatrick, William, 153
Kindergartens, 5, 120-21
Kingdom of Heaven on Earth, 3, 7, 13, 25, 34, 56,
    178, 255
Knighthood of Youth, 124
Kohs, S. C., 231
    Ethical Discrimination Test, 231-32
Kornhauser, Arthur, 186

Larrabee, W. C., 2
Lehman, Harvey, 201-02
    Play Quiz, 205
Lentz, Theodore, 200
Life Adjustment, 104, 108, 109, 127
Lindbergh, Charles, 143
Lusk Law, 100

Macintosh Decision, 102
Maller, J. B., 198-99, 206-07
Mann, Horace, 1, 8
Manson, Grace, 200
Manual training. See Training
Marxists, 4
Mateer, Florence, 158
Mathews, Ellen, 225-27
May, Mark, 76-77, 198-99, 200, 203-05, 233-36
McFadden, John, 180-81
McGrath, Marie Cecelia, 178
McGrough, Irene, 170
McMurry, Charles, 8, 11
Meritocracy, 50, 56, 137
Mirick, George, 112
Montefiore School, 143-44
Mosley School, 143-44
Moral(ity)
    decline in, 19, 104
    relativity of, 149-50, 153, 155, 257, 259
    secularized, 7, 13, 34, 50, 62, 256
    State sanctioned, 30, 74, 86, 106, 127, 149,
        153, 198, 256, 260
    training, 1, 5, 16, 18, 21, 22, 23, 24, 25,
        33, 54, 61, 81, 86, 111, 132

301

302.

About the Author

Stephen Yulish is an assistant professor in the Department of Educational Foundations and Administration at the University of Arizona. His academic background includes a B.A. in physical anthropology from Case Western Reserve University and an M.A. and Ph.D. in the history of American education from the Department of Education Policy Studies at the University of Illinois. A former teacher in an inner city school in Cleveland, Ohio, he has also taught graduate education courses on the Navajo Reservation. Professor Yulish, wife Debi, and their three sons reside in Tucson, Arizona.